CW01271565

Michael B. Barry

THE FIGHT FOR IRISH FREEDOM
An Illustrated History of the War of Independence

Andalus Press

Published by Andalus Press
Dublin, Ireland.

info@andalus.ie
www.andalus.ie

THE FIGHT FOR IRISH FREEDOM
An Illustrated History of the
War of Independence

ISBN 978-0-9933554-6-2
© Michael B. Barry 2018
Michael B. Barry asserts the moral right to be identified as the author of this work.

All rights reserved. No part of this publication may be reproduced, stored in a retrieval system, or transmitted in any form or by any means, mechanical, electronic, recording, photocopying or otherwise, without the prior permission of the publisher.

By the same author:
Across Deep Waters, Bridges of Ireland
Restoring a Victorian House
Through the Cities, the Revolution in Light Rail
Tales of the Permanent Way, Stories from the Heart of Ireland's Railways
Fifty Things to do in Dublin
*Dublin's Strangest Tales (*with Patrick Sammon*)*
Bridges of Dublin, the Remarkable Story of Dublin's Liffey Bridges (with Annette Black)
Victorian Dublin Revealed, the Remarkable Legacy of Nineteenth-Century Dublin
Beyond the Chaos, the Remarkable Heritage of Syria
Homage to al-Andalus, the Rise and Fall of Islamic Spain
The Alhambra Revealed, the Remarkable Story of the Kingdom of Granada
Málaga, a Guide and Souvenir
The Green Divide, an Illustrated History of the Irish Civil War
Courage Boys, We are Winning, an Illustrated History of the 1916 Rising

Jacket Images
Front flap: t Military Archives; b Bibliothèque nationale de France. Front cover: tl Cork Public Museum; tm Irish Capuchin Provincial Archives; tr Old Photos of Cork; b National Library of Ireland. Back cover: t South Dublin Libraries; b Irish Capuchin Provincial Archives. Back flap: b Kilmainham Gaol Museum; Author photogrph, Veronica Barry.

Jacket design by Anú Design.
Book design by Michael B. Barry.

Printed by Białostockie Zakłady Graficzne SA, Poland.

Contents

Acknowledgements and Illustration Credits		5
Chronology		6
Introduction		9
Chapter 1	A Phoenix Arises, 1916-1918	11
Chapter 2	Ruthless War Begins as Dáil Meets, 1919	43
Chapter 3	The Struggle Intensifies, 1920	65
Chapter 4	Ambushes, Truce and Treaty, 1921	181
Bibliography		297
Glossary		300
Index		302

In memory of my father, Michael Barry (1892-1961) who
lived through the War of Independence

Acknowledgements

This book benefited from the help, insights and scholarship of many kind people. Thanks are due especially to:

Dr Brian Kirby, Irish Capuchin Provincial Archives; Aoife Torpey, Kilmainham Gaol Archives; Derek Jones; Ernest McCall; Louise Mulcahy; Mick O'Dea; David Power, South Dublin Libraries; Seán Hogan, Department of Housing, Planning and Local Government; Lisa Dolan, Adrian Short, Hugh Beckett and Noelle Grothier, Military Archives, Cathal Brugha Barracks.

The following were very helpful to me: Tony Roche, Photographic Unit, National Monuments Service, Department of Culture, Heritage and the Gaeltacht; Daniel Breen, Cork Public Museum; Dr Lydia Ferguson, TCD; Francis Twomey; David Byrne; Bernie Metcalfe, Glenn Dunne, Mary Broderick, National Library of Ireland; Mícheál Ó Doibhilín, *kilmainhamtales.ie*; Mark Kennedy; Debra Wenlock; Jackie Dermody, Clare County Library; Seán Reynolds, Irish Prison Service; Tommy Mooney; Lar Joye; Donal Buckley; Robert Porter; Ray Bateson; Tom O'Neill; Bernard Minogue; Jeff Larkin; Colin Kirsch, Las Fallon; Pádraig Óg Ó Ruairc; Pearse Lawlor; Tony Kearns; Gerald Burroughs; Damian Shiels; John Borgonovo; Marcus Howard; Angus Mitchell; Tom Corbett; Declan Dunne; Mark Humphrys; Anthony Leonard; James Langton; Cormac O'Malley; Michael Curran; Diarmuid O'Connor; Tony McGettigan; Michael Forde; Martin MacDevitt, *irishpapermoney.com*; Peter McGoldrick, *irishconstabulary.com*; Joanne Clarke, Croke Park Museum; Vicki Hopson, Soldiers of Gloucestershire Museum; Joe Gannon, *thewildgeese.com*; Mark Platts, *thehistorybunker.co.uk*; Anne Boddaert, Crawford Art Gallery; Jim Horgan, Military Museum, Collins Barracks, Cork; Lt.-Col. Colin Bulleid, the Royal Hampshire Regiment Trust; Trevor McCarthy, Kilmallock Tours; Garry O'Brien, *irishvolunteers.org*; Michael Pegum, *irishwarmemorials.ie*; Ivor Hamrock, Mayo County Council; Harry Hutchinson, Kevin Kavanagh Gallery; Sophie Donaldson, *Irish Independent*; Nicholas J. Lilly, Warwick & Warwick Ltd; Simon Cook, The Rifles Berkshire and Wiltshire Museum; Finbarr Connolly, National Museum of Ireland; Peter Rigney, Ciaran Cooney, Norman Gamble, Irish Railway Record Society; and Dr Mary Clarke, Dublin City Library & Archive.

Paula and Dermot O'Doherty generously gave their advice. Lastly, but most importantly, providing essential and much valued support: Veronica Barry and Patrick Sammon.

Illustration Credits

Images on the specified pages are courtesy and copyright of the following (abbreviations for top, bottom, left, middle, right, respectively, are: t, b, l, m, r):

An Phoblacht: 59m; Author's collection: 15t, 15b, 51t, 79b, 93b, 94, 106tr, 171b, 172r, 185t, 192b, 194t, 199t, 230; Bibliothèque nationale de France: 76-77t, 86t, 89t, 111, 114b, 125t, 176t, 195b, 249b, 278b; Board of Trinity College, the University of Dublin: 16t, 60tr, 69, 83, 87t, 90b, 113b, 120t, 133t, 139t, 153b, 155m, 155b, 156-157t, 166b, 170b, 174b, 178b, 182t, 183b, 202t, 221b, 239t, 280b, 281bl, 293b, 295t; British National Archives: 231b; British Newspaper Archives: 240b, 267b; Brother Allen Collection, Military Archives: 18t AL-SB-02, 18b AL-SB-08, 18m AL-1916-129, 19t AL-1916-127, 19b AL-IMG-105, 153t AL-1920-56; Cashel Folk Museum: 160t, 270br; Ciaran Cooney: 31b, 53bl, 210tl; Clare County Library: 131b, 288t; Clew Bay Heritage Centre: 254b, and with Cormac O'Malley, 193bl; Cork Public Museum: 117t, 133bl, 204b, 219t; Crawford Art Gallery, Cork: 113t, 116t; Damian Shiels, Rubicon Heritage: 270t, 270b; David Byrne: 88b; Debra Wenlock: 97t; Derek Jones: 56tl, 62-63b, 80b, 87tl, 102b, 107t, 202mm, 223, 292-291t; Diarmuid O'Connor: 225bl, 237bl; Dublin City Library and Archive: 14, 24b, 30b, 35b, 37, 44b, 49t, 51m, 57m, 58bl, 58br, 61, 63b, 64t, 64m, 66, 72tr, 73bl, 76b, 77b, 78t, 79tl, 79t, 80t, 81, 82t, 84t, 85t, 9ct, 101, 103b, 104t, 105b, 112, 113bl, 114t, 115, 119bl, 125b,126b, 133b, 134t, 136b, 138, 145t, 147b, 152, 156t, 157tl, 16t, 161m, 164t, 164m, 166t, 168, 174-175t, 178t, 179t, 183t, 198br, 201b, 203, 208b, 212br, 218, 227, 237b, 240t, 241t, 241m, 248, 256, 278t, 279t, 280t, 280br, 281t, 282b, 284t, 285b, 286t, 287, 294b, 295b; Ernest McCall: 108t, 160b, 214b; Francis Twomey: 31t; Gerard Burroughs: 109b, 157rr; Imperial War Museum: 167b, 196t, 206t, 220t, 269b, 272, 273t; Irish Capuchin Provincial Archives, Dublin: 12t, 13t, 22tr, 27t, 34b, 36b, 40, 45tl, 46t, 53t, 53br, 56m, 72l, 110, 116b, 118t, 120b, 120br, 134b, 137, 140b, 141bl, 189m, 210tr; *Irish Independent*: 52t, 247t, 294t; Irish Prison Service: 121, 122-123, 200-201t; Irish Railway Record Society: 84tr, 84b, 188m, 188b, 197b, 209b, 266t; Irish Volunteers Commemorative Organisation, Pat O'Hagan: 99bl; Jeff Larkin: 88t; Joseph McGarrity Collection, Digital library@Vilanova University: 23t, 42b, 52m, 55t, 269t; Kilmainham Gaol Museum: 16b, 127t, 132b, 155t, 159b, 177t, 193br, 200b, 217b, 261t, 238bl, 275b; Las Fallon: 85b; Library of Congress: 13b, 24t, 32b, 33t, 35t, 54, 55br, 55bl, 145b, 176b, 179ml, 179bl, 214t; Mark Humphrys: 52b; Michael Curran: 70b; Mícheál Ó Doibhilín: 246t, 279b, and with the Dublin Fire Service, 249t; Mick O'Dea: 99tl, 142-143, 211t, 244b, 253t, 257t, 271t; Military Archives, Ireland: 17 CD 4/8/5c, 20b CD 119/3/5, 22tl CD 227/7/A1c, 22tr CD 227/7/A1g, 22b CD 227/7/A1d, 23b CD 227/7, 24b P-11-01, 24t CD 4/4/2, 25t CD 227/7, 26t CD 9/2/2, 27bl CD 105/8/7, 27b, 29b CD 216/1, 29bl CD 266/7/1, 32t CD6/28/3, 33bl CD 258/8/4, 34t CD 4/8/4, 34m CD 4/10/7, 36t CD 178/3/2, 39b P-9-003, 41b 1918.11.30_Vol_I_No_7_An_t-Óglach-1, 42t CD 256/3, 45t MA-HS-A-0862, 47b CD 103, 48br CD 131/3/4d, 50b MA-ACPS-GPN-232-1, 50t CD 264/38/3b, 56tr CD/188/02/2, 57b P-28-004, 62b CD 256, 78b CD 6/16/2, 81bl CD 227/35, 92b CD 6/31/6, 96b CD 6/31/6, 104b CD 29/5/7, 117b CD 6/29/7, 128t MA-169-039, 128m CD 250/3/5, 140tl CD 6/31, 140tr CD 627/6, 144t CD 227/35, 154b CD/006/291/1/P2, 159r PRCN-1050-01-01-01, 161 MA-P-39-002, 170t CD 6/9/16e, 173b CD 276/3, 174b CD 264/41/2, 179b WS 1713p6, 180b CD 75/6/7, 182m CD 13, 184b CD 227/35, 187b MSP34REF4903FRANKBUSTEED038, 189b P-14-001N, 211b MSPC-RO-327 004, 229b CD 29/5/6b, 232t 1921.06.03_Vol_III_No_11_An_t-Óglach-4, 232b CD 284/1, 234b CD 331/1, 236b CD 286/4, 238b CD 331/3, 249bl CD 188/4/6, 260 CD 227/35, 264t CD 227/35, 264b CD 227/35, 265t CD 227/35, 265m CD 227/35, 265b CD 227/35, 265bl CD 227/35, 266b CD 280/2/1, 267bl CD 11, 268 CD 227/39/1c, 276t CD 11, 276b 1921.05.01_Vol_III_No_6_An_t-Óglach-2, 277b CD 284/1/4, 283t CD 284/1/6, 283b MAMSPCA6 a & b, 285t CD 227/21/J3, 289r P-29-001, 289b CD 308/3/2; Military Museum, Collins Barracks, Cork: 67t; Military Museum, The Curragh: 67m, 89b, 90t, 90b, 93t, 94, 207t, 225m; Mulcahy Family: 21t, 21b, 29tr, 29tl, 58tr, 64b, 242b, 244b, and with the National Museum of Ireland, 277t; Museum of Technology, Lincolnshire: 207m, 235mt, 236t; National Archives of Ireland: 296; National Library of Ireland: 30t, 33br, 44t, 45b, 56b, 58t, 60tl, 60br, 71t, 75t, 79m, 86b, 119b, 129, 135t, 153m, 156m, 169, 171t, 172b, 182b, 191, 193t, 194b, 202ml, 221t, 224t, 228b, 245t, 281b, 282t, 286b, 290-291, 292b; National Monuments Service, Department of Culture, Heritage, and the Gaeltacht: 244t, all 251; National Museum of Ireland: 82b, 158t, 173t, 215b, 226t, 238t, 239b, 288m; Old Photos of Cork: 262t; Online Bicycle Museum — www.Oldbike.eu: 220b; Pádraig Óg Ó Ruairc: 267t; Pearse Lawlor: 124t, 235b; Police Museum, Belfast: 107b; Rifles (Berkshire & Wiltshire) Museum: 103t; Robert Porter: 109tl, 109t; Royal Hampshire Regiment Museum: 253; Royal Fusiliers: 198b, 208t, 209t; Soldiers of Gloucestershire Museum: 252; South Dublin Libraries: 20t, 26b, 46b, 92t, 119t, 158b, 202mr, 212b, 213t, 239tl, 246b, 247b, 250, 257t, 275, 284b; Swedish Army Museum: 207b, 235t; *The life and tragic death of Winifrid Barrington*/Angus Mitchell: 226br; Tom Corbett: 191tl; Tommy Mooney: 219b, 288b; Tony Kearns: 228t, 231t; Trevor McCarthy: 98, inset; UCD Archives: 49t; UCD-OFM partnership: 48t; Ulster Folk & Transport Museum: 90t, 96m, 97bl, 197t, 255t; Veronica Barry: 11, 43, 48bl, 65, 68b, 181, 186b; Warwick & Warwick: 99br; www.irishpapermoney.com: 51b; www.irishwarmemorials.ie: 47t, 98t, 98b, 102tr, 135bl, 153bl, 205b; www.royalirishconstabulary.com: 67b, 67mr, 71b, 97b; www.thehistorybunker.co.uk: 70t, 106b; www.thewildgeese.com (Joe Gannon): 254m.

Wikimedia Commons: 35t British Library_ F.M. Sir John French_ Commander in Chief in France (Photo 24-309).jpg, 41t Waffenstillstand gr.jpg, 47bl Soloheadbeg_proclamation.jpg_Dublin Castle RIC, 49t (inset) Frank Graham Cootes_www.whitehouseresearch.org, 67mt Rama_www.archive.org/de, 67ml Webley (Royal Irish Constabulary Revolver_Hmaag, 87b Peter Trimming_Flickr_ MarkIVFemaleTankAshfordKent.jpg, 173bl Bassano Ltd_National Portrait Gallery_ Peterstrickland.jpg, 219m Hogan's Flying Column.gif, 222b TomMaguire.jpg, Btm0330 courtesy of the Maguire Family, 222br Partry Mountains_geograph.org.uk_Oliver Dixon, 224b Bovington 021_Peerless Armoured Car_ Hohum — background has been removed, 225bm, mac eoin_ http://www.fionnbarcallanan.com/archive-McGuinness.html, 225br NLI Commons_HOGW 191; 235mb Luger P08_Askild Antonsen, 258br NMM_by Richard_Symonds_23, 271bl Art.IWM PST 5972, 283bl Loyal regiment_Wally_Wiglet.

All other photographs and maps not mentioned here are copyright Michael B. Barry © 2018.

Every effort has been made to establish copyright, but if a copyright holder wishes to bring an error to the notice of the publishers, then an appropriate acknowledgement will be made in any subsequent edition.

Chronology

1916

24 April	The Easter Rising begins in Dublin. The Irish Republic is declared. On 29 April Patrick Pearse surrenders to Brigadier-General Lowe.
3–12 May	Execution of leaders of the Rising.
23 December	Staged release of first internees begins with the Volunteers interned at Frongoch camp.

1917

3 February	Count Plunkett wins North Roscommon by-election.
9 May	Joseph McGuinness wins South Longford by-election.
March	National Executive of Irish Volunteers re-established.
10 June	Sinn Féin hold a rally at Beresford Place to protest against conditions of Republican prisoners in Lewes Jail in Britain. The DMP attempt to break up the meeting. In the fracas, DMP Inspector John Mills is struck on the head by a hurley wielded by a member of Na Fianna Éireann. Mills dies later of his injury. This is the first Crown forces fatality since the Easter Rising.
10 July	Éamon de Valera wins East Clare by-election by a landslide.
25 July	Opening of an Irish Convention to discuss how Ireland is to be governed. Discussions end in April 1918 with no agreement on Home Rule.
10 August	WT Cosgrave wins Kilkenny by-election.
25 September	Thomas Ashe dies in Mountjoy Gaol after a hunger strike. It is followed by a huge funeral procession in Dublin.
25 October	Éamon de Valera is elected President at the Sinn Féin annual convention.

1918

4 January	Two soldiers from Donegal, arrested for desertion, are being transported by train under military escort to detention to a barracks at Derry. They are rescued by Irish Volunteers at the station at Kincasslagh Road.
March	The General Headquarters staff of the Irish Volunteers are established. Appointed are: Richard Mulcahy as Chief of Staff; Michael Collins as Adjutant-General. By the end of the year, the Irish Volunteers begin to be generally known as the Irish Republican Army.
17 March	Volunteers raid the RIC barracks at Eyeries, Co. Cork and seize rifles.
13 April	The RIC barracks at Gortatlea, Co. Kerry, is attacked, resulting in the death of two Volunteers.
16 April	Following a huge assault by the Germans on the western front, a Military Service Bill is passed in Westminster enabling conscription in Ireland. This leads to universal opposition in Ireland. Two million people sign a national pledge against conscription.
11 May	Lord French, promising a firmer approach, is appointed as Lord Lieutenant and arrives in Dublin.
17 May	Sinn Féin leaders are rounded up as part of a supposed 'German Plot'.
11 November	An Armistice is signed. WWI hostilities cease.
14 December	A General Election is held. In Ireland, Sinn Féin win 73 seats; Unionists 26; and the previously dominant Irish Parliamentary Party a mere 6.

1919

21 January	The first meeting of *Dáil Éireann* is held at the Mansion House in Dublin. A Declaration of Independence and also a message to the 'Free Nations of the World' are read out. A 'Democratic Programme' is issued. The same day an ambush at Soloheadbeg results in the shooting dead of two RIC constables escorting a consignment of gelignite.
3 February	De Valera and two others escape from Lincoln Prison.
6 April	An attempt to free a prisoner from a prison hospital in Limerick results in an RIC man and the prisoner being killed. The Limerick 'Soviet' (workers council) calls a general strike on 13 April, in protest against military restrictions.
10 April	The Dáil authorises a boycott of the police, as well as a bond sale of £500,000.
13 May	Seán Hogan is rescued from a train at Knocklong, Co. Limerick, two RIC men are killed.
11 June	De Valera arrives in the USA intending to marshal support for Irish independence.
23 June	D/I Hunt is shot in Thurles.
July	A 'Squad' is formed by Michael Collins, now IRA Director of Intelligence.
30 July	Detective-Sergeant Smyth is shot in Drumcondra by the Squad and dies weeks later. Detective Hoey is shot dead at Townsend Street on 12 September.
7 September	An IRA unit led by Liam Lynch attacks a military party at the Wesleyan Chapel in Fermoy. The military later respond by looting the town.
Autumn	Isolated RIC Barracks in the south and west are evacuated. The larger barracks are transformed into bastions.
October	A British cabinet committee is established, chaired by a former Unionist leader, to draft a new Home Rule Bill. In December a 'Government of Ireland' bill is introduced in the House of Commons, with provision for northern and southern parliaments.
November	Approval is given to reinforce the RIC with ex-servicemen recruited in Britain.
26 November	Dublin Castle proscribes Sinn Féin and associated organisations.
December	Inspector-General Byrne of the RIC is superseded by an acting replacement.
19 December	There is an attempt to assassinate Lord French at Ashtown railway station, as he was returning from the country. Volunteer Martin Savage is killed in the ensuing gunfight.
December	A bond drive for the 'Republic of Ireland' starts in the US, promoted by de Valera.

1920

January	Enrolment of ex-servicemen to the RIC begins. In time these become known as 'Black & Tans'.

3 January	Carrigtwohill RIC Barracks are attacked and the occupants surrender. This is followed by a wave of attacks on barracks across the country.
15 January	In local elections, Sinn Féin (and supporters) gain control of 172 out of 206 borough and urban districts.
21 January	Assistant-Commisioner Forbes Redmond, sent to reorganise the 'G' Division of the DMP, is shot dead in Harcourt Street, Dublin.
2 March	A British spy, John Byrne, is shot in Dublin by the Squad.
20 March	Tomás Mac Curtain, Lord Mayor of Cork, is assassinated in his home at Blackpool by men with blackened faces. In retaliation, the Cork IRA kills D/I Swanzy, in Lisburn, Co. Antrim on 22 August.
26 March	Alan Bell, successfully investigating Sinn Féin finances, is shot dead in Ballsbridge.
Easter	The IRA burn 180 abandoned RIC barracks.
5 April	Republicans arrested in mass-round ups in January go on hunger strike demanding political status. There are huge demonstrations in Dublin. In a confused move, the authorities release the prisoners.
April	A review of the Irish administration leads to a shake-up: Sir Hamar Greenwood is appointed as Chief Secretary in early April; Major-General Sir Henry Tudor is appointed Police Advisor in May.
May	The 'Munitions Crisis' starts as railway workers refuse to transport soldiers and equipment. It continues until December.
28 May	A large attack is made on Kilmallock RIC Barracks. Two RIC and one Volunteer are killed.
June	Courts are authorised by the Dáil and become established all over Ireland.
15 June	D/I Lea-Wilson is shot dead in Gorey, Co. Wexford.
26 June	Brigadier-General Lucas is captured near Fermoy by the IRA. He escapes weeks later.
May	The Auxiliary Division of the RIC is authorised. Ex-officers are recruited and trained and in the months that follow are deployed in what are regarded as the 'hot' areas in Ireland. A total of 2,264 are eventually recruited.
13 July	In an attack on a patrol at Dingle, Co. Kerry, two RIC are killed.
17 July	Lieutenant-Colonel Gerald Smyth is shot in Cork. This followed the RIC mutiny at Listowel on 19 June 1920, where Smyth told the constables that no policeman would get into trouble for shooting any man. Sectarian riots ensue after Smyth's funeral in Banbridge, Co. Down.
30 July	Denis Lacey leads an attack at Oola, near Limerick Junction – two soldiers are killed. Later he leads an attack at Thomastown where six military are killed.
30 July	Frank Brooke, director of the D&SER, is shot dead at Westland Row (now Pearse) Railway Station by Squad members, Paddy O'Daly and Jim Slattery.
12 August	Terence MacSwiney, Lord Mayor of Cork, is arrested and begins a hunger strike. He is transferred to Brixton Prison. He dies after 74 days on hunger strike. There are enormous processions in London and Dublin. MacSwiney is buried amidst huge crowds in Cork on 31 October.
16 August	Reprisal at Templemore after the shooting of an RIC Inspector.
18 August	Seán Mac Eoin leads a successful raid on the military barracks in Longford.
20 September	Volunteer Kevin Barry is arrested at an attack on a British rations party. He is court-martialled and sentenced to hang. Large crowds pray outside Mountjoy Prison on 1 November as Barry is executed.
20 September	Balbriggan is sacked and burned by Crown forces after RIC D/I Burke and his brother are shot. Two Volunteers are arrested, bayonetted and their bodies dumped.
22 September	An RIC patrol is ambushed by the Mid-Clare IRA at Rineen. Five RIC are killed. Brutal reprisals ensue in Ennistymon, Milltown Malbay and Lahinch.
27 September	Reprisal at Trim, Co. Meath.
28 September	Volunteers force their way into the military barracks at Mallow and seize weapons. A sergeant is killed. The following night Mallow is torched by Crown forces.
October	Reprisals at Listowel, Tralee, Tubbercurry, Tuam and other towns.
12 October	Major George Osbert Smyth (brother of the assassinated Lieutenant-Colonel Gerald Smyth) is shot dead while raiding the hideout of Dan Breen and Seán Treacy in Drumcondra.
12 October	Five Volunteers, manufacturing bombs, are killed in an explosion at Kearn's Quay, Saltmills, Co. Wexford.
14 October	Seán Treacy is killed in a shoot-out on Talbot Street.
25 October	Three RIC are killed in an ambush at Moneygold, Grange, Co. Sligo.
31 October	D/I Philip Kelleher is shot dead in the bar of the Greville Arms Hotel in Granard, Co. Longford. Granard is burned by Crown forces, but Seán Mac Eoin's Volunteers repel a similar attack on Ballinalee.
1 November	Auxiliaries shoot Mrs Ellen Quinn as she was sitting on the lawn front of her farmhouse at Kiltartan, Co. Galway
12 November	An engagement with Auxiliaries at Ballymacelligot, near Tralee, resulted in two Volunteers dead. British propaganda led to filming of faked scene at Vico Road, Killiney, purporting to be the 'Battle of Tralee'.
17 November	Killing of an RIC Sergeant in Cork city. It results in a wave of 'tit-for-tat' killings.
18 November	Sir Hamar Greenwood, in the House of Commons, reads out an alleged captured document indicating that the IRA was considering spreading typhoid among British troops.
21 November	The IRA set out to assassinate suspected British spies across Dublin. Fourteen are shot dead. Later Crown forces fire on a crowd at a football match at Croke Park. Seven are shot dead, with five dying later and two trampled to death. Prisoners Conor Clune, Dick McKee and Peadar Clancy are murdered in Dublin Castle that evening. There was a massive roundup of Republicans in the weeks that followed.
28 November	Ambush at Kilmichael, Co. Cork, where 17 Auxiliaries are killed, with three IRA dead.
11 December	Cork city centre is burned and looted.
16 December	An ambush at Kilcommon Cross, Co. Tipperary, results in four British soldiers being killed.
23 December	De Valera returns from the USA.
23 December	The 'Government of Ireland' Bill becomes law.
27 December	Martial law is proclaimed in Cos. Cork, Tipperary, Kerry and Limerick – extended to Clare, Waterford, Kilkenny and Wexford on 5 January.
29 December	The first official reprisal occurs in Midleton after an ambush. Seven houses are demolished. Other official reprisals soon follow.
End December	The Dublin ASU is formed. Attacks on Crown forces in the city soon intensify.

1921

20 January	An attack on the RIC travelling in a Crossley Tender at Glenwood, Co. Clare leaves a D/I and five RIC dead.
21 January	One Volunteer dies of his wounds after a failed ambush at Tolka Bridge in Drumcondra. Five Volunteers are captured — four of these are later hanged.
28 January	An ambush laid at Dripsey, Co. Cork is foiled. Two Volunteers die and eight are captured. Mrs Mary Lindsay (and her chauffeur), who had informed on the IRA ambush, is seized and later killed after five of the Dripsey prisoners are executed by firing squad.
2 February	Auxiliaries are ambushed by Seán Mac Eoin and the North Longford flying column at Clonfin, Co. Longford. Four Auxiliaries are killed.
3 February	An attack on RIC in tenders at Dromkeen, Co. Limerick, results in eleven RIC dead.
11 February	An attack on a train carrying troops at Drishanbeg, near Millstreet, Co. Cork. Two British soldiers die.
14 February	Ernie O'Malley and two other prisoners escape from Kilmainham Gaol.
15 February	An attack on a train carrying troops at Upton, Co. Cork, results in eight civilians and three IRA killed.
20 February	At Clonmult, Co. Cork, a house where the IRA are billeted is surrounded. Twelve Volunteers are killed.
25 February	An ambush at Coolavohig, near Macroom leaves three Auxiliaries dead.
5 March	An ambush occurs at Clonbanin, near Banteer. Brigadier-General Cumming and three soldiers are killed.
7 March	The Mayor of Limerick and his predecessor are shot dead at their homes by men in civilian dress.
7 March	Seán Mac Eoin is arrested at Mullingar Railway Station.
11 March	Crown forces attack an IRA training camp at Selton Hill, near Mohill, Co. Leitrim. Seán Connolly and five other Volunteers are killed.
14 March	Six Volunteers are hanged in Mountjoy Jail. Three more are hanged over the following months.
19 March	A large British sweep at Crossbarry is resisted by the IRA under Tom Barry. The large engagement results in ten British soldiers and four IRA killed.
21 March	The IRA mount an ambush on a train with troops at Headford Junction, Co. Kerry. Eight British soldiers, two civilians and two IRA are killed.
23 March	Crown forces are ambushed at Scramogue, Co. Roscommon. Four (including two officers) are killed. Two Black and Tans are captured and later executed.
Spring	Formation of the 1st Southern Division, IRA.
11 April	Attack on 'Q' Company, ADRIC base at the L&NWR Railway Hotel, North Wall. One Volunteer is killed.
14 April	Sir Arthur Vickers is killed at Kilmorna House, Co. Kerry. The following day Major McKinnon of the Auxiliaries is shot on Tralee golf course.
23 April	The RIC encircle a farm near Clogheen, Co. Cork. Six Volunteers are shot dead.
2 May	A joint bicycle patrol of troops and RIC surprise an IRA flying column at Lackelly, Co. Limerick. Four Volunteers are killed.
3 May	The IRA ambushes the RIC at Tourmakeady, Co. Mayo, resulting in four dead. As British troops make a sweep over the Partry Mountains, the IRA Adjutant is killed in an exchange of fire.
4 May	The body of a tramp is used to lure the RIC to an ambush outside Rathmore, Co. Kerry — eight RIC are killed.
14 May	The IRA hijack an armoured car in a daring but failed attempt to rescue Seán Mac Eoin from Mountjoy Jail.
15 May	The local IRA lay an ambush and shoot D/I Biggs and Winifrid Barrington at Coolboreen, near Newport, Co. Tipperary.
15 May	At Ballyturin House, near Gort, Co. Galway, D/I Blake and his wife (and two British officers) are shot dead after a tennis match.
19 May	Five IRA are killed after an engagement with a police patrol at Kilmeena, Co. Mayo.
24 May	Elections are held under the 'Government of Ireland Act'. Unionists win 40 of the 52 seats for the 'Northern Ireland' Parliament. No polling takes place for the 'Southern Ireland' Parliament – all candidates are returned unopposed. Sinn Féin win 124 of the 128 seats.
25 May	The IRA seize the Custom House in Dublin, which is burnt, as planned. Four Volunteers as well as four civilians are killed. An estimated 107 Volunteers are captured.
31 May	A mine explodes as the band of the 2nd Battalion Royal Hampshires march at Youghal. Seven bandsmen are killed.
2 June	At Carrowkennedy, Co. Mayo, eight RIC (including a D/I) are killed in an ambush.
3 June	An ambush occurs at Modreeny, Co. Tipperary. Four RIC are killed.
16 June	At Rathcoole (on the Millstreet-Banteer road) two Auxiliaries are killed in an ambush. Mines placed on the road put armoured trucks out of action.
13 June	A consignment of 495 Thompson submachine guns bound for Ireland is seized on a ship at Hoboken, New Jersey. (A few Thompsons had previously been smuggled to Dublin.)
22 June	King George V makes a conciliatory speech at the opening of the 'Northern Ireland' Parliament
24 June	A troop train (carrying Hussars and horses) is derailed at Adavoyle. Three soldiers and many horses are killed.
1 July	An ambush on an RIC cycle patrol at Culleens, Co. Sligo, results in the death of two RIC men.
4 July	Discussions begin at the Mansion House, Dublin, between Éamon de Valera and southern Unionists on a call by Lloyd George for talks in London. Another meeting is held with General Macready on 8 July. Terms for a truce are agreed.
10 July	On the eve of the Truce, an ambush at Castleisland, Co. Kerry, leaves four British soldiers and three Volunteers dead.
11 July	A Truce comes into force. Under its terms, the British were to end manoeuvres, raids and searches. The IRA were to cease attacks on Crown forces.
12 July	De Valera and a delegation arrive in London. He later meets with Lloyd George. There is little meeting of minds.
9 September	The Dáil cabinet agrees to send a delegation to London for discussions with the British.
11 October	The Irish plenipotentiaries arrive at Downing Street and weeks of negotiations ensue.
6 December	The plenipotentiaries, under severe pressure to sign the Treaty or face renewed war, fail to consult Dublin and sign the document. It results in a Brexit of a kind, with the British departing from the 26 counties of 'Southern Ireland'. There is limited freedom, but no Republic. Six months later, a Civil War ensues in Ireland.

Introduction

In the period after the Rising of Easter 1916, the British wished to resolve the 'Irish question', but naturally on their own terms. They were hampered by a constricted view of the world, seen through the prism of Empire. Lloyd George had no sympathy or feeling for Ireland. He wrote a letter in September 1920 saying 'Ireland was a hell's broth – *Potas y Diafol* (Devil's broth).' Most of those leading the British side during the War of Independence had colonial experience. They were noted for their arrogance and condescension, sustained by a strong element of racism towards the Irish. This elite, constrained by the attitudes of its class, did not understand the views of the population of Ireland and were unable to analyse the problem clearly, or deal with it in an effective manner. Indeed the British Government's direction of its war against the independence of Ireland over the period 1919 to 1921 was incompetent, marked by rapid changes in direction, alternating between coercion and nervousness.

In May 1916, in the aftermath of the Rising, Irish independence seemed a distant dream. However, the ruthless and drawn-out executions of the leaders that followed proved to be a public relations disaster in Ireland for the British, creating much public sympathy for the Republican cause. When the Germans made their last-ditch offensive in Spring 1918, the British panicked and made the grave error of proposing conscription in Ireland – which immediately radicalised the Irish public. At the same time, the Irish Convention (set up to discuss how Ireland was to be governed, against the background of the conflicting wishes of Unionists and Nationalists) fizzled out. Intriguingly, during the proceedings, there had been fleeting agreement by Unionists to a mild form of all-Ireland Home Rule. In the event, this proposal was torpedoed by a Catholic bishop.

Sinn Féin, now more radical than before the Rising (in which they had played no part), surged and won by-elections throughout 1918. They won 73 seats in the post-war general election of December 1918. This gave them democratic legitimacy and facilitated the establishment of the First Dáil in January 1919, which duly ratified the Republic, proclaimed in 1916.

When did the War of Independence begin? There is no simple answer. The first fatality, among the Crown forces, after the Easter Rising was in June 1917, when a DMP Inspector died after being hit by a hurley in Dublin. There was early action when Volunteers rescued two men from a military escort in Donegal on 4 January 1918. The RIC were attacked in several sporadic incidents during 1918. Two Volunteers were killed in the attack on the RIC barracks at Gortatlea on 13 April 1918. However, the ambush at Soloheadbeg on 21 January, resulting in two RIC deaths (an action unauthorised by IRA GHQ), marked a loss of innocence. As attacks by the IRA began to gain in intensity over the rest of 1919, Soloheadbeg can arguably be said to mark the real start of the War of Independence. From this point on, the struggle was country-wide and more ruthless, in contrast to the simpler narrative of the week-long, Dublin-centred Rising.

The IRA, as the Volunteers became known, were fortunate in having exceptional leaders at GHQ, such as Richard Mulcahy and Michael Collins. Collins saw clearly the overriding importance of intelligence and the need to maintain security by eliminating spies, who had sunk every previous Irish attempt at independence. Throughout the country there was much 'subsidiarity' (using today's EU-speak) among the IRA. These mostly decided their own actions, albeit within a framework of directives from GHQ in Dublin – which were sometimes ignored. Guerrilla warfare has been called the method of the weak versus the strong. Through trial and error, the IRA developed in an ad hoc manner a form of guerrilla war that proved (in the areas that actually saw the fighting) to be particularly effective.

As 1919 moved into 1920, for the British the news from Ireland got worse. The RIC, up to then the effective garrison for the British in Ireland, came under severe assault. They were boycotted, RIC barracks were attacked. Morale plummeted, there were many resignations and recruitment came to a halt. The British response was to bolster the RIC, as they maintained that this was purely a police action dealing with malcontents and criminals. Thousands of ex-servicemen were recruited in Britain – the 'Black and Tans' now arrived in Ireland. In addition, an elite paramilitary force of ex-officers, the Auxiliaries, was recruited. However as the situation worsened, the military were also ambushed and the British Army began to play a fully active role.

On pages 178-9, details are given of the curious case of the alleged Typhoid Plot. Papers belonging to Richard Mulcahy, IRA Chief of Staff were captured in a raid on 16 November 1920. The British claimed that a discussion document on the use of bacteriological warfare against the British Army was amongst these papers. The reaction at the time was to discount the British claim as black propaganda – Dublin Castle press officers had form in this. Hamar Greenwood read the captured document in parliament. 'Sinn Féin Plot to Spread Typhoid Among Troops' ran the press headlines and the British protested loudly, which was ironic given that the British Army had gassed rebels in Mesopotamia in 1920. However, James O'Donovan, IRA Director of Chemicals, in a later Witness Statement said that he had given consideration to the possibility of infecting horses and men of the British Army during the Conscription Crisis of 1918.

Richard Mulcahy's papers include an 1962 interview where he discusses the raid. He noted that Dr Pat McCartan had sent a discussion paper on typhoid to Michael Collins, who had passed it on to

Mulcahy, writing: 'this is your department'. Mulcahy added that: 'this was a joke as far as Mick and myself were concerned' and that the paper had been destined for the wastepaper basket at the time it was captured in the raid. Thus the document was real, but had already been dismissed by the IRA leadership.

There was a post-war deadline on the parliamentary front – the all-Ireland Home Rule Act, passed into law in 1914 (and deferred during the war) was due to come into force. Lloyd George responded to Unionist pressure and the British Cabinet crafted a new Orange-tinted Home Rule bill which specified the partitioning of Ireland. Over the course of 1920 this bill slowly made its way through parliament, becoming law in December of that year. Thus, by an act of the British Parliament, for the first time in history, Ireland was partitioned.

In 1921 the news was even darker for the British as the number of Crown forces killed every month continued to increase. The IRA (although grievously short of arms) mounted ambushes that became increasingly sophisticated. Despite this, senior army officers optimistically reported that victory was just around the corner. Reprisals, unofficial at first, became official in the martial law areas, marking a new low in the campaign by the Crown forces. The British began to earn an international reputation for brutality, in what was, after all, a part of the 'United Kingdom'. By mid-1921, oscillating between a policy of flooding Ireland with troops and instituting peace talks, the British opted for talks. The Truce was duly signed. The IRA, bolstered in their struggle by the tide of international public opinion, thus had opened the first chink in the British Empire.

In the months that followed, negotiations led to the Treaty of December 1921, which resulted in a limited form of independence for the 26 counties. This Dominion status, as opposed to a Republic, granted under the Treaty, was the principal cause of the Civil War, which broke out six months later.

Estimates of the casualty figures of the War of Independence have varied widely – more research is required. One approximation gives a figure of around 1,450 killed (comprising 261 British Army, 428 Police, including Auxiliaries, 550 IRA Volunteers and around 200 civilians). These figures are painful in a small country, but pale when compared with, for example, the daily fatalities in the Battle of the Somme.

I was brought up in Ballydehob on the Mizen Peninsula in West Cork and have some personal resonances with the War of Independence (and no, I am not related to Tom Barry, nor to Kevin Barry). I heard about that time from my father – regrettably, at the age of eleven, I did not have any curiosity, and I took these stories as part of the normal background of life, and did not probe further. In 1919-21 the Mizen Peninsula was not as 'hot' as other areas of Cork during the War of Independence – but it was infinitely 'hotter' than a good number of other counties, where there was little real or effective IRA activity. As I went around West Cork with him in his car, he would point out a field where a man was shot at random by a passing group of 'Black and Tans'. Further along was a house burnt out by the Tans. He recalled that once soldiers had charged into our premises, led by the distinctive Major Arthur Percival, who later earned notoriety when he surrendered Singapore to the Japanese. On another occasion, the Crown forces rousted the inhabitants of Ballydehob, and made them kneel down in the square and say a decade of the rosary for the English king – nothing as savage as, for example, the burning of Balbriggan, but a humiliating event which further etched resentment into the local psyche.

This volume completes my trilogy of illustrated histories that cover the Irish Revolution, 1916-1923. (The previous books are *Courage Boys, We are Winning* on 1916 and *The Green Divide* on the Civil War) Due to the unique style that I developed when writing these books, they have garnered public approval and appreciation. This approach presents the events in a richly visual manner, using a mix of old photographs and documents, along with contemporary photographs and specially-created maps. Despite the necessary constraints of space, due to the caption format, I endeavour to tell the full story in a comprehensive, easily understandable yet nuanced way.

As usual I carried out deep and wide research in Ireland and abroad. I also sourced largely unseen material from many generous people. Amidst the many images presented here (an unprecedented 650), some are familiar but many have never been published before. In a sea of black and white images, several illustrations were sourced from continental magazines that described the conflict in full colour (albeit in a *'Boys-Own'* style of derring-do).

The book is set out chronologically. Chapter One gives the context to the war – the renaissance of Republicanism, post-Rising 1916 to 1918. Chapter Two tells of the First Dáil and the development of a new streak of ruthlessness in the struggle for freedom. The length of Chapter Three, covering 1920, is testimony to the increased tempo of the war at that time. Chapter Four is equally long and, if anything, reflects a higher intensity of the conflict up to the Truce in July 1921. The chapter ends with the Treaty of December 1921. Thus within these pages are set out the events from after the 1916 Rising until 1921, one of the most pivotal episodes in the history of Ireland.

Michael B. Barry
Dublin, September 2018

Chapter 1
A Phoenix Arises
1916-1918

After the suppression of the Rising in Easter 1916, it appeared that the British could return to concentrate on winning the 'Great' War. However, the execution of the rebel leaders led to a rise in sympathy for the cause of independence. As the rebels were released from detention in Britain they joined Sinn Féin which then successfully won a wave of by-elections. Under severe pressure from a German assault, the British miscalculated and proclaimed conscription in Ireland. This generated universal opposition. The Irish Volunteers re-organised with a new purposeful and practical direction. An 'Irish Convention' assembled all shades of opinion, save Sinn Féin, to discuss the governance of Ireland. A mild form of an agreed all-Ireland Home Rule faltered under the opposition of a Catholic Bishop – and the convention petered out. The British called off conscription as they were winning the war but the damage was done. Senior Sinn Féin leaders were arrested under the 'German Plot' leaving Michael Collins and others to pursue a more militant course. As the war ended, a long-deferred General Election was held. In Ireland, Sinn Féin gained a commanding 73 seats, resoundingly eclipsing the Irish Parliamentary Party with a mere six seats. The Unionists took 26 seats.

Above: May 1916 – the Easter Rising by the Irish Volunteers and the Irish Citizen Army had been defeated and central Dublin was in ruins. With the rebels defeated, Britain could now return to concentrate fully on the struggle against the Central Powers.

Left: the burial ground at Arbour Hill. The leaders of the Rising had been executed with dispatch and buried in quicklime, without ceremony, here in what was an obscure yard at the back of Arbour Hill Detention Barracks.

Right: en route to the docks. In the aftermath of Easter Week the 'Sinn Féiners' were rounded up en masse across the country, and sent to detention in Britain.

Right: the proposition that the Rising was a temporary aberration was widely promulgated. Here a cartoon portrays the events of 1916 (dubbed the 'Sinn Féin Revolt'), with the hopes for an Irish Republic in ruins. Helpfully, it shows a rifle that was made in Germany.

THE ILLUSTRATED LONDON NEWS

No. 4020   VOL. CXLVIII.   SATURDAY, MAY 6, 1916.   SIXPENCE.

THE REAL IRELAND, AS OPPOSED TO THE FALSE DOCTRINES OF THE SINN FEIN REBELS: CAPTAIN WILLIAM REDMOND, MR. JOHN REDMOND'S SOLDIER BROTHER, LEADING IRISH TROOPS.

The few misguided fanatics who engineered the Sinn Fein rebellion are in no sense representative of Irish feeling. The real Ireland is rather to be found among the gallant Irish troops at the front. In March last year Mr. William Hoey Kearney Redmond, M.P., brother of Mr. John Redmond, and here seen marching at the head of his men, was gazetted a Captain in an Irish regiment. In this connection we may recall what Mr. John Redmond said as to " the opinion of the overwhelming majority of the Irish people " regarding the Allied cause : " This was the opinion which thousands of Irish soldiers have sealed with their blood by dying in the cause of the liberty of Ireland and of the world " ; and, regarding the rebellion, " Is it not an additional horror that on the very day when we hear that men of the Dublin Fusiliers have been killed by Irishmen in the streets of Dublin, we receive the news of how the men of the 16th Division—our own Irish Brigade, and of the same Dublin Fusiliers—had dashed forward and by their unconquerable bravery retaken the trenches that the Germans had won at Hulluch ? "

Drawn by S. Begg from the War Office Official Film.

Right: the struggle for victory in the 'Great War' was all-pervasive in British eyes. In such dire straits, the proposition was that the Irish were an integral part of the cause of the British Empire. In this piece entitled 'Triumphs of British Science and Invention in the War', the Germans are presented as inferior in intellect to (the invented concept of) the 'Anglo-Celtic races'.

Left: the 'Great War' still raged on. There was an urgent need to present Irishmen fighting in the British Army as 'loyal'. Here, in the 'Illustrated London News' of May 1916, Captain William Redmond (long-time Parnell supporter, MP for East Clare and John Redmond's younger brother) is shown leading his men. The caption reads: "The real Ireland as opposed to the false doctrines of the Sinn Féin rebels".

Right: a commission on the rebellion concluded that amongst the reasons were poor intelligence and tolerance of militias. It stated that the system of government in Ireland was ineffective and inefficient. In reality, this dysfunctionality was to continue throughout the subsequent War of Independence.

> PUNCH, OR THE LONDON CHARIVARI.—May 24, 1916.

THE GOLDEN MOMENT.

Erin (to Mr. Redmond and Sir Edward Carson). "COME, MY FRIENDS, YOU'RE BOTH IRISHMEN; WHY NOT BURY THE HATCHET—IN THE VITALS OF THE COMMON ENEMY?"

By the end of May 1916, in the aftermath of the Rising, Lloyd George, then Minister for Munitions, was tasked by Asquith to resolve the Irish question. He met separately with the Unionists as well as with the Irish Parliamentary Party (IPP). An agreement appeared to be in sight: implementation of the 1914 Home Rule Bill, with exclusion of six northern counties. Lloyd George, with characteristic ambiguity, gave the impression to the IPP that the exclusion was temporary, thus gaining their initial acceptance. However, he assured Unionists that the exclusion was permanent. When this permanency became apparent to the IPP, the negotiations collapsed. *Above left*: Punch heralds the great initiative.

With martial law declared after the Rising, the commanding officer General Maxwell was now effectively ruler of Ireland. On 6 May 1916, he wrote to Bishop O'Dwyer of Limerick asking him to restrain two nationalist priests. This rebounded spectacularly on the general. The bishop replied, referring to the executions: 'I regard your action with horror, and I believe that it has outraged the conscience of the country.' *Left*: Bishop O'Dwyer.

The broad spread of Irish public opinion had not initially supported this rebellion by a group of advanced nationalists. However, after the May executions, sympathy grew, leading to a shift in favour of the insurgents and their ideals.

HIS EASTER OFFERING.

Right: the dream of 1916 hadn't gone away. In this poster the Easter Rising is portrayed in a semi-mystical setting.

Above and left: North Camp, Frongoch. Immediately after the Rising over 2,500 Republicans had been arrested and shipped to various prisons in Britain. Later on the bulk of the detainees (those who had not been tried) were transferred to the bleak Frongoch Camp – a former POW camp in North Wales.

Frongoch and other locations became a university for the Volunteers – there was time to consider, discuss and plan afresh a redoubled struggle for independence. Networks were established between men from all parts of Ireland. They were able to imbue some of the essence of military life: discipline, order and communal living.

Left: South Camp in the grain store of an old distillery at Frongach.

Above: life in a hut at North Frongoch.

Right: Michael Collins (arrow) at Stafford Detention barracks. Transferred to Frongoch at the end of June 1916, Collins's irrepressible energy and organising skills came to the fore there. He reflected on the Rising, referring it as: 'bungled terribly, costing many a good life... (with) a great lack of essential organisation'. The Irish Republican Brotherhood (IRB) became for him the efficient vehicle for organisation. He was elected Head Centre of the Frongoch IRB.

In December 1916 there was a general amnesty. Those from Frongoch were released, arriving in Dublin on Christmas Eve. The arrival was low-key, as the British had not publicised the releases in advance. The last batch of prisoners (those who had been tried and convicted) were released in June 1917. Above: the later releases were greeted by large crowds as seen in this gathering on the quays near Liberty Hall.

Left: the ruined Liberty Hall forms a backdrop as members of the Irish Citizen Army meet in 1917.

Sinn Féin at the time of Easter 1916 was a minority 'moderate' separatist grouping and its leader, Arthur Griffith (right), had not supported an armed uprising. Yet, paradoxically and mistakenly, the British press universally dubbed the rebels 'Sinn Féiners'. As the prisoners came home they drifted into Sinn Féin and it began to regroup. With this new influx of radicalised veterans, coupled with a rise in nationalist sentiment post-Rising, Sinn Féin began to embody a more militant nationalism.

The 1910 British Parliament's term had been prolonged due to the War. By 1917, several of the more elderly IPP MPs had died, thus sparking an unusually high number of Irish by-elections. The incumbent MP for North Roscommon died, which led to a by-election on 3 February 1917. Papal Count George Noble Plunkett (father of the executed Joseph Plunkett) stood for Sinn Féin and won by a large margin.

Kerry Appeals to Longford!

The Kerry County Council has adopted the following resolution:

THAT WE, THE MEMBERS OF THE KERRY COUNTY COUNCIL, REALISING THAT REPRESENTATION AT THE PEACE CONFERENCE IS A MATTER OF VITAL IMPORTANCE FOR OUR COUNTRY HEREBY CALL UPON THE ELECTORS OF SOUTH LONGFORD TO RETURN JOSEPH MacGUINNESS AS THEIR REPRESENTATIVE, AS WE BELIEVE THAT THE PRESENT IRISH PARLIAMENTARY PARTY HAVE SIGNALLY FAILED IN THEIR DUTY TO OUR COUNTRY AND THE TRUST SO LOYALLY PLACED IN THEIR HANDS.

Vote for MacGuinness

Issued for Joseph MacGuinness by his authorised Election Agent, P. J Hannon, Solicitor, Longford, and Printed by Patrick Mahon, Yarnhall Street, Dublin.

MEN OF SOUTH LONGFORD,
WHO WILL YOU FOLLOW?
THE MAN WHO FOUGHT FOR YOU IN DUBLIN DURING

Easter Week
JOE MacGUINNESS,

Or the Men who would have sent you to Meet German Guns—:

John E Redmond, M.P., Thomas P. Smyth, M.P., F. E. Meehan, M.P., Joseph Devlin, M.P., Thomas O'Donnell, M.P., and thirty other M.P.'s.

Who Stumped the Country to Get Recruits for the British Army.

They Are Now Appealing for Your Votes.

ASK THEM WHEN AND WHY THEY STOPPED RECRUITING.

Up MacGuinness!

Cork's Appeal to South Longford!

The following is Copy of a Resolution passed unanimously by the Guardians of the Cork Union at their meeting held on Thursday, 3rd May, 1917:

RESOLVED—"That we, the Cork Board of Guardians, respectfully but firmly demand that the English Home Secretary grant the Countess de Markieviecz a daily visit from an outside friend; that in view of Councillor Partridge's statement, that 'confinement and insufficient food is killing my comrades at Lewes,' which receives confirmation by the release of himself and another prisoner, 'medically labelled for the scrap heap,' we hereby demand that our fellow-countrymen now convicts in Lewes prison be either liberated or treated as prisoners of war, and **that we appeal to the patriotic people of South Longford to force England to open the dungeon doors, in response to a weapon more effectual than mere protests.**"

(Signed)   M. AHERN, J.P., Chairman.
                J. COTTER, Clerk.

The Cork Corporation at last meeting, 27th April, 1917, Lord Mayor Butterfield presiding, passed unanimously a similar resolution.

FELLOW-COUNTRYMEN OF SOUTH LONGFORD!

Do you repudiate the men who died for Ireland in Dublin, and will you desert those poor victims of British rule who suffer the slow torture and degradation of penal servitude, and will you, in the words of the **Bishop of Limerick,** "allow them to linger and rot in English jails without a protest which the world will hear?" **If so, vote for Redmond's nominee.**

Do you desire to gladden the heart of the Irish exile and every generous-minded lover of freedom the world over, and incidentally frustrate another attempt to enforce Conscription with a worthless settlement on the Irish people? If you do, **VOTE FOR THE MAN IN JAIL,** and shame England by having for your member

JOSEPH McGUINESS, "M.P.- Convict,"

Lewes, England.

Above: Joseph McGuinness in Volunteer uniform. The death of the IPP member for South Longford, an old Fenian in his late seventies, led to another by-election in May 1917. A reluctant Joseph McGuinness, veteran of the Four Courts garrison and convicted prisoner in Lewes Prison, was proposed by Michael Collins. He defeated the IPP candidate by a narrow margin.

Left: some of the pamphlets, including appeals from County Councils, distributed by the, by now, well-oiled Sinn Féin election machine. These powerfully raised the issues: eliciting sympathy for the dead of Easter Week; the opportunity to force England 'to open the dungeon doors' and opprobrium piled on John Redmond and his party for their role in recruiting for the British Army.

The next by-election, that in East Clare, was due to the death of John Redmond's MP brother, William. He had died on 7 June 1917, not of old age, but of his wounds after leading a charge at the Messines Ridge. Above: he is remembered in a memorial to fallen barristers of WWI at the Law Library in the Four Courts.

Right: Éamon de Valera, Commandant of the 3rd Battalion at Boland's Bakery, had been sentenced to death but this was commuted to penal servitude for life. After incarceration in English prisons, he was released with others on 16 June 1917. They returned to a tumultuous welcome in Dublin. De Valera was nominated as the Sinn Féin candidate in the East Clare by-election.

Right: a Sinn Féin handbill presents de Valera as a 1916 hero against the IPP candidate, Patrick Lynch (who had been senior crown prosecutor in Kerry). De Valera won decisively, with 71% of the vote. Lynch joined Sinn Féin a year later.

WHICH?

VOTE FOR DE VALERA, A Felon of Our Land

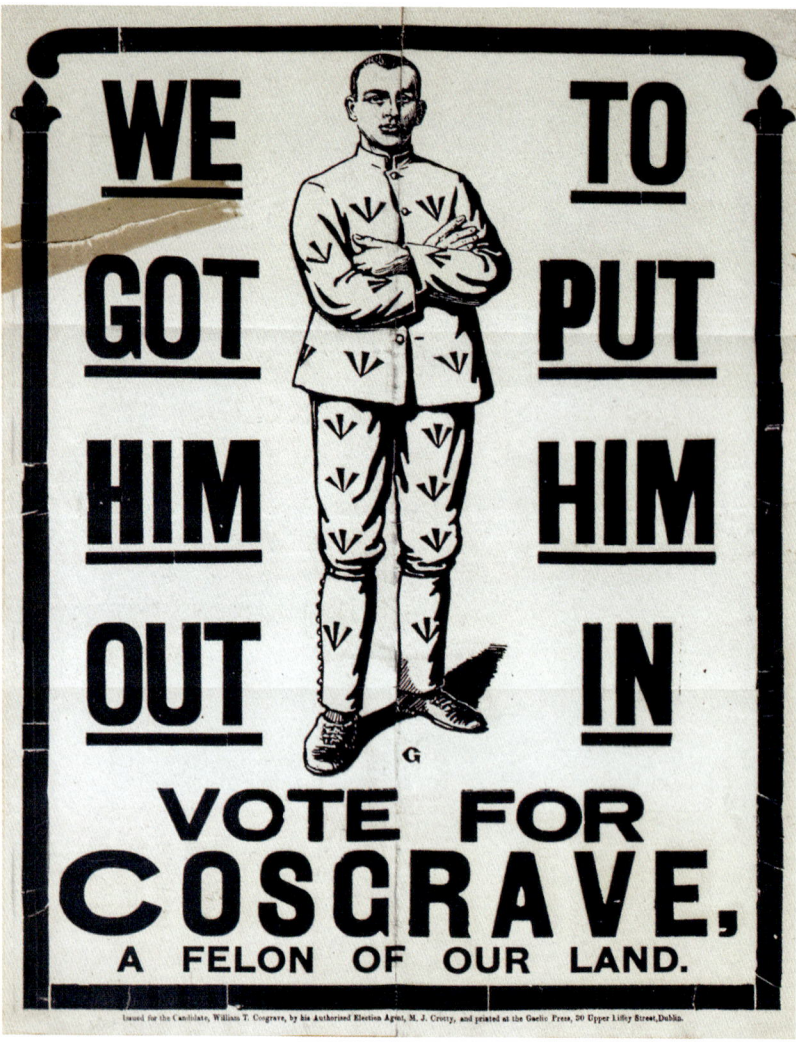

Left: the branding of 'felon' was proving to be a powerful vote winner, as was the phrase 'we got him out to put him in'. Another elderly IPP MP, the member for Kilkenny City, died in July. Sinn Féin selected William T. Cosgrave as the candidate for the resulting election. He had been sentenced to death, commuted to life imprisonment. After incarceration in English prisons, he had just been released in June 1917. Sinn Féin were on a roll. It mounted a strong campaign with large numbers of supporters, many of these Volunteers, swamping the efforts of the IPP.

In the election held on 10 August, WT Cosgrave won twice as many votes as his IPP opponent. Bonfires were lit and celebrations followed. Left: Cosgrave makes a speech from the balcony of Kilkenny Courthouse after being elected. His fellow MP, Éamon de Valera, looks on.

Right: each election was a stepping stone to freedom – the premise was that the road to freedom was through Sinn Féin. The party had adopted the principle of abstentionism from the London parliament. The Sinn Féin victories sounded the death knell for the old order, namely the Irish Parliamentary Party, which over the decades had tried to secure advantage for Ireland, working through the British parliamentary system.

In May 1917, amidst the political volatility, Lloyd George (Prime Minister since December 1916), proposed a forum to discuss how Ireland might try 'hammering out an instrument of government for her own people'. The Irish Convention was convened in July 1917. Participants included the Ulster Unionists, southern Unionists, the Irish Catholic hierarchy and the IPP. Significantly Sinn Féin declined to attend, on the basis that the terms of reference provided that in any solution, Ireland must be 'within the Empire'.

Right: delegates arrive at Trinity College on 25 July for the opening of the Irish Convention.

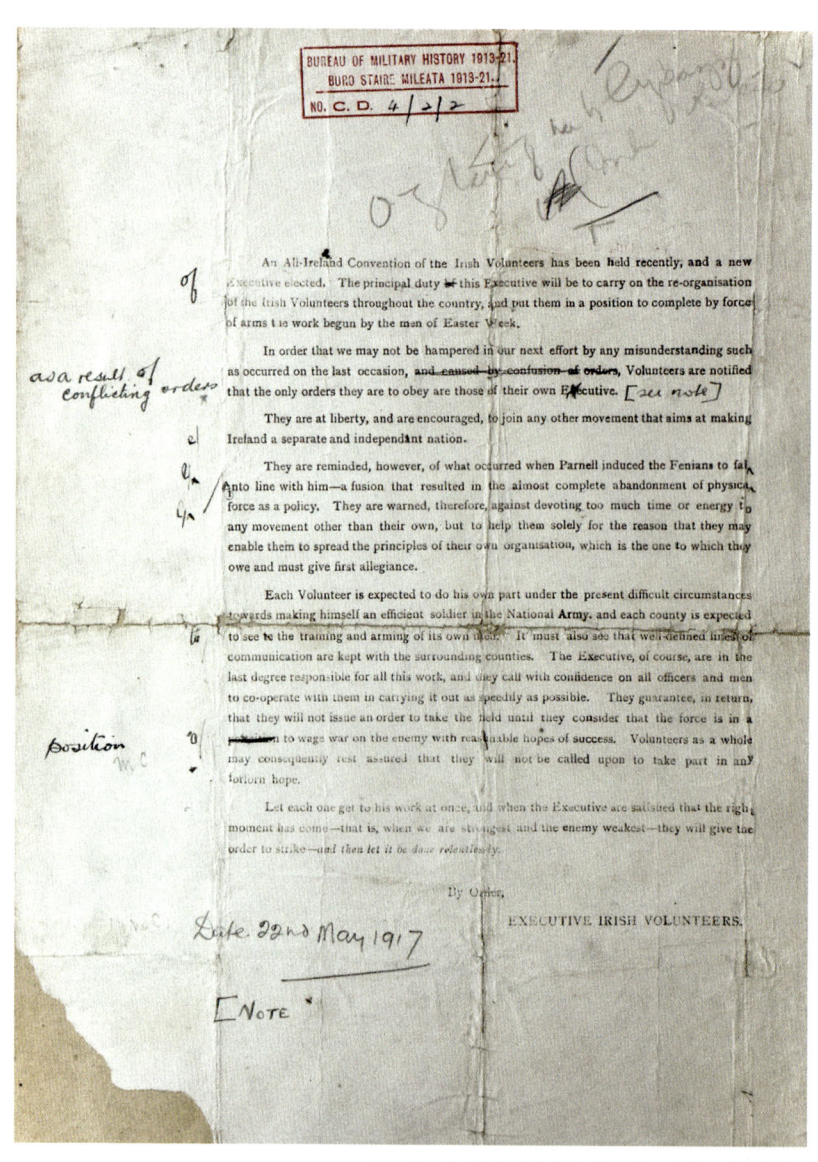

Kathleen Clarke, widow of Tom Clarke, had established the Republican Prisoners' Dependants' Fund. Impressed by Michael Collins, released from Frongoch at the end of 1916, she put him in charge. Collins's drive and energy ensured that he soon became a leading force in Sinn Féin and the renascent Volunteers. A convention was held in March 1917 and a Volunteers' Executive formed.

Left: a proof of a handbill explaining the role of the Executive and the task ahead, written by Collins and marked up with his corrections.

Below left: funeral of Thomas Ashe. This energetic man had been Commandant of the Fingal Battalion of the Volunteers, victors in the successful engagement at Ashbourne during the Rising. Like his fellow commandant, de Valera, Ashe's death sentence was commuted. He had been released in June 1917. Later he was convicted for making a seditious speech and went on hunger strike. He died on 25 September after a clumsy attempt at force-feeding.

Right: Ashe, seen with his jailers at Mountjoy Prison. Ashe's funeral on 30 September 1917 was a huge manifestation of support for the Irish revolution. It was a replay of O'Donovan Rossa's funeral in 1915, where Pearse gave the oration. The coffin was carried in a cortège through large crowds on Dublin's streets, flanked by na Fianna Éireann, Cumann na mBan and Volunteers.

Below right: Volunteers fire a volley at Glasnevin. Michael Collins gave a brief graveside oration: 'Nothing additional remains to be said. That volley which we have just heard is the only speech which it is proper to make above the grave of a dead Fenian'. Not the soaring rhetoric of Pearse two years before, but these few words matched the mood post-Rising and were a harbinger of Collins's future actions: direct and ruthless.

Below: a badge from the funeral.

On 25 October 1917, the Sinn Féin annual convention was held in the Mansion House, Dublin. Éamon de Valera was elected President. This was immediately followed by an Irish Volunteers' convention in Drumcondra. Demonstrating the close links and interchangeability between the two organisations, de Valera was also elected President of the Irish Volunteers.

Left: monument to the Irish Volunteers at Phibsboro, Dublin.

At the Volunteers' convention, Michael Collins (near right), was appointed director of organisation. Richard Mulcahy (far right) was director of training. In March 1918 the Volunteers GHQ was set up. Collins was made Adjutant-General and Mulcahy was appointed Chief of Staff.

Cumann na mBan, the women's auxiliary organisation linked with the Irish Volunteers, also reorganised after the Rising.

Right: an early Cumann na mBan meeting.

Below: a Cumann na mBan cycle company at a Wolfe Tone Commemoration at Bodenstown.

Left: the Irish Convention meets in Regent House, Trinity College. (Inset: Regent House today.)

Over the months, amidst the debates, extensive efforts had been made to promote agreement. Intriguingly, a form of mild 32-county Home Rule gained fleeting acceptance by the Unionists but foundered on opposition by the Catholic Bishop O'Donnell.

Left: John Redmond, leader of the IPP. Redmond's death on 6 March 1918 was one of many setbacks (the conscription crisis was another) for the convention. The convention ended in impasse shortly afterwards. In its report, a majority recommended Home Rule with special provisions for Unionists. However, the Unionists inserted their dissenting minority report.

Inset: the Report of the Irish Convention, signed on 8 April 1918.

Right: there are several claimants to being the location of the first armed action by the Irish Volunteers, post-Rising. The plaque here states: 'the first (barracks) capture...after 1916'. The Castletownbere Battalion raided the Royal Irish Constabulary (RIC) barracks at Eyeries, Co. Cork, on 17 March 1918 and seized five carbines.

> 1916 – 2016
> IN THIS BUILDING ON THE 1st OF JANUARY 1916
> TERENCE MACSWINEY PARADED THE FIRST
> COMPANY OF IRISH VOLUNTEERS IN BEARA.
> THE COMPANY WAS MOBILIZED FOR ACTION
> ON EASTER SUNDAY 1916,
> AND ON ST. PATRICK'S DAY 1918
> RAIDED THE EYERIES POLICE BARRACKS,
> THE FIRST SUCH CAPTURE IN IRELAND AFTER 1916.
> I gcuimne ar ár laochra
> a troid ar son saoirse dúinn.
> Cumann Staire Béarra
> agus Cumann Béarra Boston.
> Erected by
> Beara Historical Society and Boston Beara Society 2016.

Right: the former railway station at Gortatlea, Co. Kerry (on the Mallow-Tralee line). On the night of 13 April 1918, Volunteers seized the adjacent RIC barracks, advancing from the railway line. They only had shotguns and one revolver. Two Volunteers died as a result of gunshots fired into the barracks by an RIC patrol which had just returned.

Left: a cartoon by Ernest Kavanagh (who was killed by a bullet during the Easter Rising) on the need for Irish cannon fodder to fight the Hun. Recruitment from Ireland into the British Army for the war was a constant preoccupation of the authorities. Conscription was introduced in Britain in January 1916 under the Military Service Act. This was an extremely sensitive subject in Ireland, which was exempted from this legislation.

Left: a multitude of well-crafted and emotive posters endeavoured to lure Irishmen to the front. There had been a surge of Irish recruits at the outbreak of WWI, but as the slaughter of the trenches became evident, recruitment tailed off as the war ground on. The signing of the Brest-Litovsk treaty between Germany and Bolshevik Russia on 3 March 1918 allowed the Germans to move around 50 divisions from the east to the western front. It was a desperate gamble to gain victory before the arrival of the American expeditionary force. The Germans made a series of massive attacks beginning on 21 March 1918 and made deep incursions through Allied lines.

Right: a touch of desperation? Just 100,000 men needed to answer the call.

Reeling from the German assault and with a dangerous shortage of troops, the British made a fevered cost-benefit analysis: the number of loyal troops that might be raised by conscription in Ireland versus the numbers that would be required to enforce it. Despite being warned by the then Chief Secretary, HE Duke, that he 'might as well recruit Germans', Lloyd George announced on 9 April that a new bill would extend conscription to Ireland (linking it with the sweetener of a simultaneous introduction of Home Rule). A Military Service Act was passed on 16 April and the IPP stormed out in protest.

Below far right: anti-conscription cartoon.

Near right: the threat of conscription sparked opposition across the spectrum of political and public life in Ireland (apart from the Unionists). Here is a 'Protestant Protest' (albeit a minority one) against conscription.

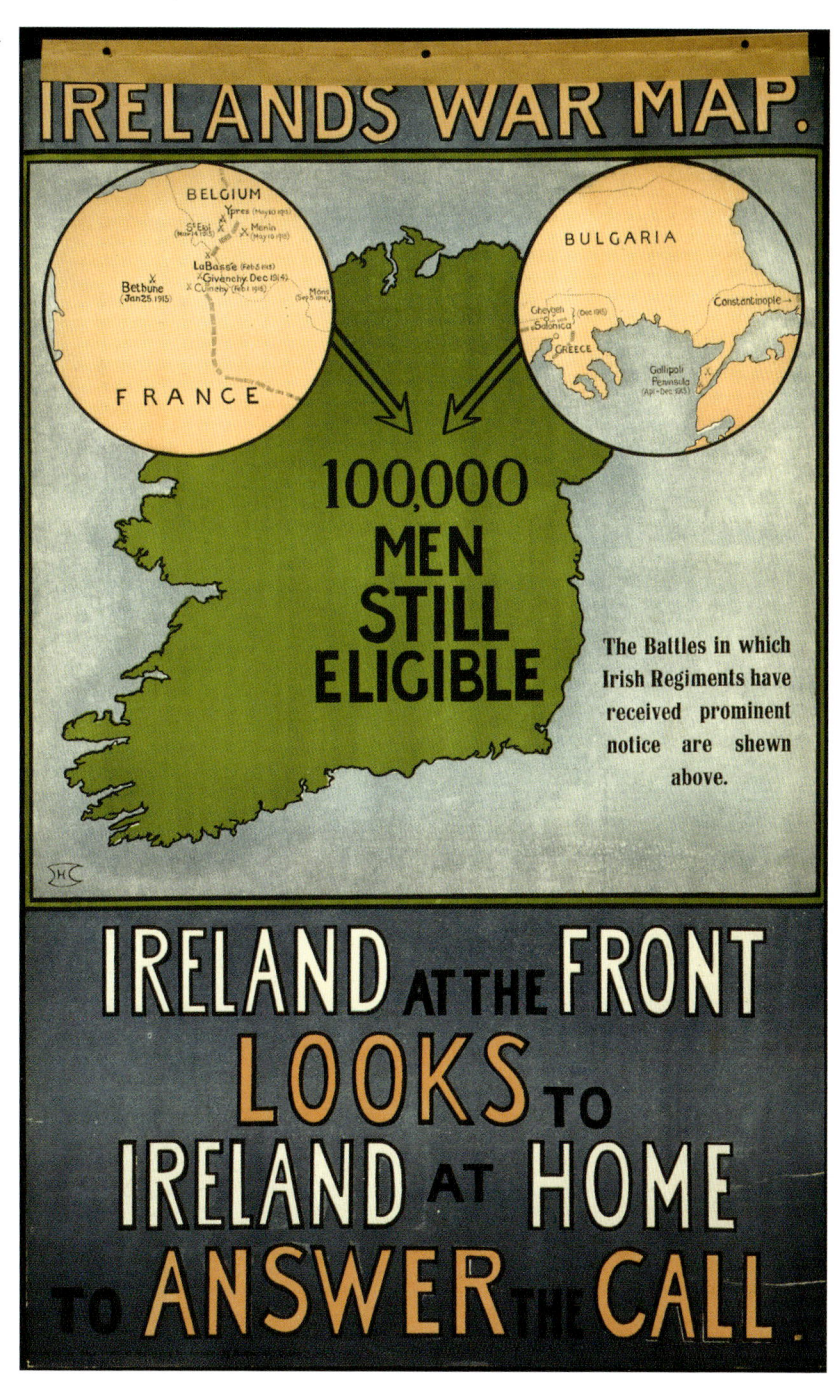

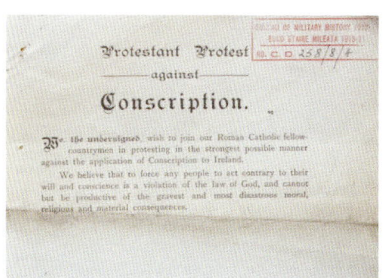

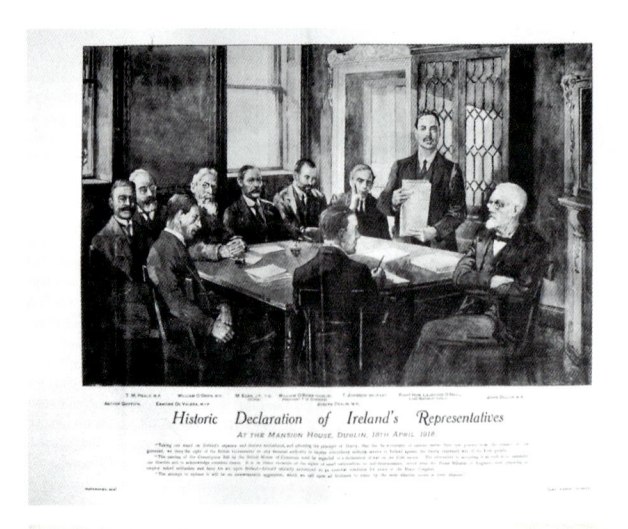

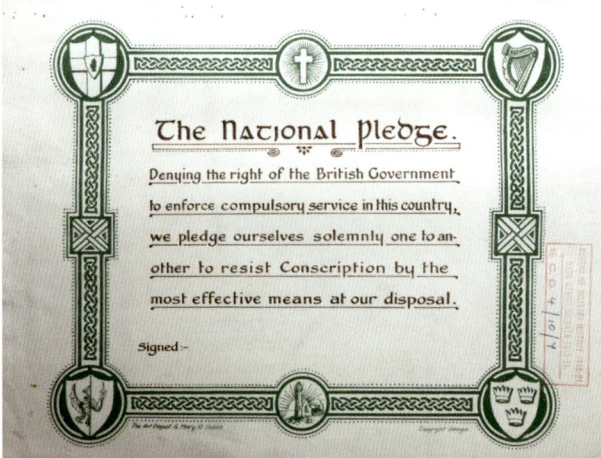

Left: there was almost universal opposition to conscription. Sinn Féin, the IPP, Labour, trade unions, and others met on 18 April 1918 in the Mansion House to plan resistance to conscription. They drafted a pledge and sent it to a special meeting of Catholic bishops.

Left: the bishops called for resistance to conscription 'by the most effective means at our disposal'. On Sunday 21 April the 'National Pledge' was declaimed at church doors across Ireland. Two million people signed the pledge. In the event, conscription was never implemented. Initially it was postponed to 3 June 1916, and then to October – and by then the war had been won. The botched attempt to introduce compulsory military service in Ireland by the British government, which led to universal opposition, was a huge miscalculation. The historian AJP Taylor said that this was the decisive moment 'at which Ireland seceded from the Union'.

Left: signing the pledge.

Above: Field Marshal Lord John French, first Earl of Ypres and former Commander of the British Expeditionary Force. He had been bullish on conscription – suggesting sending armoured cars and planes to Ireland to enforce it.

Right: David Lloyd George who, after becoming Prime Minister in December 1916, was to have a decisive role in shaping Ireland's destiny over the following years.

In the midst of the conscription uproar in Ireland, Lloyd George had decided to shake up its moribund administration. Field Marshal Lord French was appointed Lord Lieutenant. The intention was that he would act with more firmness, in effect as military supremo.
Right: Lord French arrived in Dublin on 11 May 1918 and later that day, accepted the oath of the new Chief Secretary, Edward Shortt, at Dublin Castle.

Left: pages from the Army HQ Southern District Intelligence Report of 30 April 1918. It notes the theft of gelignite and the attack on Gortatlea barracks. Also 'there is only one subject which occupies the mind of nine-tenths of the people...how...to avoid the conscription'. It finishes with an account of Joseph Dowling, arrested by the naval authorities.

In these febrile times, a 'German Plot' emerged. Dowling was arrested after landing on an island off the Clare coast on 12 April. Interrogated in London, it emerged that he had been a Connaught Ranger, who, after capture by the Germans, had joined Casement's Irish Brigade. He admitted that he had arrived in a German submarine with instructions to establish contact with Sinn Féin leaders. Dublin Castle considered that Sinn Féin had plotted with the Germans. The British cabinet decided to 'put down with a stern hand the Irish-German conspiracy'. Lack of any hard evidence did not stop a round-up of prominent Sinn Féiners starting on 17 May 1918.

Left: Dowling's death sentence. This was later commuted to penal servitude for life.

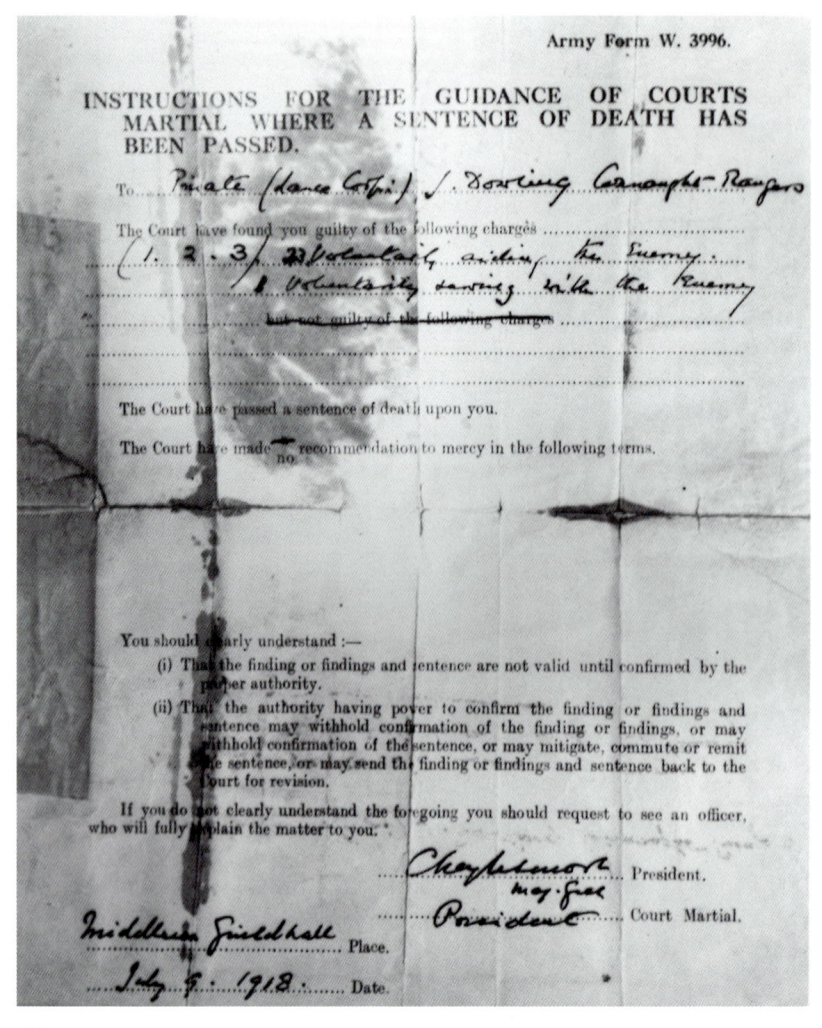

Right: some of the arrested. Many in the upper echelons of Sinn Féin were rounded up. Michael Collins had heard in advance, from his informant Ned Broy, of the planned roundup, and avoided arrest. He had warned de Valera – who declined to go into hiding and was arrested at his home in Greystones. Many of those arrested were at the more political end of Sinn Féin. The more radical cadre, such as Collins, Richard Mulcahy and Harry Boland, were still free. This was an ominous portent for the British, as this cadre encouraged a more militant approach amongst the nationalist movement.

ARRESTED IN IRELAND: THE COUNTESS MARKIEVICZ.

A NOVELIST SINN FEINER ARRESTED: MR. DARRELL FIGGIS.

A SINN FEINER ARRESTED IN IRELAND: MR. JOSEPH McGUINNESS, M.P.

A PROMINENT SINN FEINER ARRESTED IN DUBLIN: COUNT PLUNKETT, M.P.

THE SINN FEIN LEADER ARRESTED AT GREYSTONES: MR. EDMUND DE VALERA, M.P.

ONE OF THE ARRESTED SINN FEINERS: MR. JOHN McGARRY.

SON-IN-LAW OF COUNT PLUNKETT: DR. THOMAS DILLON, ARRESTED.

THE TREASURER OF THE SINN FEIN MOVEMENT ARRESTED: MR. WILLIAM COSGRAVE.

Right: surrounded by RIC and soldiers, in a country location, some of the arrested are escorted to a train for Dublin. Once again, Irish nationalists were shipped to Britain for incarceration in a variety of prisons.

Above: the wild and isolated terrain at Béal a' Ghleanna. On 7 July 1918 a group of Volunteers lay in ambush by the road here between Ballingeary and Ballyvourney in Co. Cork. As a horse and side-car conveyed two RIC policemen, the ambushers confronted them. A policeman was injured in the scuffle and the Volunteers escaped with two Lee-Metford carbines and ammunition.

Left: memorial at the ambush site, unveiled by Taoiseach Jack Lynch in 1970.

Right: the Cyclist Company, 4th Battalion, Irish Volunteers, parade at Sallins, Co. Kildare on 23 June 1918. All over Ireland the Volunteers recruited, organised, drilled and trained. They were bedevilled by lack of arms, which was to be a constant problem throughout the War of Independence.

Left: card from Countess Markievicz and Kathleen Clarke in Holloway Jail, December 1918. Those arrested in the 'German Plot' were still languishing in British jails.

Love & all good wishes from Constance de Markievicz I.R.A & Kathleen Clarke

Holloway Jail Dec 1918

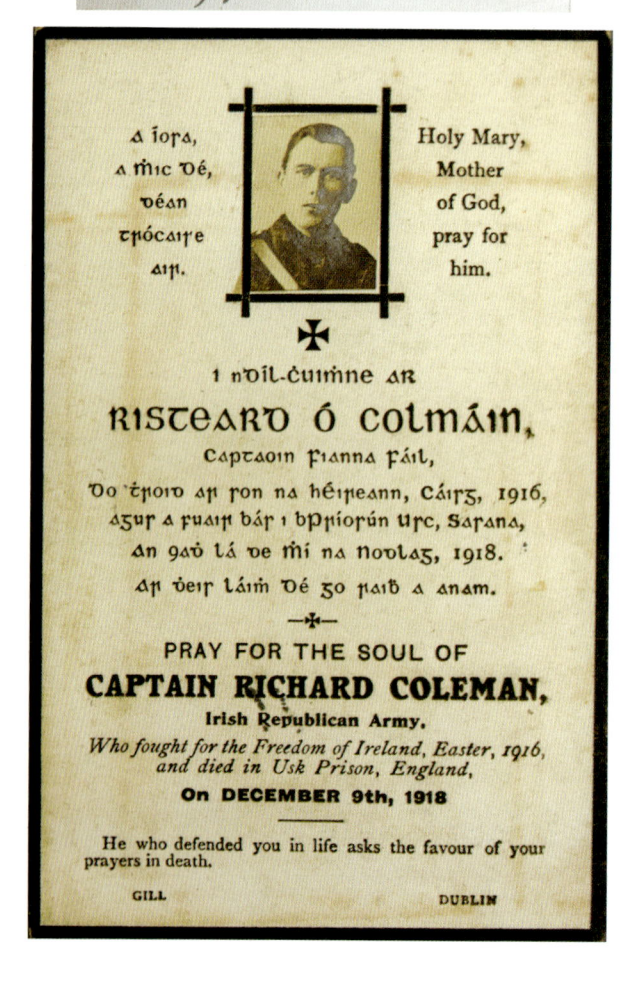

Left: memorial card for Richard Coleman. During Easter 1916 Coleman, from Swords, had been a member of the Fingal Battalion and was one of a group of Volunteers sent to Dublin by Thomas Ashe where he saw action in the Mendicity Institute under Sean Heuston. One of the 'German Plot' detainees, he was sent to Usk prison. In the cold and damp conditions he contracted the Spanish flu (the influenza pandemic which was raging across Europe.) He died on 9 December 1918. His body lay in state in St Andrew's Church, Westland Row. Over 100,000 people filed past – his funeral generated as big a crowd as that of his former commanding officer, Thomas Ashe.

A Íosa, a Mhic Dé, déan trócaire air.

Holy Mary, Mother of God, pray for him.

†

I ndíl-chuimhne ar

RISTEARD Ó COLMÁIN,

Captaoin Fianna Fáil,

Do throid ar son na hÉireann, Cáirg, 1916, agus a fuair bás i bpríorún Urc, Sarana, an 9adh lá de mhí na Nodlag, 1918.

Ar deis láimh Dé go raibh a anam.

—✠—

PRAY FOR THE SOUL OF

CAPTAIN RICHARD COLEMAN,

Irish Republican Army.

Who fought for the Freedom of Ireland, Easter, 1916, and died in Usk Prison, England,

On DECEMBER 9th, 1918

He who defended you in life asks the favour of your prayers in death.

GILL   DUBLIN

Right: on 11 November 1918 an armistice was signed between the Germans and the Allies in a railway carriage in the forest of Compiègne in France. With the war now at an end, the British Government immediately called a General Election – to be held on 14 December 1918. This election was more democratic than in the past – the franchise was now extended to include all men over 21 (previously only householders could vote) and women over 30. Thus it practically tripled the electorate. Foreseeing the election, Sinn Féin had selected its candidates by the end of November. Michael Collins and Harry Boland had a large influence – as a result the IRB was well represented among the candidates.

Right: an tÓglach was the periodical of the Irish Volunteers since 1914. It continued its theme of exhortation and technical instruction after the Rising. Here the edition of 30 November 1918 notes that the Great War is over but 'the seven-hundred year old war between Ireland and England goes bitterly on'. It laconically adds that 'during the next fortnight political activities will largely occupy the time of Irish Republicans'.

An tÓglác

OFFICIAL ORGAN OF THE IRISH VOLUNTEERS.

Vol. I. No. 7]   30th November 1918.   [Price Twopence.

NO ARMISTICE.

THE great war that for over four years has convulsed the world is now officially "ended"; but the seven-hundred year old war between Ireland and England goes bitterly on. An armistice has been signed in France; but in Ireland there is no armistice. All the military forces of the enemy are now as ever employed with the utmost rigour against those who are fighting for a free Ireland. The pretence that "peace" has come, as far as this country is concerned, is the most audacious falsehood. Some 200,000 enemy troops, equipped with all the resources which British military ingenuity and efficiency can provide, are located in our midst to hold our country for the enemy. They represent the claim of England to rule this country. Every mean device, every form of lying and treachery, every resource of bribery, every employment of traitors in our midst, every savage repression and petty persecution that can be safely carried out are resorted to by the enemy against all who stand for Irish independence. But the real essential fact at the back of all this is the 200,000 armed British soldiers, slaves employed to enforce slavery. They are England's one real argument in support of her claim to Ireland; and that argument may prove a rotten and worthless one.

For against these soldiers of England stand the young manhood of Ireland, enrolled in the Irish Volunteers to fight for the freedom of Ireland. Not slave soldiers are these men, but Volunteers! Not cowardly conscripts, led to the slaughter because they have not courage to resist the military service they loathe, but men who voluntarily accept discipline and danger in the cause of the country they love. No pale, puny anæmic products of English factory towns, but the pick of Irish manhood, the product of our Irish soil, clean-limbed, strong and wholesome. We, too, are armed and drilled; on any fair field one Irish Volunteer is a match for four of such British soldiers as we have seen in Ireland—creatures rather to be pitied than hated as the pitiful products and slaves of a capitalistic Imperialism justified in the exploitation of the many for the benefit of the few.

The British soldiers in Ireland represent the claim of England to hold this country of ours for her own use and benefit. The Irish Volunteers represent the claim of the people of Ireland to own their own country. Of the two arguments we think our argument is the sounder.

For the system on which England's "argument" is built up is in a process of disintegration. Everywhere in Europe, Imperialism, and all that it stands for, can be seen cracking and crumbling away. England remains its last stronghold; and even there its days are numbered. The ideal the Irish Volunteers stand for remains intact. The true principles of national liberty have more adherents to-day than at any time since the war started. Our fight for independence must be fought on our own soil; and our willingness to *fight* for it, not figuratively but literally, our readiness to shed our blood if need be in the enforcement of our claim to liberty, is an essential condition to success. People who are not prepared to fight for their liberty do not deserve to get it. But it is a heartening thought that never since the outbreak of war could we count on so many friends throughout the world as at the present day in our fight for liberty.

During the next fortnight political activities will largely occupy the time of Irish Republicans; but the soldiers of Ireland will not on that account relax their military activities. Important as the General Election is in regard to the securing of Irish freedom, the efficiency of the Irish Volunteers is even more important. When and where that efficiency may be next tested is unknown; the only thing for Volunteers is to be prepared *for all* contingencies. There is no armistice in Ireland. Our troops are at present like soldiers "in the trenches," confining their offensive to raids on a small scale; but ready, at any time, to take the offensive on a large scale. We have been in the trenches for a long time now; and have

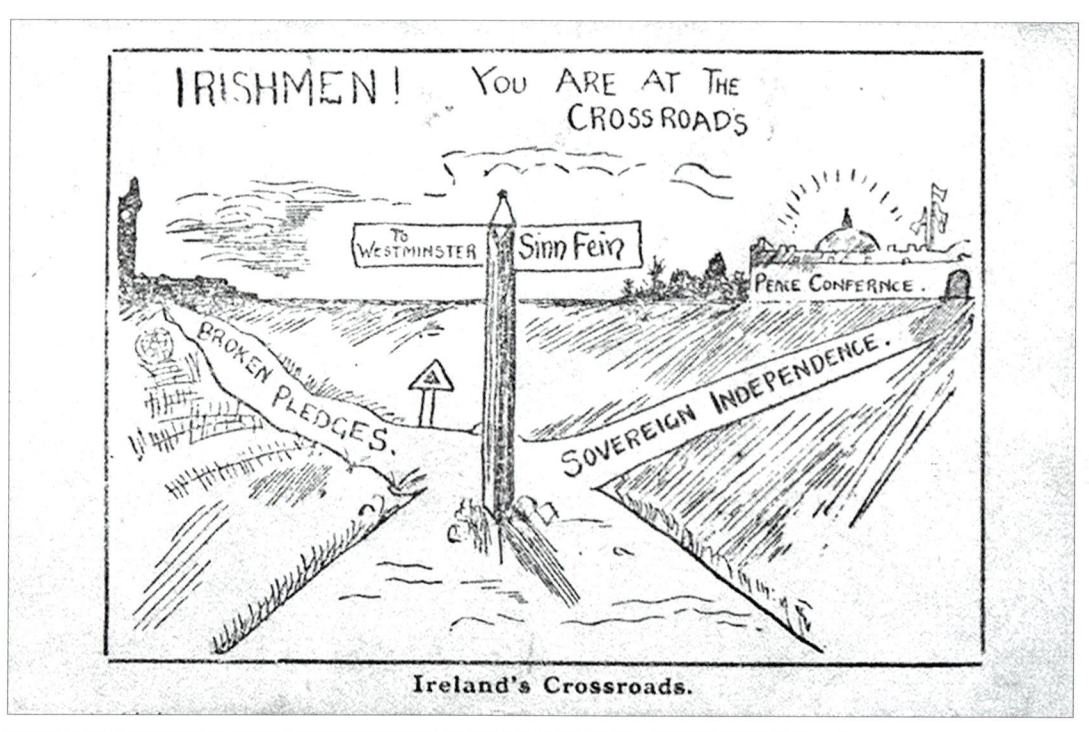

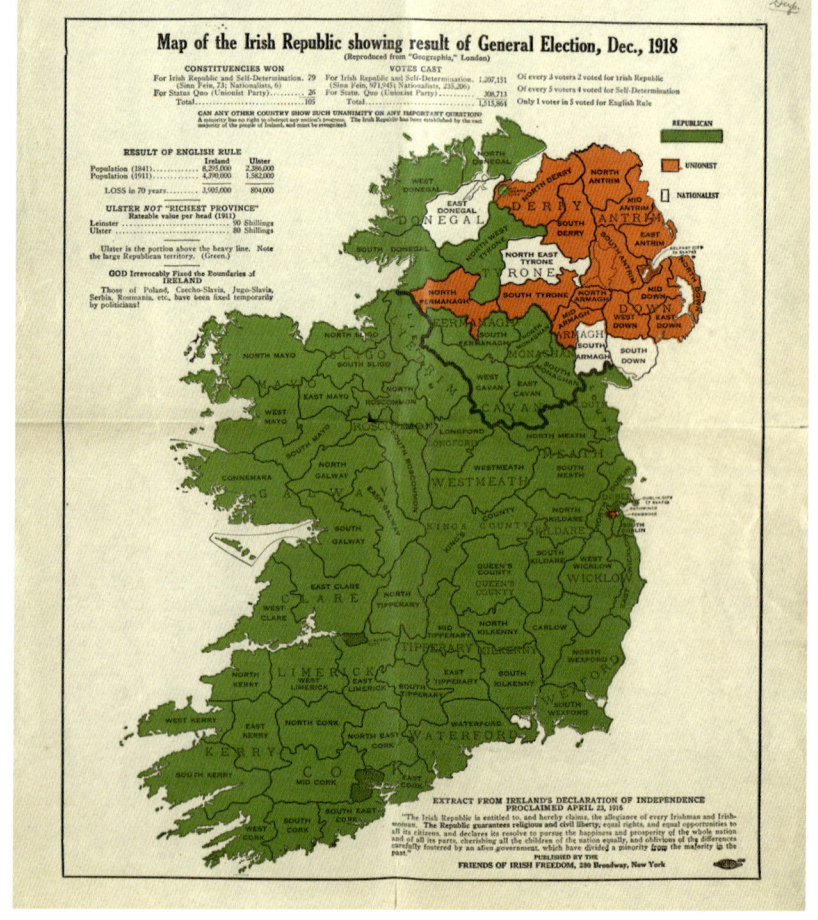

Above: a Sinn Féin postcard presents the choice at the 1918 election. The party offered abstentionism, with a hope of obtaining Ireland's sovereign independence at the post-war Peace Conference in Paris. Significantly, Sinn Féin's manifesto committed to using 'any and every means available to render impotent the power of England to hold Ireland by subjection by military force or otherwise'.

Left: overwhelmingly green – the map details the results of the general election in Ireland. It heralded the end of the IPP, which won only six seats. Unionists won 26 seats and Sinn Féin won by a landslide, gaining 73 seats.

Chapter 2
Ruthless War Begins as Dáil Meets
1919

The first Dáil Éireann, held in January 1919, ratified the Irish Republic, declared in Easter 1916. It also sought recognition of Ireland at the Paris Peace conference, but the delegation sent there was shunned. An ambush by Volunteers at Soloheadbeg, coincidentally on the same day as the first Dáil, resulted in two RIC deaths. This caused disquiet in senior Republican circles, but in reality the ambush marked the start of a ruthless phase of the war for independence. Several escapes of Republican prisoners from prisons ensued, particularly that of Éamon de Valera from Lincoln Prison. Reflecting the new purposeful struggle, Michael Collins established the 'Squad' whose mission was to eliminate spies, scourge of previous Irish independence movements. The DMP 'G' Division, effective gatherers of intelligence on Dublin Republicans, were neutered. Across the country, the effectiveness of the RIC, eyes and ears of the British grasp on Ireland, was diminished as they were boycotted. They were withdrawn from smaller, more vulnerable barracks in the face of increased attacks. As 1919 ended, an ambitious (but failed) attempt to assassinate the Viceroy, Lord French, in Dublin shook the British authorities.

Above: the first meeting of Dáil Éireann at the Mansion House on 21 January 1919. All elected were invited but the Unionists and IPP MPs did not attend. Seventy-three Sinn Féin deputies had been elected, but only 28 could attend as the rest were in detention in Britain. Other deputies answered the roll call for Michael Collins and Harry Boland, to mask the fact that they had just left for England to organise prison escapes. *Left:* a view of the proceedings.

Above: an admission pass signed by Count George Noble Plunkett.

Right: deputies who attended the first Dáil, with Cumann na mBan members. Cathal Brugha (arrow) was elected Ceann Comhairle, or Speaker.

The Dáil issued a 'Declaration of Independence'. Noting that the Irish Republic had been proclaimed on Easter Monday 1916, the Dáil ratified the establishment of this and pledged to bring the declaration into effect. It also issued the 'Democratic Programme'. In recognition that Labour had stood aside to allow Sinn Féin a free run at the election, Thomas Johnson, the Labour Party leader, assisted in the drafting. Approved without much scrutiny, it espoused social and economic ideals.

Right: the Dáil also issued a message to the 'Free Nations of the World', calling them to support the Irish Republic 'by recognising Ireland's national status and her right to its vindication at the Peace Congress'.

Ireland's Address
TO
THE FREE NATIONS OF THE WORLD

OFFICIAL ENGLISH TRANSLATION

HAVING PROCLAIMED HER INDEPENDENCE AT THE FIRST MEETING OF
DÁIL EIREANN
HELD IN THE MANSION HOUSE DUBLIN
TUESDAY, 21st JANUARY, 1919
THIS HISTORIC ADDRESS WAS THEN SENT OUT TO THE FREE NATIONS OF THE WORLD

Published by Fergus O'Connor, Dublin.

Left: the Soloheadbeg ambush site.

The South Tipperary Brigade planned to seize a consignment of gelignite being conveyed to the quarry near Soloheadbeg (around six kilometres north of Tipperary town). They had resolved the RIC escort would be shot if they gave armed resistance. On 21 January 1919, after several days of lying in wait, the Volunteers saw the cart approach with two council workers, followed by two RIC men. The shout went out: 'hands up'. Constables O'Connell and McDonnell raised their rifles. A second call for surrender was to no avail and the policemen were shot dead. The ambushers made off with the council horse and cart, loaded with the RIC rifles and 50kg of gelignite.

There had been skirmishes with the RIC during 1918, all random and unapproved by GHQ. Soloheadbeg was yet another such operation – but which resulted in sudden death.

Left: a wanted poster for Dan Breen. He, together with Séamus Robinson, Seán Hogan and Seán Treacy had led the ambush. South Tipperary was declared a Special Military Area (under the Defence of the Realm Act).

Right: plaque at Soloheadbeg.

There was general outrage at the death of the policemen.

Richard Mulcahy, Chief of Staff, IRA, later wrote of the incident: '...it had many regrettable and unwarranted features; it took place on the day the Dáil was being assembled...bloodshed should have been unnecessary in the light of the type of episode it was...'.

Right: the Sinn Féin Rúnaí (Secretary) replies to a letter requesting condemnation of the killing of the policemen. There is an element of prevarication: 'we have no idea as to who should be condemned'. In reality the ruthlessness at Soloheadbeg represented a loss of innocence – it was a foretaste of the bitter war that was to ensue in the years that followed.

Below: a proclamation offering a reward, pardon and protection, for help in catching the Soloheadbeg ambushers.

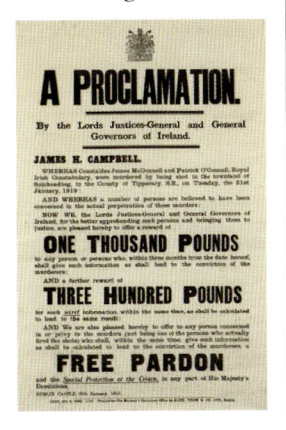

Sinn Féin

6 HARCOURT ST., DUBLIN.

6 Sráid Fearcair, Át Cliat.

27th Jan., 1919.

A chara,

    I am in receipt of your letter of the 24th inst. Sinn Féin cannot undertake to prejudge the case of the two armed policemen doing garrison duty for the English Government in Co. Tipperary who lost their lives. I think it is an extraordinary thing for any responsible person to inviate this Organisation to issue a condemnation when we have no idea as to who should be condemned. So far as we can judge at the moment, the position of the country is menaced and the lives of the people in it are menaced by, and only by, the forces of the English garrison. At all events, the moral responsibility for the loss of life to members of hostile enemy forces does not lie with the people who seek to defend their own population against them. I presume the two armed English policemen did not carry loaded arms for the sake of preserving life.

Mise,

RUNAIDHE.

Mr M.U. O'Shaughnessy,
Woollen & Linen Draper,
Kilfinane.

A PROCLAMATION.

By the Lords Justices-General and General Governors of Ireland.

JAMES H. CAMPBELL.

ONE THOUSAND POUNDS

THREE HUNDRED POUNDS

FREE PARDON

Left: Christmas postcard sent by Seán McGarry from Lincoln Prison. A key, made according to the scale shown here, was smuggled in inside a cake – however, the key did not fit.

De Valera, imprisoned at Lincoln, had made a wax impression of the chaplain's key. A replica was smuggled in but again the key didn't work. Finally Peter de Loughry, a locksmith and Mayor of Kilkenny, made a copy of the master key. It worked and de Valera, together with McGarry and Seán Milroy managed to escape on 3 February 1919. A waiting Michael Collins and Harry Boland brought them by taxi to safe houses.

De Valera reached Dublin and on 24 February took refuge in the gate lodge of the Archbishop's House in Drumcondra.

Near left: a memento autographed by de Valera dedicated to the priest who sheltered him at Drumcondra. He added 'ex loco refugii nostri', ('from our place of refuge') adapted from the introit of a Mass he had attended there.

Far left: Lincoln Prison.

Right: President Wilson (inset, portrait) speaks at the Paris Peace Conference, which opened on 18 January 1919, where the Allied victors discussed the peace terms for the war. A year before, Wilson had expounded his idealistic Fourteen Points. To the discomfort of the colonial powers, Britain and France, one of these called for 'adjustment of colonial claims' where the 'interests of the populations concerned must have equal weight...'.

Seán T. O'Kelly, delegated by Sinn Féin and the First Dáil, arrived in Paris on 8 February, to request support for Ireland's independence. In the event, Wilson, an Anglophile, who detested Irish-America, curtly refused to meet O'Kelly. The Chairman of the conference, French Prime Minister Clémenceau also ignored the Irish delegation. The victorious powers did not want to irritate Britain, or consider listening to a movement that had seemingly sided with the Germans in 1916.

Right: a rather optimistic postcard showing Uncle Sam welcoming Ireland to put its case for independence at the Peace Conference. The reality turned out to be radically different.

49

Above: postcard issued after Robert Barton's escape. Barton, a TD, had been arrested for making a seditious speech in February 1919. Using a file provided by Richard Mulcahy, he escaped from Mountjoy Jail on 16 March. He left a note for the Governor – 'owing to the discomfort', he 'felt compelled to leave'; he would send for his luggage later. Two weeks later, adding to the embarrassment of the British, 20 Volunteers escaped from the prison, using a rope ladder.

Left: a 1920s view of Collinstown aerodrome (now Dublin Airport). On the night of 19 March 1919, Volunteers poisoned the guard dogs, overpowered the guard and made off with 75 rifles.

Volunteer and trade unionist, Robert Byrne, detained for gun possession, was rescued from a Limerick hospital on 6 April 1919 by the IRA. In the fracas, an RIC guard was killed. Byrne died from wounds later that day. Thousands attended his funeral.

In a panic, on 9 April, the British declared a Special Military Area covering parts of the city, with the Shannon as a northern boundary.

Above right: troops, barbed wire and a Mark IV tank (the first intervention by tanks in Ireland) barricade a bridge.

Right: checking for passes – these were needed to enter the military area.

In protest at the military area and the inconvenience of passes, the Trades Council called a general strike on 13 April, delegating control to a committee. The committee, or 'Soviet' (workers' council) as it became known, managed the city in a peaceful and skilful manner, while the military were boycotted. After pressure from the local bishop and mayor, and with tepid support from the rest of the country, the strike ended two weeks later.

Right: in response to a shortage of money, the strikers printed their own.

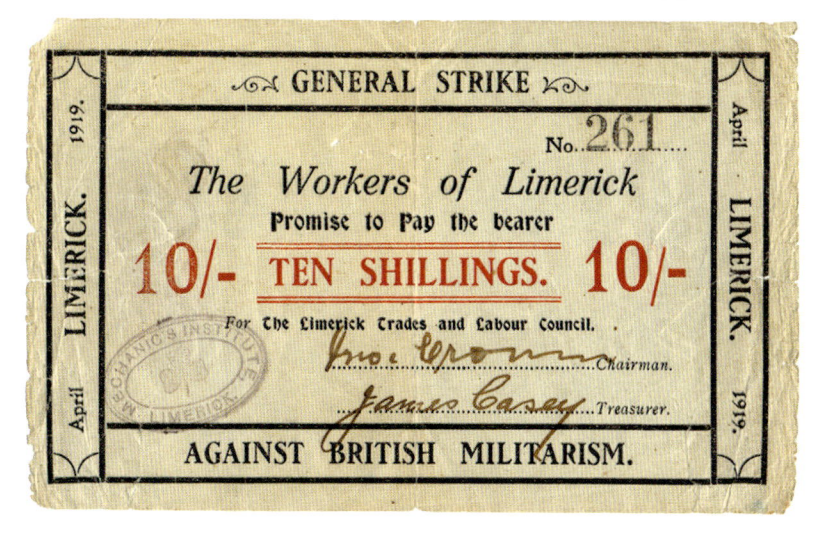

Left: Boland, Collins and de Valera in jovial mood outside the Mansion House.

Dáil Éireann sat on 1 April 1919 in private session at the Mansion House. It was a fuller attendance as the 'German Plot' arrestees had been released. De Valera was elected as President of the Council of Ministers; ministers included Collins in Finance and Cathal Brugha in Defence. On 10 April the Dáil authorised a bond sale of £500,000, as well as a boycott of the police.

Left: a proof of a $50 bond issued by the Irish Republic in the US.

Below left: Collins issued bond certificates to Republican personages (here, Eóin MacNeill) at St Enda's (Pearse's school). It was masterful propaganda – Collins arranged for the ceremony to be filmed; the attendance included the widows of the 1916 leaders.

Below: symbolic. Collins signed upon this butchers block, reputed to have been used when Robert Emmet was beheaded.

Above: 'X' indicates where Seán Hogan was rescued at Knocklong station, Co. Limerick.

Right: Seán Hogan. One of the Soloheadbeg volunteers, he had been captured by the RIC and was being escorted to prison in Cork. On 13 May 1919, his comrades, including Dan Breen and Seán Treacy, stormed Hogan's carriage in the Cork train as it stopped at Knocklong. After a gunfight, Hogan was rescued, Breen and Treacy were injured and two RIC men were killed.

Below: Knocklong today. The station closed in 1977.

Left: de Valera, flanked by Judge Daniel Coholan and veteran Fenian, John Devoy (right).

As the hopes of Irish success at the Peace Conference evaporated, Éamon de Valera took the view that salvation lay in harnessing American support. He set off as a stowaway in a cargo ship and arrived in New York, the city of his birth, on 11 June 1919.

As 'President of the Irish Republic' he embarked on a series of mass meetings across the United States making the cause for Irish independence. He launched a bond drive with a $5 million target.

Left: there was much coverage in the American Press when de Valera visited the Chippewa reservation in Wisconsin. He was made a chief, sympathising with the native Americans, as 'we are making a similar fight'.

Below: advertisement announcing a meeting.

DE VALERA MADE CHIEF BY THE CHIPPEWAS

THE REAL FACTS ABOUT
IRELAND
DeVALERA
President of the Irish Republic
—At the—
ARMORY
Sunday, Oct. 19
8 P. M.
SEATS WILL BE PROVIDED FOR ALL

Right: rarely seen in such a domestic setting, de Valera (with his aide, Harry Boland) poses with children. The children's father, JJ McGarrity (standing), a Philadelphia businessman, was a steadfast ally of de Valera when a split developed between him and Coholan and Devoy over the bond drive and interpretations of Irish independence.

Below right: a 'Hindu revolutionary' (in fact a Sikh) presents a sword and flag in San Francisco. De Valera, a supporter of freedom for subject peoples everywhere, proved an inspiration for Indian nationalists.

Below: sovereignty and sunrise in Seattle – a view of freedom dawning.

Sword Ceremony at Meeting of Valera and Hindu Revolutionary

Gopal Singh, Hindu revolutionary leader, under sentence of deportation, presenting sword and flag to Eamonn de Valera, Irish leader. In center stands Jajat Singh, independence advocate

55

Left: Frank Thornton and Tom Cullen, who, along with Liam Tobin, were close intelligence associates of Michael Collins, appointed IRA Director of Intelligence in January 1919. As he developed his extensive intelligence network, Collins correctly identified that Britain's control was founded on its spy network: while soldiers were replaceable, spies with their knowledge were not – and he now planned to eliminate these.

Left: the new assassins – the initial 'members of the Squad'. From left – Mick McDonnell, Tom Keogh, Vinnie Byrne, Paddy O'Daly and Jim Slattery. This group of tough young men had been selected from the Dublin Brigade of the IRA. Collins reminded them that previous Irish independence movements did not have an intelligence system which dealt with spies and informers; this was now going to be rectified.

Left: Squad victims – 'G' men Detective Daniel Hoey (tall, back to camera) and Detective-Sergeant Smyth (centre, facing camera). Smyth was shot on 30 July 1919 at Drumcondra and died weeks later. Hoey was shot in Townsend Street on 12 September.

Right: the Wesleyan Chapel, Fermoy. On Sunday, 7 September 1919, it was the turn of the British military to be attacked – a first in the present conflict. The Cork No. 2 Brigade, led by Liam Lynch and armed only with six revolvers, intercepted a party of soldiers who were marching to attend service at the chapel. Lynch called on the soldiers to surrender – a soldier swung his rifle and was shot dead. The attackers made off with a haul of rifles. In a foretaste of things to come, soldiers later emerged from the barracks, and looted shops in the town.

Right: last days of glory? Men of the RIC who fought in WWI, in the Victory march in Belfast, with Lord French taking the salute. The RIC was to bear the brunt of the increase in violence as the months rolled on.

Below: men of the RIC pose for the camera. The force was being militarised – new weapons were issued to counter the assault on the police.

R.I. Constable.—"Hands up! Who goes there?"
Loyalist (who has knocked up the barracks).—"Friend."
R.I. Constable.—"Friend be d——d; we haven't a friend in the country."

Above: the Irish Constabulary chase Fenians in Tipperary in 1867. Queen Victoria granted it the prefix 'Royal' for their efforts in suppressing the Fenian uprising. The RIC had been the efficient means by which the British maintained their control of Ireland, their eyes and ears across the country.

Left: cartoon showing the new reality of a constabulary under siege, boycotted and attacked. One source says that graffiti on walls ran: 'Join the RAF and see the World — Join the RIC and see the Next'.

Left: at the end of 1919 the RIC was withdrawn from small isolated barracks. The larger ones were transformed into bastions, with steel plates over windows and loopholes.

Right: map of Ashtown ambush

On 19 December 1919, the Viceroy, Lord French, was returning by train from his country house in Co. Roscommon. Volunteers (including Soloheadbeg veterans), led by Mick McDonnell, intended to assassinate him as he travelled in a convoy from Ashtown station to the Viceregal Lodge. The plan was that a cart would be pushed onto the road near Kelly's public house at Ashtown Cross, after the first car (assumed to be just an escort) passed by. As planned, they attacked the second car, but French was actually in the first car. A furious gunfight ensued. Martin Savage was killed. Dan Breen as well as several RIC men were wounded.

Right: taken in the aftermath, a postcard, looking south.

Below: all change today. Ashtown Cross looking north.

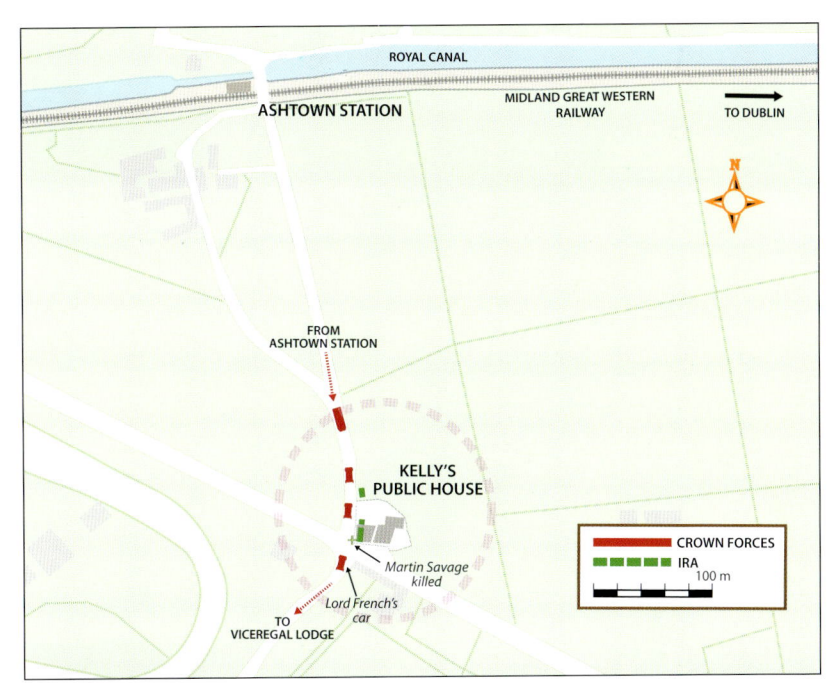

Above: the location where Martin Savage was shot at Ashtown.

Left: Lord French had a narrow escape – a bullet hole in the back of his car.

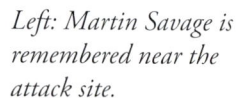

Left: Martin Savage is remembered near the attack site.

Below left: monument to Savage at Ashtown Cross.

Below: memorial card. Savage was only 21 when killed. A 1916 veteran who had been imprisoned in Britain, he was given a funeral with full military honours at his native Ballisodare, Co. Sligo.

Above: Inspector-General of the RIC, Brigadier-General Sir Joseph Byrne (a veteran of the Boer War), had been appointed in August 1916. A Catholic from Co. Derry, he encountered sectarianism at a high level. The ills of the RIC were blamed on him. At the end of 1919, as part of what has been called the 'Ulsterisation' of the police, an Orangeman, TJ Smith, was brought in as acting replacement.

Right: Lloyd George and some of his cabinet (Winston Churchill is seen immediately behind him). An element of gloom prevailed in the autumn of 1919. There was bad news from Ireland – although, in reality, not the nightmare it was to became in 1920. Fifteen police and one soldier had been killed in 1919 – apart from the shocking news of the attack on Lord French. Many new initiatives were discussed and begun, including reinforcement of the police.

Above: the South Lancashire Regiment at Wellington Barracks, June 1919. A large body of troops was stationed in Ireland, but up to now had been confined to providing support to the civil authorities.

At the end of 1919 the British Cabinet considered that Ireland was being afflicted by a criminal conspiracy, not a war. Thus the foremost necessity was to use the police, rather than the army, to defeat what they saw as the Sinn Féin 'murder gang'. In November (after the de facto departure of Inspector-General Byrne, who had opposed the measure), approval was given to greatly enlarge the RIC and recruit ex-soldiers.

Left: a recruitment flier. By year's end, recruiting for the RIC had begun in Britain. At a time of high unemployment, ex-servicemen were being invited to join 'the Finest Constabulary Force in the World' with an attractive pay of ten shillings a day.

The 'Home Rule' Act of 1914 had provided for an all-Ireland Home Rule parliament. Suspended during the war, and with the Peace Treaty concluded in Paris now in place, it was due to come into force. However in October 1919, in what was presented as 'a fresh attempt to solve the Irish problem' Lloyd George established a cabinet committee, chaired by Walter Long, former leader of the Unionists, to draft a new bill as a replacement. The resulting 'Government of Ireland' bill was introduced in December 1919. This new attempt at Home Rule (the fourth) had a decidedly orange tint: it was partitionist, proposing an Ireland divided into two separate self-governing territories: 'Northern Ireland' and 'Southern Ireland'.

Right: the man who crafted the partition of Ireland – Walter Long, with some of his committee colleagues.

On 26 November 1919, Dublin Castle proscribed Sinn Féin and allied organisations: the Irish Volunteers, Cumann na mBan, and for good measure, the Gaelic League (mistaken for the Gaelic Athletic Association). Dáil Éireann had previously been banned in September.

Left: the Sinn Féin headquarters, 6 Harcourt Street, after the proscription.

Left: Second Lieutenant Frederick Boast.

The year ended with a bizarre incident in the Phoenix Park, illustrating the trigger-happiness of the Crown forces. On the night of 27 December, just a week after the attempt on Lord French's life, Lieutenant Boast was in charge of the guard at the Viceregal Lodge. At around 1:30 in the morning, the guard said they heard shots. Boast and two soldiers went to investigate. At a point near the polo ground, they encountered a man, a farm labourer. The soldiers shot him, with Boast also being shot. A jury later recorded a verdict that Boast was killed by his own soldiers and condemned the military for shooting the civilian.

Left: Lord French's official residence in 1919 – the Viceregal Lodge, now Áras an Uachtaráin.

Chapter 3
The Struggle Intensifies
1920

As the IRA assailed the RIC, a wave of new recruits, soon known as 'Black and Tans', were dispersed across the country. A paramilitary force of ex-officers, the Auxiliary Division, was also established and assigned to the 'hottest' areas. Their brutal approach generated fear and incurred the hatred of the local population. A hunger strike by prisoners in Dublin ended with a botched release by the authorities. The refusal by railwaymen to transport Crown forces lasted until the end of 1920. March saw the Lord Mayor of Cork assassinated by masked men – the RIC Inspector accused of instigating this was killed in Lisburn, sparking sectarian riots. By mid-year, the IRA switched to ambushes of mobile patrols. Reprisals by Crown forces continued. The next Lord Mayor of Cork, Terence MacSwiney went on hunger strike after being arrested. His death sparked a world-wide wave of sympathy. Kevin Barry, a young Volunteer, was executed in November amidst mass protests. Later that month, the IRA assassinated many British spies across central Dublin. November ended with an ambush in Kilmichael where 17 Auxiliaries were killed. In December, Cork city centre was burned by Auxiliaries and the war reached a new intensity.

THE SINN FEIN RAID ON CARRIGTWOHILL POLICE BARRACKS THE WRECKED BUILDING AND A CAPTURED SINN FEIN CAR.

Above: following pressure from No. 1 Cork Brigade, GHQ authorised attack on three RIC barracks. On the night of 3 January 1920 they attacked at Carrigtwohill. They breached the barracks wall using gelignite and charged in. The occupants surrendered.

Left: a dazed-looking young constable sits in the Carrigtwohill barracks amidst devastation. The raiders made off with rifles and revolvers. Shortly afterwards, the barracks was evacuated by the RIC

Right: RIC ceremonial parade helmet. The insignia is a harp surmounted by the British crown. Throughout the first half of 1920, there was a wave of IRA attacks on RIC barracks.

Following their armed suppression of the 1867 Fenian uprising, the RIC had changed more towards being a more traditional police force. Now, the force had to revert to a paramilitary role. The weapons issued to the RIC were essential for their new battle.

Right: the RIC handgun was the Webley and Scott (break-top) Mk VI .455 calibre revolver.

Below near right: an earlier revolver, the Webley RIC 1886 model.

Far right: easier to conceal – the Webley MP Model .32 automatic issued to DMP detectives.

Below right: a Martini-Henry carbine. This had been issued to the RIC in 1899. A carbine (a shorter rifle) was easier for a constable to carry while on a horse – or bicycle.

Bottom right: a Lee Metford bolt-action carbine (with a six-cartridge magazine). These (along with similar Lee Enfield carbines) were surplus, converted to take bayonets and issued to the RIC in 1904 (replacing the Martini-Henrys).

67

Left: fixed in granite, a Dublin Metropolitan Police constable on the front of Great Brunswick (now Pearse) Street Barracks.

By the end of 1918, the 'G' Division of the DMP, had been losing its effectiveness under severe pressure from Collins's men. Detective-Inspector WC Forbes Redmond was brought from the north and appointed Assistant Commissioner to reorganise 'G' Division. Michael Collins assigned Frank Thornton to travel to Belfast, where he stole a photograph of Redmond from a district inspector's office. Now the Squad took up the chase. On 21 January 1920, Redmond, heading to his hotel, was killed on Harcourt Street by Paddy O'Daly. It was a single shot to the head as they knew Redmond was wearing a bulletproof waistcoat.

Left: a DMP detective's steel bullet-proof waistcoat (National Museum of Ireland collection) – sketch.

The RIC had suffered many resignations. From early 1920 onwards it was being bolstered by ex-servicemen, hurriedly recruited in Britain.

Right: this 'Punch' cartoon of May 1920 articulates British sympathy for the RIC, reeling under attack.

HOMAGE FROM THE BRAVE.

"Old Contemptible" (*to Member of the Royal Irish Constabulary*). "WELL, MATE, I HAD TO STICK IT AGAINST A PRETTY DIRTY FIGHTER, BUT THANK GOD I NEVER HAD A JOB QUITE LIKE YOURS."

Left: a modern-day replica of the motley 'Black and Tan' uniform.

Enrolment of the new ex-service recruits (mostly British but some Irish) in early 1920 was initially slow – the pace quickened around mid-1920 after the RIC got a big pay rise. There was a shortage of RIC dark green cloth – so the recruits were clad in a mix of military khaki and RIC uniform, but with an RIC hat. Soon they earned the soubriquet 'Black and Tans' (after the Kerry beagles of the Scarteen Hunt, Co. Limerick) – a name sometimes confusingly also applied to the separate paramilitary force of Auxiliaries. Later in 1920, batches of RIC cloth arrived and all the new constables received full RIC uniforms. The original idea had been to recruit an RIC special reserve of temporary constables, but it did not turn out to be so. In the event, the new recruits were assigned to RIC barracks around the country as ordinary constables. They soon gained a reputation for indiscipline.

Left: in this photograph issued by Dublin Castle, the new variegated uniform is explained.

Above: a ubiquitous presence. RIC constables on patrol observe from the doorway of a Cork shop.

In mid-1920 the first contingent of British policewomen arrived in Ireland to serve as searchers. They accompanied the Crown forces on raids and roadblocks and searched women suspects.

Right: a 'Lady police searcher' with 'G' Company Auxiliary Division, RIC (ADRIC) at Killaloe.

Above: happier days – Mac Curtain and his family.

Left: Tomás Mac Curtain, elected (since January 1920) Sinn Féin Lord Mayor of Cork. He was a Frongoch veteran and O/C of Cork No 1 Brigade.

Early in the morning of 20 March 1920, a group of men with blackened faces burst into his house at Blackpool, a northern suburb of Cork. Two raced upstairs and shot Mac Curtain dead in front of his wife.

Below: plaque at St Finbarr's Cemetery, Cork where Mac Curtain is buried.

Right: Mac Curtain lies in state at City Hall with a Volunteer guard of honour.
Below right: thousands line the route of what was called the 'most impressive funeral ever seen in Cork'.

On 17 April the inquest jury issued the unanimous verdict that 'the murder was...carried out by the RIC, officially directed by the British Government'. They returned a verdict of wilful murder against Lloyd George, Lord French, the head of the RIC, and two RIC Inspectors including District Inspector Oswald Swanzy – who was immediately transferred to Lisburn. Collins sent a team from Cork Brigade to work with the Northern IRA. On 22 August, they shot Swanzy in Lisburn. Sectarian riots broke out in the area and over a thousand Catholics had to flee.
Right: burned-out Catholic premises in central Lisburn.
Below: District Inspector Swanzy.

There was outrage at the shooting in Dublin on 26 March 1920 of Alan Bell, dubbed 'an elderly Resident Magistrate'. However, it turned out that he had an interesting past and present. He had been an RIC District Inspector, later a Resident Magistrate. There were dark allegations that he had been implicated in the 'Piggott Forgeries' case of 1887 where Parnell was purported to have backed the 1882 Phoenix Park murders (the fatal stabbing of the Chief Secretary for Ireland, and the Undersecretary).

Bell was a member of a secret committee in Dublin Castle, set up by Lord French in November 1919 to rejuvenate the intelligence system. Bell was said to be directing several agents including Assistant-Commissioner Redmond (shot on 21 January) who had been brought in to reorganise the 'G' Division of the DMP.

Bell had also been conducting an enquiry into the location of Sinn Féin funds. In this enquiry Bell summoned bank managers to appear before him and was forensically interrogating them on the location of the Dáil loan funds.

Left: Alan Bell's grave at Deansgrange Cemetery, Dublin.

Above: 'X' marks the spot at Merrion Road, Ballsbridge, where Alan Bell was shot.

Bell was commuting by tram from his Monkstown home to his enquiry in central Dublin. He had left his bodyguard behind at home and was unguarded on the tram. As the tram passed Ballsbridge, Mick McDonnell of the Squad tapped Bell on the shoulder and said: 'Come on, Mr. Bell, your time has come'. He was dragged from the tram onto the road and shot. His demise was primarily because his enquiry had come too close to the bone. Bell had already confiscated over £70,000 after a raid on the Sinn Féin Bank. However, unlike other Ministers of Finance, Michael Collins had an assassination squad at his disposal.

Right: the location of the shooting, today

The IRA GHQ issued orders to burn income-tax offices and abandoned RIC barracks across Ireland. Around 30 tax offices were burnt as well as over 180 barracks.

Left: debris being removed from a burnt-out income-tax office in Dublin.

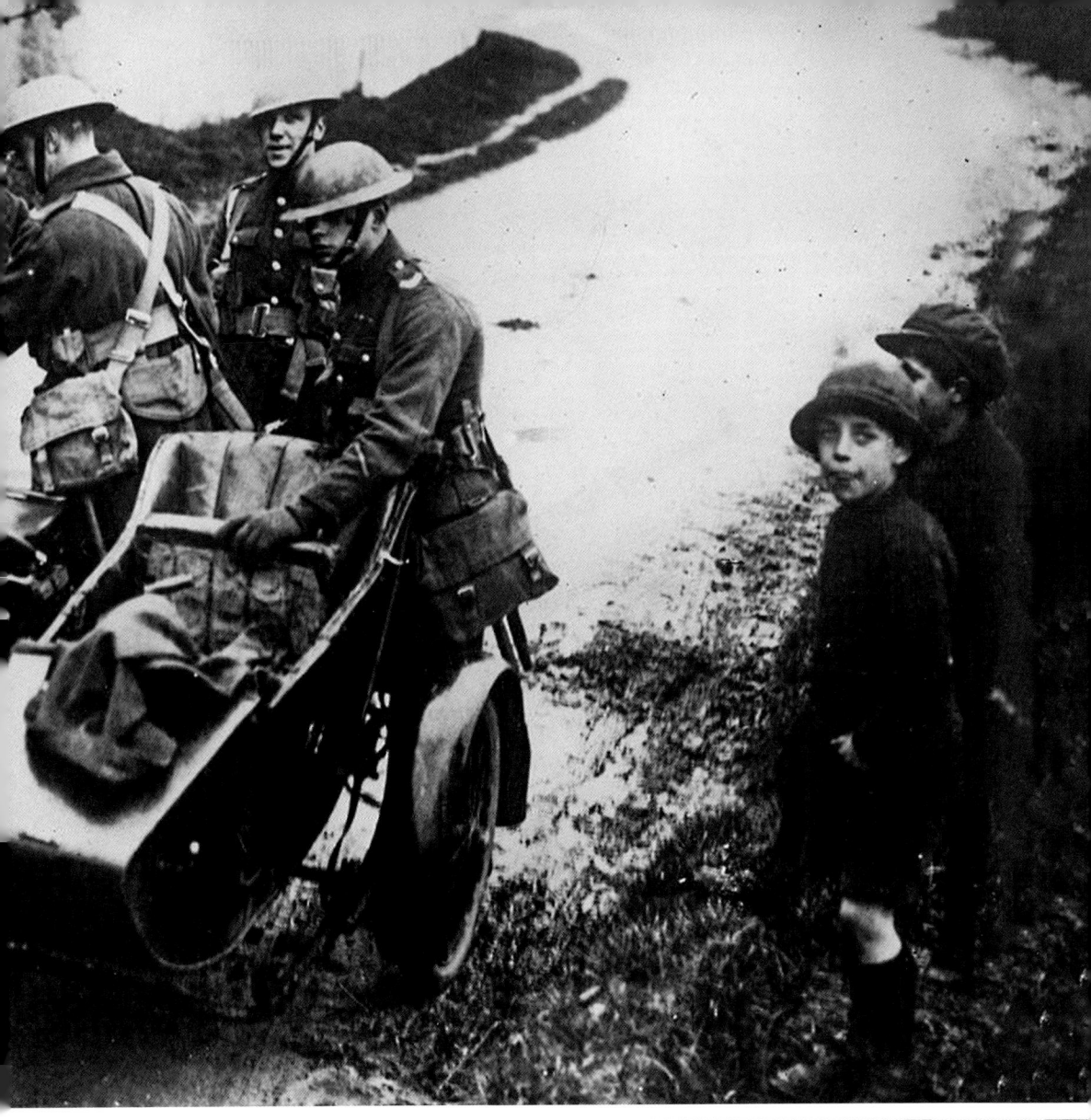

Above: a civilian being searched at an approach road to Dublin during Easter 1920. Nervous that a show of force would be mounted on the anniversary of the Easter Rising, the authorities blanketed the city with troops.

Right: all vehicles entering and exiting the city were stopped.

NOTICE.

All persons committed to prison are informed that they will not be able by wilful injury to their bodily health caused by refusal of food or in any other way, to procure their release before their discharge in due course of law.

(4803.)Wt.8312—2000.3/18.A.T.&Co.,Ltd.

Above: soldiers with bayonets hold back thousands protesting outside Mountjoy Jail during the hunger strike of April 1920.

Mass round-ups of 'Sinn Féiners' by police and military commenced at the end of January 1920. Hundreds were interned in British and Irish jails under the Defence of the Realm Act.

On 5 April 1920 republican prisoners (led by Peadar Clancy) in Mountjoy went on hunger strike demanding prisoner-of-war status. Mass demonstrations ensued. A general strike began on 13 April, to continue until the hunger strikers were released.

Left: notice issued to prisoners that a hunger strike will not 'procure their release'.

Above: illustrating the desperation of the authorities, the Royal Air Force had been asked to buzz the crowds.

Above right: one of several tanks deployed.

Right: an Austin armoured car near Mountjoy, with 'Up Sinn Féin' chalked on.

On 14 April, in an embarrassing volte-face, the authorities decided, under overwhelming pressure, to release the hunger strikers. In some confusion, both internees and convicted prisoners were released.

Below: 'L'Illustration' shows hunger strikers recovering in the Mater Hospital.

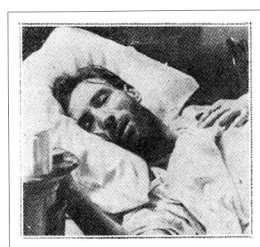

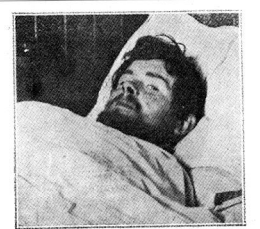

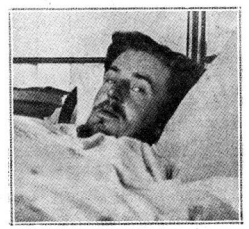

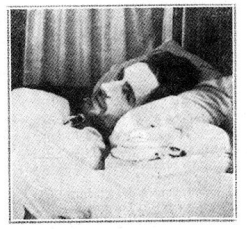

W. Byrne, de Dublin. Michael Maunsel, de Kerry. Michael Flynn. P. O. Reilly, de Dublin

Quatre des Irlandais. « affamés » volontaires, soignés dans les hôpitaux de Dublin après leur libération.

79

Left: General Sir Nevil Macready, previously Commissioner of Police in London.

In the first of a series of initiatives to strengthen security, he was appointed Commander in Chief of the army in Ireland. Significantly, he had experience of directing troops during the miners' strike in the Rhondda valley.

It was a period of change for the Irish Administration, perceived by London as being dysfunctional. The process had already started, but was accelerated by the debacle at the end of the April hunger strike, when convicted prisoners were maladroitly released along with internees. The head of the British civil service, Sir Warren Fisher, was asked to investigate Dublin Castle. His conclusions were damning: the administration was 'quite obsolete' and 'woodenly stupid'. It was to be all change at high level.

Left: new brooms, 1920. An autographed photograph, taken in the safety of Dublin Castle grounds. Seated, from second left, are a competent troika seconded from Whitehall: Alfred Cope (Assistant Undersecretary), Sir John Anderson (Undersecretary) and Mark Sturgis (Assistant Undersecretary).

Right: Sir Hamar Greenwood and his wife at their residence in the Phoenix Park. Greenwood, an MP, had been appointed Chief Secretary (a not-much-sought-after position) on 2 April 1920. Some were not impressed by him – Lord Oranmore noted in his journal: 'a Canadian bagman and a windbag at that'.

Below: Major-General Sir Henry Tudor. In May 1920 Tudor was appointed 'Police Advisor' (and in November became known as 'Chief of Police' after the retirement of the head of the RIC). With no police experience, most of his military career had been in the colonies (where he met Winston Churchill and became a life-long friend). During WWI he was an innovative artillery commander.
Tudor brought a pugnacious approach, with little feeling for political realities, to the task of directing the police in crushing the 'outrages'.

In mid-May 1920, dockers in Dublin refused to handle a cargo destined for the military. The Royal Engineers had to intervene and operate the dockside crane. The Irish Transport and General Workers' Union decided to apply the embargo to all members. Soon the action spread spontaneously to other ports and the railways – it became known as the 'Munitions Crisis'.

Left: soldiers lift off a truck at the dockside.

It was not a railway general strike, rather the workers' policy was that no train which carried munitions or armed troops or police would be worked. The railway companies responded by suspending or dismissing the employees concerned. As the months passed, the railways were effectively at a standstill in many parts of the country. The British military had to resort to the roads to transport men and supplies, which caused severe difficulties.

Right; 'Punch' takes a baleful look at the railwaymen's action, helpful to the 'Sinn Féin Assassin'.

Left: the postcard succinctly summarises the situation.

IRISH ENGINE DRIVER—
"STEAM IS OFF, BLACK AND TAN. NOTHIN' DOIN'."

THE BLAMELESS ACCOMPLICE.

IRISH RAILWAYMAN (*to Sinn Fein Assassin*). "YOU'LL BE ALL RIGHT. DETESTING MURDER, AS MR. THOMAS SAYS I DO, I'VE TAKEN CARE THAT THAT FELLOW SHOULD HAVE NO AMMUNITION."

["The Irish members of the N.U.R. expressed publicly their feeling of disgust at murder and outrage."—*Mr. J. H. THOMAS.*]

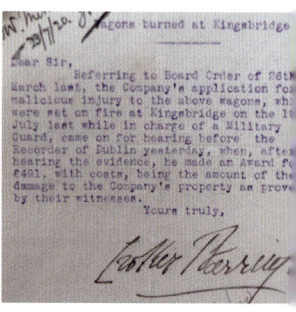

Left: in mid-June 1920, delegates of the National Union of Railwaymen and the Irish railway workers met Lloyd George at Downing Street. There was no meeting of minds, nor was there with the British labour movement which did not give any effective assistance to the Irish transport workers.

The British Government considered withdrawing the subsidy given to the railway companies – but did not enforce this. There was an appeal for funds to support the dismissed workers, whose numbers reached over a thousand by August. However, as the railwaymen's lost wages grew and the number of dismissed increased, on 21 December 1920 a railwayman's conference in Dublin voted for an unconditional return to work.

Left: a list prepared by the Great Northern Railway (I) at the end of October 1920, giving details of drivers who were suspended.

Left: memo to the GS&WR Secretary informing that the claim for the damage to the wagons burned at Kingsbridge was approved.

Right: the damage at the goods yard at Kingsbridge (now Heuston) Station. On 19 July Volunteers of 1st Battalion, 1st Dublin Brigade overpowered a military guard. They set fire to several wagons containing munitions and made off with rifles and ammunition.

Below: the Dublin Fire Brigade were called. They stopped the fire spreading but refused to save the military stores in the wagons.

DUBLIN FIREMEN GRIN AS MILITARY STORES BURN—This Dublin fire brigade enjoyed the blaze that destroyed a number of freight cars carrying military stores and munitions. Although the men refused to attempt to put out the fire, they stood by to prevent a spread of the flames to other railway property. The fire preceded a raid in which the military guard on the munitions train was overpowered and rifles and ammunition captured.

85

Above: medium Mark A Whippet tanks clatter through the mist along a Co. Clare road, in November 1919. A tank is not primarily designed to carry troops, as evidenced by the soldiers awkwardly perched on the tanks. Some of these are likely to be the crew, escaping from the unpleasant heat and fumes of the interior. Left: this 'Shemus' cartoon depicts the British juggernaut that was rolling over Ireland. A tank might not have the flexibility of an armoured car but it was a visible manifestation of military might. By late 1919 a variety of Mark IV and medium Whippet tanks was assigned throughout Ireland.

Right: members of the Royal Tank Corps stand in front of a Whippet at an Irish barracks.

The Whippets were scouting vehicles. They were, as the name suggests, faster and lighter (at 14 km/hr and 14 tonnes) than the Mark IV.

Right: 'Preserving the Peace in Disordered Dublin'. The 'Graphic' presents this Mark A Whippet tank (with prominent recognition markings) on a Dublin street, in early 1920, as an instrument of peace.

Right: a Mark IV on display at Ashford, Kent. The red and white stripes were British recognition markings used in WWI.

The Mark IV, introduced in 1917, was the much improved version of the original British tanks of WWI. Over 1,200 were built. Heavily armoured, they weighed 28 tonnes, and were correspondingly slow at 6 km/hr.

As the conflict in Ireland escalated, armoured cars were seen as more effective than tanks.

Left: a US-made variant of the Jeffery Quad armoured car, with a single rotating turret, at Pancho Villa State Park, New Mexico.
In 1915 a batch of around 40 US-made Jeffery Quad four-wheel drive truck chassis were shipped to Canada where armoured hulls were fitted. These were sent to England with the Canadian Army during WWI. The British later acquired these, shipping half to India and the rest to Ireland. By 1919, over 20 of this type were stationed in Ireland.

After the outbreak of war in 1914, the Imperial Russian Army had ordered armoured cars from the Austin Motor Company, specifying a twin turret design. In 1918 a batch of an upgraded variant could not be sent to Russia due to the revolution. Purchased by the British Army, some were sent to Ireland in 1919.

Left: an Austin armoured car in the Phoenix Park, 1919.

Above: an Austin armoured car in front of the RIC barracks at Ennis, Co. Clare in November 1919.

Right: a Hotchkiss .303 machine gun (this example is mounted on a Peerless) was mounted on each turret of the 1918-model Austin used by the British Army.

Above: a front view of a Peerless armoured car. From July 1920, the Austin armoured cars were replaced by Peerless models.

After WWI, the British, involved in 'imperial policing' around the world, were short of armoured cars. They had a surplus of thousands of US-made five-tonne Peerless trucks which were highly regarded for strength and performance. It was decided to fit an Austin armoured car body on a Peerless chassis.

Left: Peerless armoured cars at the Austin factory in 1920.

Above: the Peerless from the rear. Placing a shorter Austin body on the Peerless chassis resulted in an odd construct – the chassis now projected at the end.

Right: a Peerless in Belfast, 1920.

Weighing over seven tonnes the Peerless was ponderous and heavy. It had solid rubber tyres and could not easily travel on what were the many poor Irish country roads. It also was in danger of bogging down on softer ground – and was better suited only to the more well-paved urban roads.

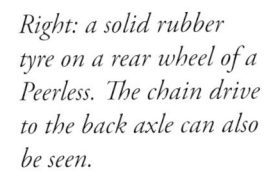

Right: a solid rubber tyre on a rear wheel of a Peerless. The chain drive to the back axle can also be seen.

Above; a broken-down Peerless tows another through a Dublin street.

Left: as the conflict escalated, Crown forces became a constant presence. Here, on Sackville (now O'Connell) Street, troops with bayonets jostle civilians with Peerless and Rolls-Royce armoured cars on hand. Clerys store (still being reconstructed after the damage of 1916) is in the background.

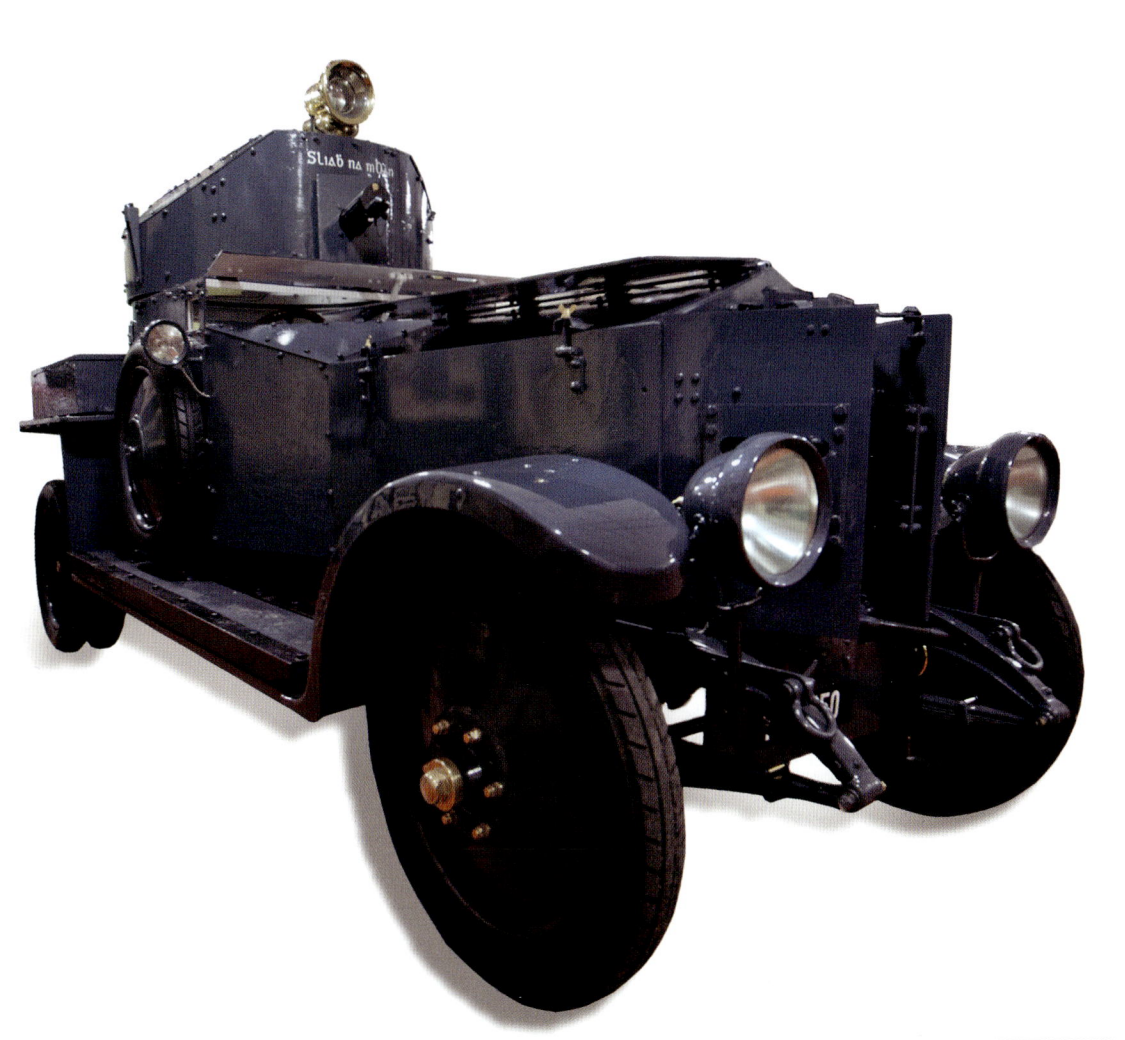

Above: the Rolls-Royce armoured car, known – due to their superb mobility – as a 'Whippet' (not to be confused with the medium tanks of the same name, see page 86). This model, Sliabh na mBan, was present at Béal na Blá where Michael Collins was shot in 1922.

Right: Rolls-Royce armoured cars had been in Ireland since 1916. Seven Rolls Royces (one seen here in a Dublin barracks in 1916) were rushed to Dublin, just as the Rising ended.

LA DOMENICA DEL CORRIERE

Anno XXII. — Num. 50. — 12-19 Dicembre 1920. — Centesimi 20 il numero.

Metodi della grande guerra che la guerra civile fa rivivere nella travagliata Irlanda. Nelle vie di Dublino: l'avanzata di una colonna di rivoltosi è arrestata da un'autoblindata con il lancio di bombe fumogene.

(Disegno di A. Beltrame).

In January 1921, a batch of a modernised version of the Rolls-Royce armoured car, which had been earmarked for Mesopotamia, was diverted to Ireland. This was a formidable machine: faster, quieter, more reliable and tougher than the Peerless.

Right: a Vickers .303 water-cooled machine gun was mounted in the Rolls-Royce turret and could fire at a withering rate of 450 rounds per minute.

Right: the cab and turret of Sliabh na mBan – it took a crew of three.

Right: refined, reliable and smooth-running – the Silver Ghost six-cylinder 7.5 litre engine.

Left: an Italian view of a Rolls-Royce armoured car in Dublin with troops and Auxiliaries.

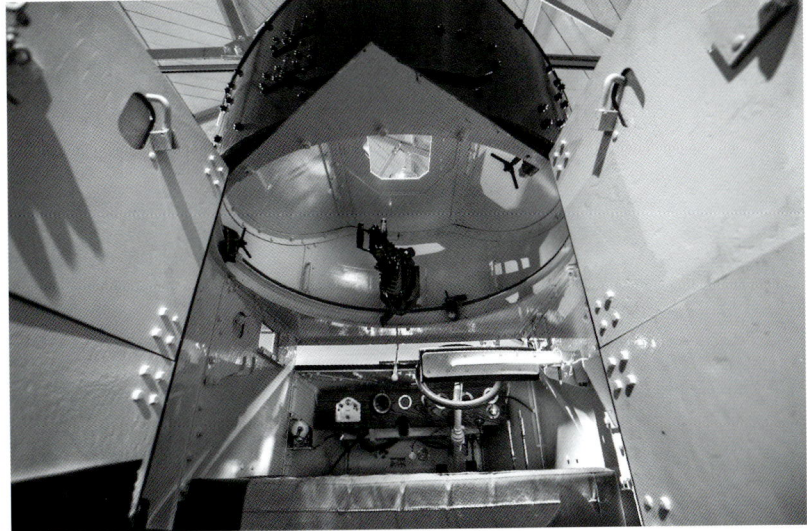

As the war escalated all over Ireland, there was an increase in road patrols by the Crown forces. Left: the Chief Secretary, Hamar Greenwood (with his wife) examines a new type of armour on a truck at Beggar's Bush Barracks.

The 'Munitions Crisis' of 1920 resulted in the Crown forces having to travel exclusively by road rather than rail. In the light of an increasing frequency of attacks, the vehicles were 'up-armoured'. Where 25mm armoured plate (adequate for machine-gun fire) was used, the vehicles were called 'tactical lorries' and those with 12mm plate (adequate for small-arms fire) were called 'protected lorries' – the latter mainly used in urban situations.

Left: a bull-nosed 1919-model Crossley 25/30 hp lorry, with experimental armour. Several vehicle types were used to transport military and police. The most ubiquitous was the Crossley 20/25 light truck, known as a 'Crossley Tender'. Proven during WWI, it had a rugged chassis, powered by a reliable 4.5 litre engine.

Left: a Crossley Tender, shielded by armour plate, transports Auxiliaries, encased under a protective wire mesh.

Right: a Lancia 'cage' armoured personnel carrier, of the Ulster Folk and Transport Museum. This (a Triota variant, introduced in 1921) served with the RUC.

Lancia IZ model trucks (made in Turin) had been used by the Allies during WWI on the Italian and Serbian fronts. The British had acquired some for their fleet and then sent surplus trucks to Ireland in July 1920. After arrival, these, a little larger than a Crossley, were armoured to provide a protected rear enclosure for the crew. An angled front enclosed the driver. A sloped mesh wire was erected on top (with a space beneath to allow firing through) to repel grenades. In 1921, the RIC and the Auxiliary Division RIC increasingly operated these vehicles for patrols in town and country.

Right: an RIC Transport Division vehicle yard.

Below: an RIC patrol in Cork in 1921.

Left: where the RIC barracks once stood in Kilmallock, Co. Limerick. The tall Carroll's building is on the left.

On 27 April 1920, the barracks at Ballylanders was attacked – the RIC within surrendered. On the night of 27 May, the IRA then attacked Kilmallock barracks (attacked by Fenians in 1867 – inset, old postcard showing the barracks, with adjacent tall house.) Like all barracks it was heavily fortified with steel shutters and sandbags. There had been extensive IRA preparation; road and rail access to the town had been cut. It was one of the biggest encounters in the war so far – 30 Volunteers were in the attack team with another 40 in support.

At around 10:00 pm fire was opened from buildings opposite. Volunteers on the roof of the adjacent Carroll's managed to punch a hole in the lower barracks roof and threw in bottles of petrol and paraffin. Eventually a Mills bomb set the building on fire. The RIC and the attackers exchanged fierce fire through the night. As the fire spread, the RIC withdrew to a fortified rear building, leaving behind two dead.

Left: memorial to Liam Scully.

Above: Mick O'Dea's painting 'The Defenders', based on a photograph of the RIC survivors at Kilmallock.

As dawn broke, the IRA, out of ammunition, withdrew from the attack. Volunteer Captain Liam Scully was fatally wounded at this point.

Left: insignia seized from the barracks by the IRA.

Right: a 1920 Irish Constabulary Medal for gallantry awarded to Constable Jonathan Holmes, one of the RIC defenders.

Left: Constable Jeremiah Mee's grave at Glasnevin.

On 19 June 1920, Lieutenant-Colonel Smyth (accompanied by Major-General Tudor), arrived at Listowel barracks which the RIC had refused to hand over to the British military. Smyth told them that there was going to be a ruthless campaign and if innocent persons were killed, then 'no policemen will get into trouble for shooting any man'. Constable Mee replied: 'You forget you are addressing Irishmen'. He placed his belt and bayonet on a table and said 'to hell with you, you murderer'. The RIC men resigned afterwards. In the months that followed, over a thousand RIC men, already under severe pressure, also resigned.

Lieutenant-Colonel Smyth's remarks made him a marked man. On 17 July 1920 an IRA party entered the County Club, in Cork, where Smyth was resident. In one account, Dan 'Sandow' O'Donovan said to him: '...your orders were to shoot on sight. Well you are in sight now, so make ready!' Smyth was shot in the head and an RIC Inspector with him was injured.

Left: the former County Club, South Mall, today.

Above: Lieutenant-Colonel Gerald Smyth was born in India, where his father was Punjab High Commissioner. He served in France where he lost an arm, and was mentioned in dispatches. In 1920 this battle-hardened soldier was seconded to the RIC as Divisional Commissioner for Munster.

Above right: the funeral service at Cork military barracks. Smyth was buried in Banbridge (where his mother was from). Train drivers in Cork had refused to man the train carrying the coffin, so it left by road.

Right: Belfast. The killing sparked the latent sectarianism there and there were riots in Banbridge and Belfast, with many fatalities.

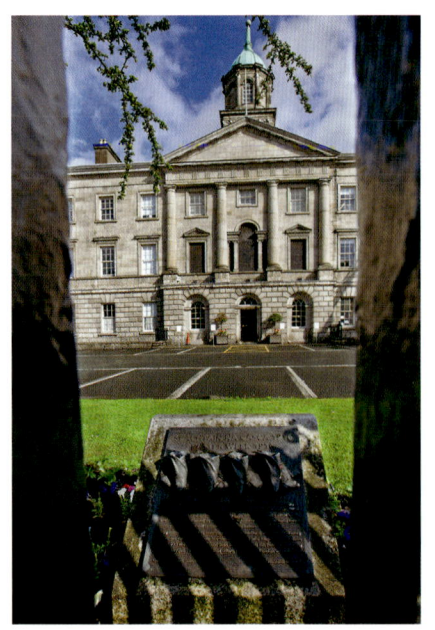

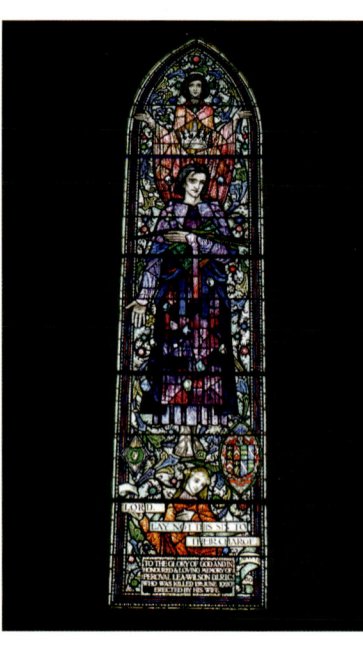

Far left; the forecourt of the Rotunda Hospital in Dublin.

Near left: stained glass memorial to Captain Percival Lea-Wilson in Gorey Church.

During the 1916 Rising, the rebels, after surrendering on 29 April, were corralled into the forecourt of the Rotunda. One of the British officers, Captain Lea-Wilson began to abuse the prisoners, particularly the crippled Seán MacDermott and the elderly Tom Clarke. Michael Collins, one of the detainees, witnessed this.

In 1920, Lea-Wilson was RIC District Inspector for North Wexford, In addition to his reputation for his 1916 behaviour, he was considered to be over-zealous in the discharge of his duties in Wexford. Michael Collins sent Liam Tobin (also bullied by Wilson at the Rotunda) and Frank Thornton of GHQ Intelligence to Gorey to assassinate him. On the morning of 15 June they shot Lea-Wilson as he walked home from the railway station.

Left: an RIC encomium to Lea-Wilson. His widow later donated a painting to the Jesuits which was eventually recognised in 1990 by an art expert as Caravaggio's 'The Taking of Christ'.

Above: Brigadier-General Charles Lucas and his captors.

On 26 June, Brigadier-General Lucas, fishing on the river Blackwater, was kidnapped by the IRA. Lucas, kept in Limerick and Clare, was well treated – reflecting the level of humanity still prevailing in mid-1920. On 30 July, he escaped, possibly facilitated by his captors.

Right: Lucas was seized at Kilbarry near this fishing lodge.

Above: a Dáil Court in Cork.

Dáil Courts, authorised by Dáil Éireann in June 1920, become established across Ireland. As the courts gained a reputation for fairness, they became a striking manifestation of the Republican counterstate, to the alarm of Dublin Castle.

Left: the record of a Republican Court held in July 1920 at Kilmallock, Co. Limerick. Batt Cronin pleads guilty to stealing 30 pairs of boots – 'but nothing else'. He admitted that his fence gave him money, and ten pints of porter every day for a week. The judgement was that he had to repay 7s 6d weekly for 11½ weeks.

Right: Westland Row (now Pearse) Station. The Dublin and South Eastern Railway (inset: D&SER insignia) headquarters were on the upper floors.

On 30 July 1920 Squad members entered the D&SER building here. They burst into the office of Frank Brooke, director, and shot him. Jim Slattery said that Paddy O'Daly asked him as they descended the stairs: 'are you sure we got him?' Slattery went back and shot him again. Brooke (a cousin of Basil Brooke, future NI Prime Minister), was a confidential advisor to Lord French and a Privy Councillor.

Irish-born Archbishop Mannix of Melbourne (inset). On 31 July, at a rally in his honour in New York he had condemned British rule in Ireland. The British government banned Mannix from landing in Ireland. A destroyer intercepted his liner en route from New York and he was put ashore at Penzance. With the Archbishop appearing victimised, Lloyd George was left looking foolish. Mannix quipped: 'The greatest victory the Royal Navy has had since Jutland, without the loss of a single sailor'.

Right: Archbishop Mannix ascends the steps of the quay at Penzance on 9 August 1920.

Join—The Corps d'élite
for Ex-Officers.

JOIN the Auxiliary Division of the Royal Irish Constabulary. Ex-Officers with first-class record are eligible. Courage, Discretion, Tact and Judgment required. The pay is £1 per day and allowances. Uniform supplied. Generous leave with pay. Apply now to

R.I.C.
RECRUITING OFFICES, Great Scotland Yard, London, W.

Full particulars will be sent by post if you wish.

Left: an advertisement seeking ex-officers for the new Auxiliary Division of the RIC (ADRIC). The pay, at £1 per day, was hugely attractive for the post-war badly-paid or unemployed ex-officers. It was double what the ex-servicemen recruited for the RIC, from early 1920, were earning.

As the conflict escalated, Winston Churchill proposed in the Cabinet in May 1920 that a 'Special Emergency Gendarmerie' be set up. There was some unease. The influential Chief of the General Staff, Sir Henry Wilson, had noted that raising ex-servicemen for the RIC was a 'panic measure of raising 8,000 scallywags'. However, Major-General Tudor, the Police supremo, pushed through a proposal for a counter-insurgency force with experienced ex-officers as temporary cadets on a six- and twelve-month (extendable) contract. Recruiting began in July 1920.

Left: in the rushed recruitment, some Auxiliaries used khaki (as happened with the ongoing recruitment of ex-servicemen to the RIC). Shortly afterwards their uniform was standardised to a dark-green RIC one, like this replica. The leather gaiters were phased out.

Above: new recruits at Beggar's Bush, wearing a mixture of khaki and RIC-green uniforms.

Right: a December 1920 postcard, with a jolly and multi-coloured line-up. From left: an RIC constable; a newly-recruited ex-serviceman constable of 1920; an ADRIC temporary cadet with (initial-issue) Tam-o'-shanter; and a constable from the Veterans and Drivers Division. The khaki uniforms in the middle were temporary — all became the RIC dark green.

THE NEW R.I.C.

Above: Beggar's Bush Barracks, Dublin. The initial batch of recruits underwent a six-week training course at the Curragh. Shortly afterwards the training was moved to Beggar's Bush, which became the ADRIC Divisional Depot HQ. By the end of August 1920, the first companies were deployed.

Left: with his Balmoral beret (standard by the end of 1920) a temporary cadet of 'F' Company carries a Winchester shotgun. ADRIC were assigned the arms and transport needed for counter-insurgency. Each cadet, going on patrol, could select from a Webley revolver or automatic pistol; a Lee Enfield SMLE rifle; a Winchester pump-action shotgun and Mills grenades. Two armoured (and caged) Crossley Tenders, and five ordinary Crossley Tenders were allocated to each company as well as two armoured cars – either Peerless or Rolls-Royce.

Above: 'Tudor's Toughs' – mural painted by men of 'B' Company, based in Sligo.

Right: a joint patrol by 'I' Company with the army in Co. Monaghan.

The ADRIC were posted mostly in the 'hot' areas, which included Dublin and the south-western counties, forming 21 companies, each with a nominal strength of 100. By the Truce in July 1921, only 2,264 men, 187 of whom were Irish, had served. This relatively small force, over the course of just one year's operation, garnered a fearsome reputation.

Right: a jovial card for Christmas 1920 from 'D' Company in Salthill, Galway. Life as a temporary cadet involved danger, but it also afforded these (mainly) young veterans, fresh from grey post-war Britain, excitement, an occasional touch of the high life, and, sometimes, opportunities for unsupervised violence and excess.

Left: Terence MacSwiney, Lord Mayor of Cork, visiting the Capuchin College at Rochestown. MacSwiney was a TD, poet and playright, as well as O/C of the Cork No. 1 Brigade. On 12 August 1920 he was meeting IRA officers in the City Hall when Crown forces raided and detained them. He immediately began a hunger strike. Tried by court martial for sedition, he was sentenced to two years and sent to Brixton Prison.

Right: 'Le Martyr Irlandais' – MacSwiney's hunger strike soon gained international attention.

Left: letter sent to Terence MacSwiney on 8 April 1920, from Richard Mulcahy, Chief of Staff. In the light of the assassination of Mac Curtain some weeks before, Mulcahy was concerned about MacSwiney's safety. He orders that simple 'brainy' protection must be arranged.

Below: happier times. MacSwiney and his bride, Muriel Murphy (of the Cork brewing family). Mulcahy is on the right.

Dublin,
8th. April, 1920.

Dear Terry,

I was alarmed to hear that you had been going about Cork during the day and even staying at home and elsewhere at night without any protection. I want you to try and realise what a blow it would be to our prestige, if, after what has happened in Cork, you should be attacked without having a scrap of protection. We could never live it down. We have adopted a system here of giving protection to all Volunteers who have received notices, and to any prominent public people so ciroumstanced, who will accept our protection. Usually in the case of Volunteers, they are required to stay away from their own homes, they have a man or two with them in whatever place they are sleeping, and a small number of men living in their immediate neighbourhood are warned to be on the alert for such attacks, and to lend a hand on the flank or in the rear in any such case.

The matter of discrimination between military raiding and murder parties might be a difficult one for people who are not cool headed, but with cool headed and intelligent protection that difficulty should not be very great. In your own particular case it is absolutely essential in view of the ciroumstances, that you should have protection not only at night, but that you should have at least a couple of men whose business it will be to follow your movements and keep you under cover every day. You will understand no doubt that there is a possibility of your being attacked during the day, and will realise how necessary it would be in such a case to have a quiet eye or two, seeing exactly what happened, and ready to take action if feasible. My messenger spoke to you about this.

A simple general instruction is being issued on this matter, but you must understand that your position is unique, and that we must be able to show in case of emergency that a simple "brainy" protection has been arranged, and something that will leave us some specimens of the attackers.

Beir Beannacht,

Le Petit Journal

SUPPLÉMENT ILLUSTRÉ

ADMINISTRATION
61, RUE LAFAYETTE, 61
Les manuscrits ne sont pas rendus
On s'abonne sans frais dans tous les bureaux de poste

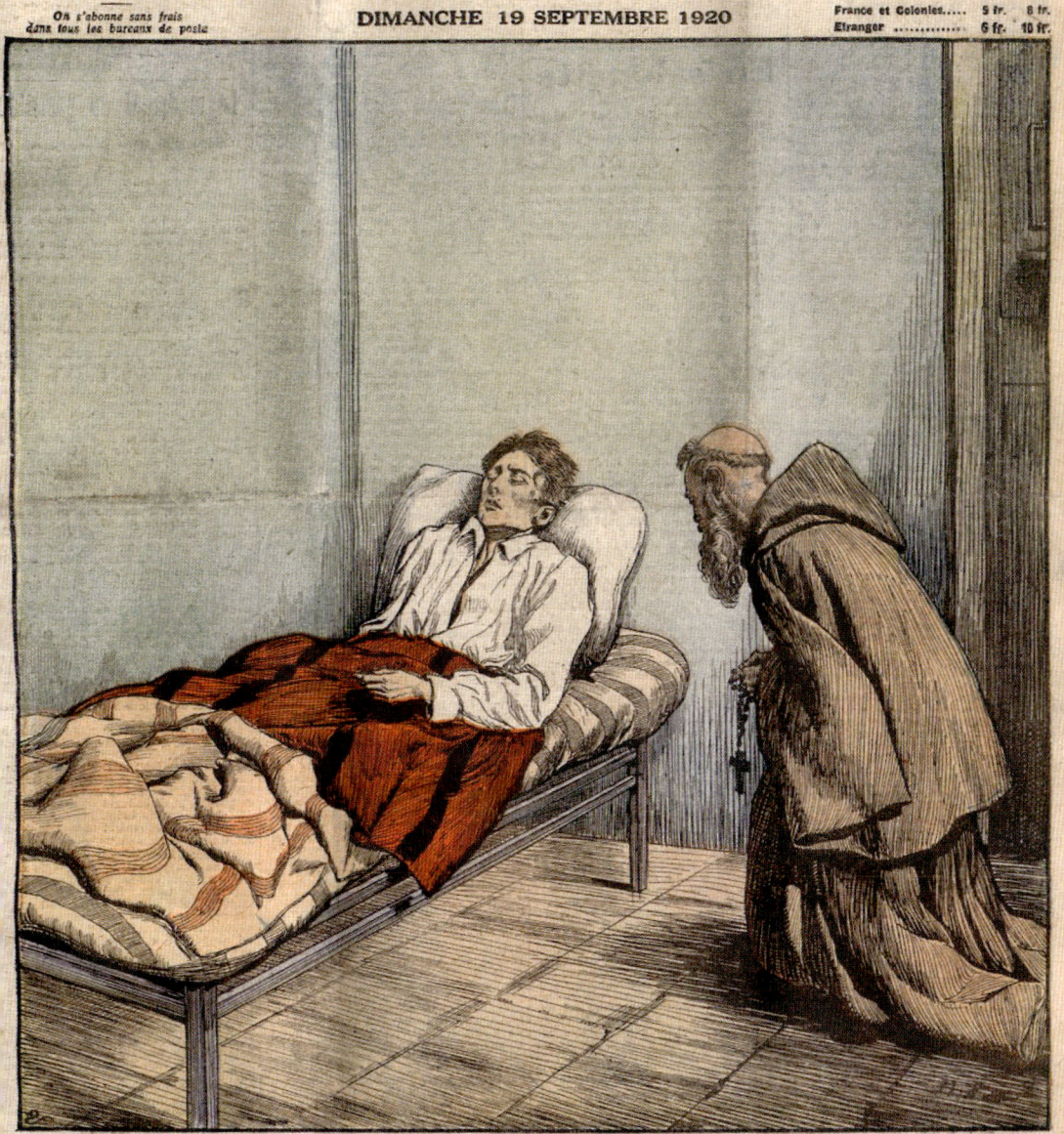

15 CENT.
31me Année

15 CENT.
Numéro 1.552
DIMANCHE 19 SEPTEMBRE 1920

ABONNEMENTS
France et Colonies..... 5 fr. 8 fr.
Étranger .... 6 fr. 10 fr.

LE MARTYR IRLANDAIS

M. Térence Mac-Swiney, lord-maire de Cork, accusé d'intelligences avec les Sinn-Feiners, refuse, dans sa prison, toute nourriture, et se laisse mourir de faim pour servir la cause de l'indépendance de l'Irlande

Left: Muriel MacSwiney, leaving Brixton Prison, after her last meeting with her husband.

At an early stage, MacSwiney had communicated to the British that if he wasn't released, his release was to be in death, then 'the British Government can boast of having killed two Lord Mayors of Cork in six months'.

As his hunger strike continued, a huge campaign developed worldwide in support of the freeing of MacSwiney. There were prayer meetings and demonstrations in Ireland, as well as in Britain. Prominent figures such as Archbishop Mannix visited MacSwiney in prison. There were also calls from influential persons in Britain supporting MacSwiney's release.

The day before MacSwiney was arrested, eleven Republican prisoners had gone on hunger strike in Cork Prison – two died in October 1920. The authorities were edgy and the military restricted the funeral of Michael Fitzgerald, hunger striker. Machine guns were mounted near the Cork church and the cemetery in Fermoy.

Left: honour and humanity – British troops salute Fitzgerald's coffin.

Right: Terence MacSwiney by Hugh Charde, Crawford Art Gallery, Cork.

The British Government was rattled by the controversy. However, mindful of what he saw as the debâcle of the mass release of hunger strikers from Mountjoy, earlier in April, Lloyd George stood firm. Hamar Greenwood, Chief Secretary for Ireland, issued a statement which said: 'None of the mercy which some seek to invoke for the Lord Mayor was shown the 80 policemen who have lost their lives in Ireland'.

On 25 October, MacSwiney died after 74 days on hunger strike. His remains lay in state at Southwark Cathedral where 30,000 mourners filed past.

Right: MacSwiney's funeral procession from Southwark to Euston station, for the planned journey home to Cork, via Dublin.

Below: defiance in London, heart of Empire – IRA Volunteers in uniform escort the hearse.

Uneasy about large demonstrations in Dublin, the authorities diverted the coffin at Holyhead onto a steamer direct to Queenstown (Cobh).

Left: undeterred, a funeral procession with an empty hearse was held in Dublin, honouring MacSwiney.

Right: the Lord Mayor's body laid in state in an open coffin at Cork City Hall.

Below: escorted by wary Auxiliaries, the arrival in Cork of the coffin (having been transferred to a tug at Queenstown).

115

Above: The funeral of Terence MacSwiney, by Sir John Lavery, Crawford Art Gallery, Cork. It shows the procession after the Requiem Mass at the cathedral in Cork on 31 October 1920.

Left: a phalanx of priests as the funeral procession moves along St Patrick's Street, amidst huge crowds, en route to St Finbarr's Cemetery. British troops saluted the coffin.

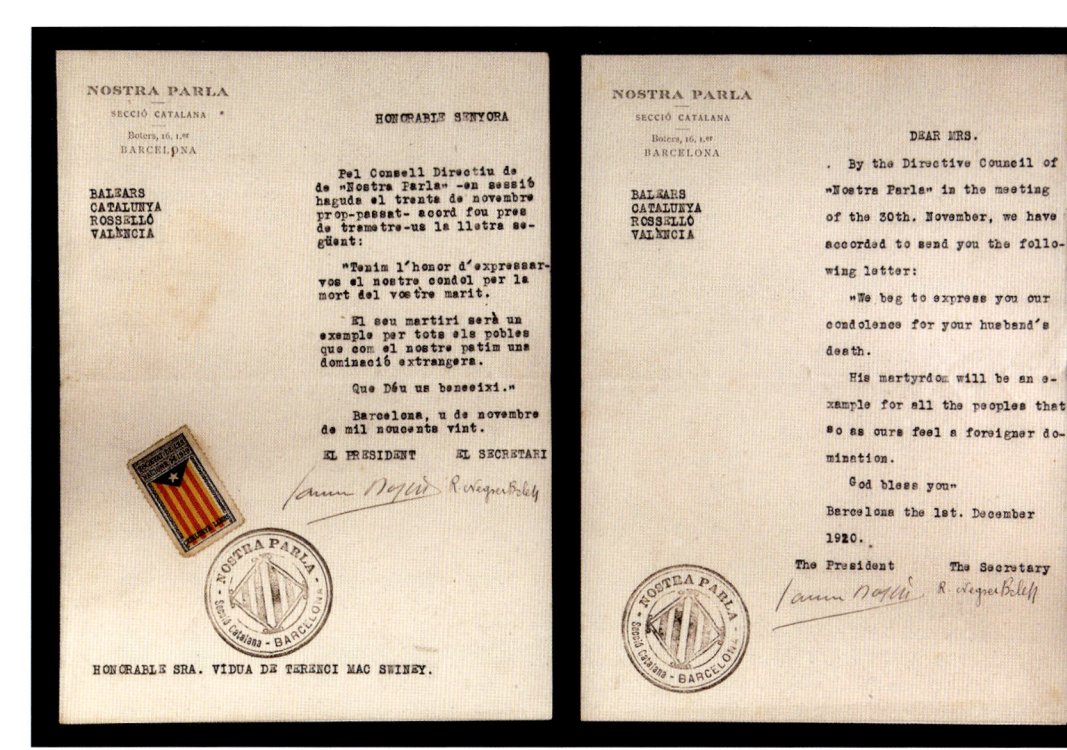

Above and right: appreciations of MacSwiney from Catalonia. His death resulted in mass demonstrations in Barcelona. In India, he proved an inspiration for both Nehru and Gandhi. Ho Chi Minh, working in Paris, said: 'a nation which has such citizens will never surrender'.

Below: MacSwiney's headstone at St Finbarr's Cemetery, where he is buried close to his fellow Lord Mayor, Tomás Mac Curtain.

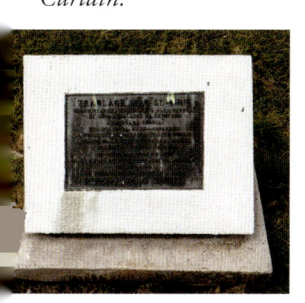

MAC SWEENEY
CONCELLER EN CAP DE CORK

Above: booklet on the life of Denis Lacey.

By mid-1920, the IRA had moved from predominantly attacking barracks to mounting ambushes.
On 30 July, Seán Treacy led an attack at Oola, Co. Tipperary where the newly-escaped Brigadier-General Lucas (coincidentally travelling in the convoy) was nearly killed (two soldiers died). Later Denis Lacey, O/C of Tipperary No. 3 Battalion flying column, led an attack at Thomastown, between Cashel and Tipperary town. Six military were killed, followed by an attack at the Glen of Aherlow that resulted in four dead Auxiliaries.

Left: statue of Seán Mac Eoin 'the Blacksmith of Ballinalee' at Ballinalee. He and his volunteers in Longford had attacked several RIC barracks during the first half of 1920. On 18 August Mac Eoin led an audacious raid on the Longford military barracks where they seized arms and ammunition.

Right: 'Just a lad of 18 summers'. Kevin Barry in a Belvedere rugby jersey.

On 20 September, Volunteers of the 1st Battalion, Dublin Brigade, intercepted a ration party (with an armed escort), as they headed to Monk's Bakery, Upper Church Street. Instructed to raise their hands and surrender their weapons, the soldiers grabbed their rifles and there was an exchange of fire. The attackers escaped, leaving one British private dead and two others fatally wounded. Kevin Barry, a first-year UCD medical student, was found hiding under the British lorry, with a Parabellum in hand and was taken into custody. On 20 October, Barry was court-martialled at Marlborough (now McKee) Barracks. Found guilty of the murder of one of the soldiers, he was sentenced to be hanged.

Right: crowds mill after the ambush (inset: plaque at Church Street.)

Below: troops escort through Dublin streets the coffins of the soldiers killed in the ambush.

Above: on 1 November 1920, the day of execution, women pray for Barry outside Mountjoy.

There was a huge outpouring of sympathy for Barry. Influential figures in Britain and Ireland petitioned for clemency, pointing out his youth. The British publicity machine responded, pointing out the youth of the dead soldiers.

Left: the hang-house at Mountjoy, a brick annex added around 1900 to the end of D wing, allowing access to D1 landing.

Below: notes by Fr Alfred, OFMCap, who had visited Kevin Barry on the eve of his execution.

Above: the 'Death Book' recording Barry's death.

Right: under the hang-house execution chamber. The platform allows a doctor to check for vital signs after a hanging.

As was the norm, an English professional hangman, John Ellis, who had hanged Roger Casement, was engaged.

Following page: the stark hang-house execution chamber where Barry was hanged (railings now surround the trapdoor for safety). The hang rope was suspended from a chain attached to beams on the underside of the roof. The condemned man spent his last night in a nearby cell. In the morning he was escorted to the chamber. The hooded and bound prisoner was placed at a chalk-mark on the trapdoor and the rope was positioned around his neck. The hangman then removed a lock-pin and pushed the lever forward, opening the trapdoor.

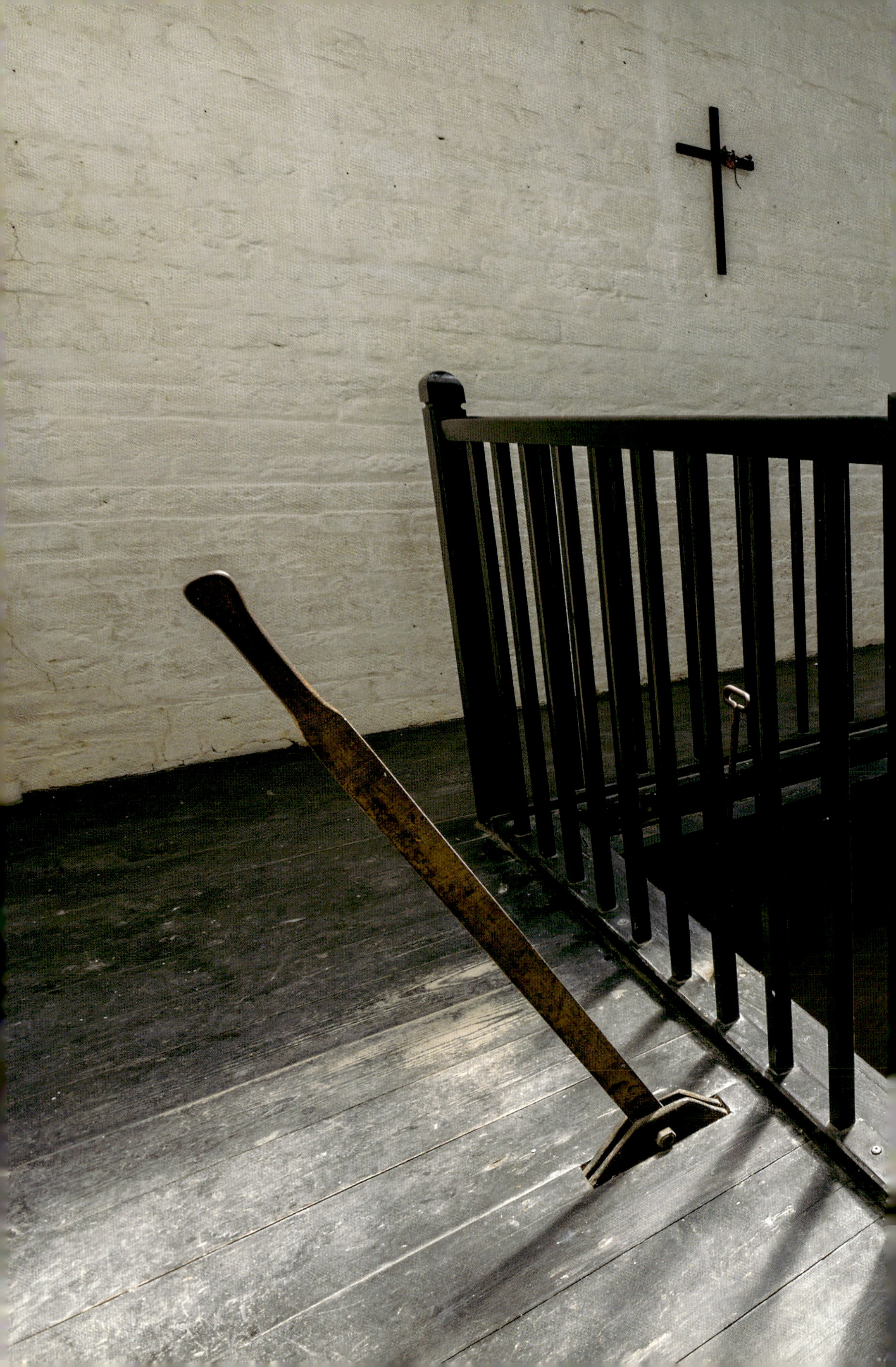

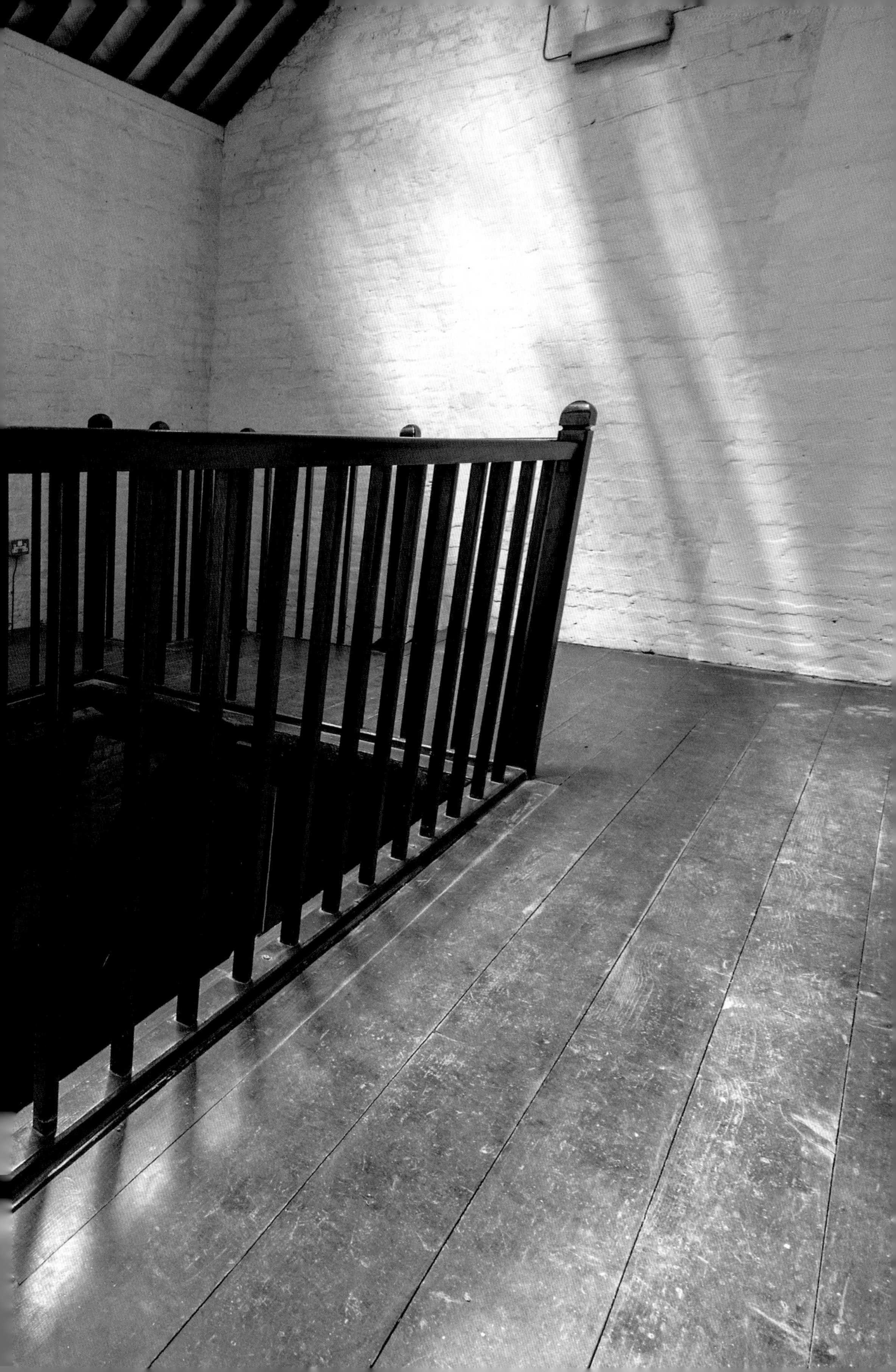

Above: a family day out. During August 1920, the parochial house in Lisburn was burnt by a sectarian mob. A group poses with children and Union Jack in front of the ruins.

Impromptu reprisals by Crown forces became the norm in 1920. Amongst others, Limerick, Thurles, Nenagh, Bantry and Fermoy suffered. On 16 August British troops attacked Templemore after the shooting of an RIC Inspector.
Left: Templemore Town Hall – a captain and a corporal died from burns as they set it alight.

Above: a summer scene. Soldiers, sleeves rolled up, one in shorts, stop and search civilians.

There had been a continuing build-up of the British Army in Ireland, and troops now participated widely in operations. Of the four battalions sent between May and June 1920, two were sent to the 6th Infantry Division, covering most of Munster, regarded as the most 'lawless' region.

Right: the Devonshires (bound for the 6th Infantry Division) embark on the 'Czaritza' at Devonport.

On 20 September 1920 RIC District Inspector Burke and his brother (a sergeant) were shot dead in a Balbriggan public house. At around 11 pm that night lorries laden with temporary cadets and RIC from the nearby Gormanston Camp raced into town where they began an orgy of violence.

Left: townspeople flee the town.

Above, Clonard Street, Balbriggan, Co. Dublin, today.

Right: twenty houses were burnt out on Clonard Street.

In a night of terror, the Auxiliaries laid waste to the town. Scores of houses were destroyed. Local businesses were destroyed and public houses were looted and burnt.

Left: ruined machinery at the Deeds and Templar hosiery factory, Balbriggan. Employing 120 people, it was completely destroyed.

Right: 'Il terrore in Irlanda'. 'La Tributa Illustrata' depicts the fleeing Balbriggan population.

Left: members of the British Labour Commission to Ireland inspect the damaged hosiery factory.

There was widespread publicity about the atrocity. However, Hamar Greenwood said later in the Commons: 'I have yet to find one authenticated case of a member of this Auxiliary Division being accused of anything but the highest conduct characteristic of them'.

Two Volunteers (James Lawless and John Gibbons) were brought to the town barracks. They were beaten up, bayonetted and their bodies dumped.

Left: memorial on Bridge Street.

LA TRIBUNA ILLUSTRATA

Supplemento settimanale de " LA TRIBUNA "

Anno XXVIII - N. 48 ‡ 28 novembre-5 decembre 1926

DIREZIONE E AMMINISTRAZIONE
ROMA — Via Milano 37 — Telef. 10-634
Un anno L. 10.– — Estero L. 13.–
Un numero Cent. 20 — Arretrato Cent. 30
INSERZIONI: Sponti di cronaca L. 6 — Pubblicità finanziaria L. 6 — ogni spazio di linea di corpo 6, su una colonna. Rivolgersi all'amministrazione de La Tribuna, Via Milano 37, Roma. Avvisi commerciali L. 2. – ogni millimetro di altezza, su una colonna. Rivolgersi all' Unione Pubblicità Italiana, Via Tritone 62, Roma e sue succursali — Ai suddetti prezzi va aggiunta la tassa governativa — Pagamento anticipato.

IN QUESTO NUMERO:
Molti chilometri di spavento
La settimana in fotografia
Perduto nel Marocco - Due novelle - Lettere alla sorella brutta - Il mondo dei capricci - Le risposte degli astri - Giuochi a premio, ecc.

Il terrore in Irlanda

La popolazione della città irlandese di Balbriggan abbandona le proprie case, trasportando i mobili e le masserizie potute salvare dal saccheggio delle truppe inglesi.

(Disegno di A. Minardi)

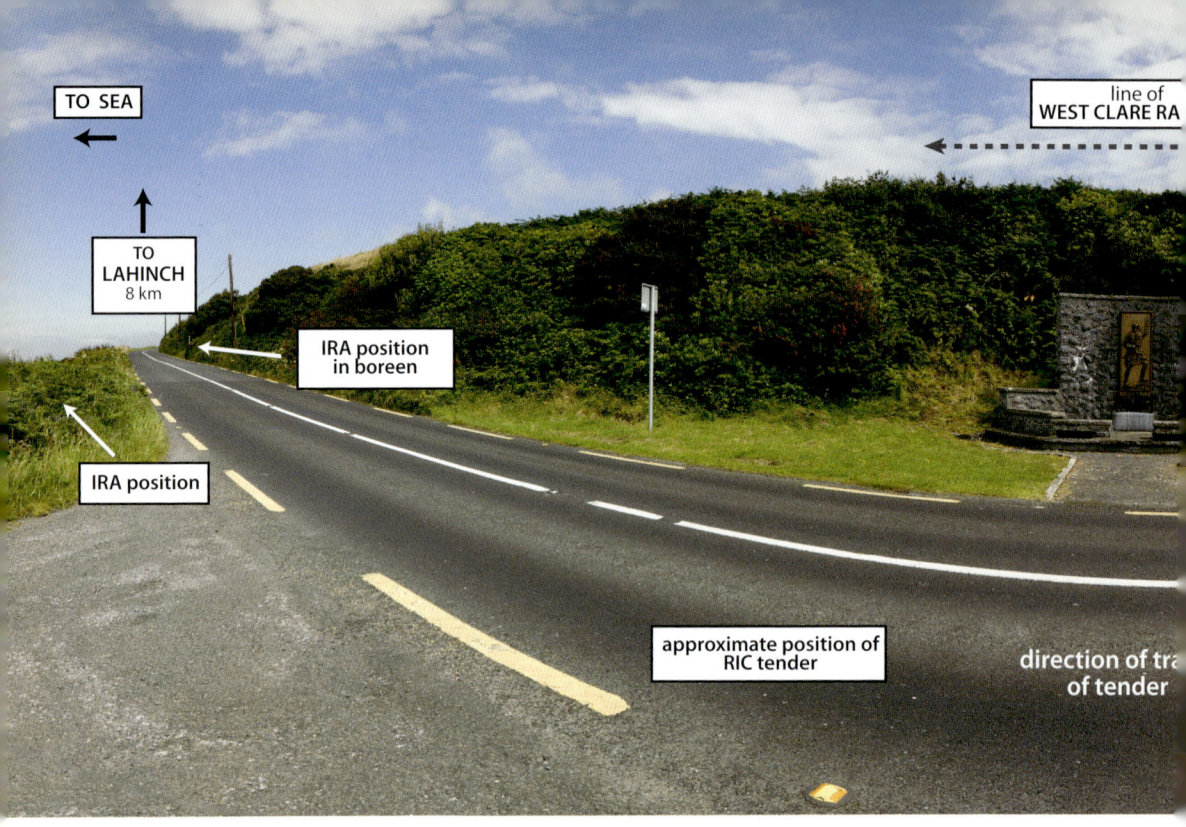

Above: a fish-eye view of the ambush site at Rineen, Co. Clare.

On the morning of 22 September the Mid-Clare IRA were spread along here, in preparation for an ambush of the regular RIC weekly patrol between Ennistymon and Milltown Malbay. In the afternoon, a Crossley Tender, on its way back from Milltown Malbay, was ambushed. After throwing two grenades at the tender, the IRA poured heavy fire on it. Five of the RIC constables were killed. Another fled and was shot as he headed towards the sea.

Left: the monument at Rineen.

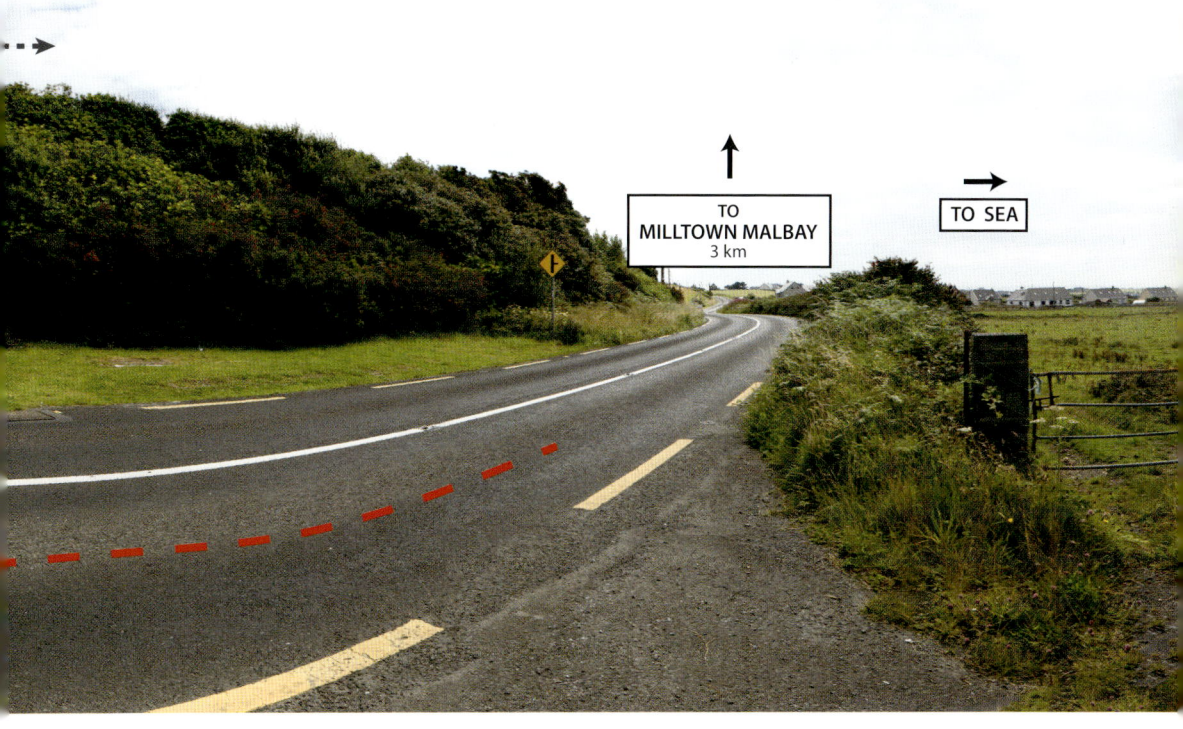

Army trucks, which had been used in a search for an officer missing from an earlier ambush about 18 kilometres distant, came on the scene. The British opened heavy fire (including from a machine gun) on the retreating Volunteers, who made their escape.

This ambush resulted in the heaviest Crown casualties in the conflict to date. Immediately afterwards, the Crown forces sacked Milltown Malbay, Ennistymon and Lahinch. Several civilians were murdered. Right: the burnt-out house of Tom Connolle, Ennistymon. Connolle, local secretary of the ITGWU, was shot and his body thrown in the flames.

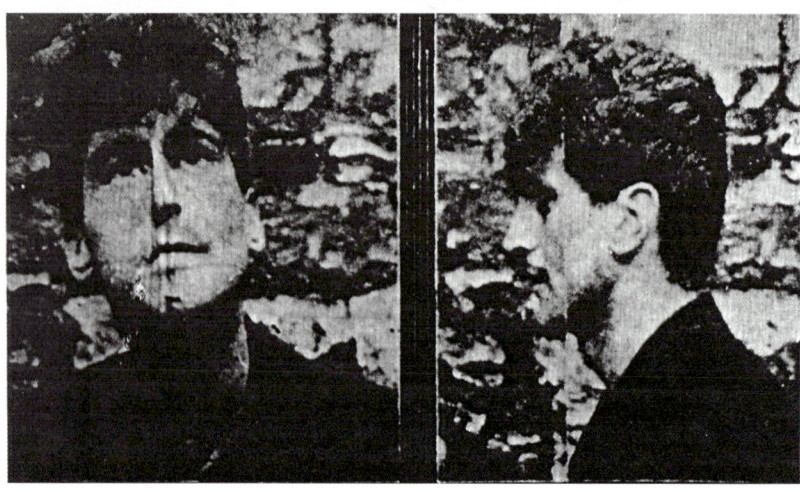

Above: a boundary wall at the former Military Barracks, Mallow.

Left: plaque marking the capture of the barracks.

On 28 September, Volunteers led by Ernie O'Malley and Liam Lynch approached the barracks. Two Volunteers on the civilian staff had related that most of the 17th Lancers garrison regularly left to exercise the horses. O'Malley approached the wicket gate with a fake letter. The Volunteers then forced their way in and overpowered the 15 soldiers within. The sergeant in charge was mortally wounded in the fracas. With a haul of 27 rifles and two Hotchkiss machine guns, the IRA withdrew.

Left: a mugshot of O'Malley, in captivity.

Right: Mallow after the reprisal.

On the night after the attack the terror began. Lorries conveyed troops from barracks at Buttevant and Fermoy, who joined their Lancer comrades in torching Mallow. They started with the Town Hall. Petrol was poured over it and it went up in flames. Next came other premises – a hotel, factory, garage and stores. Terrified townsfolk ran down the burning main street seeking refuge.

There was international outrage. The London 'Times' spoke out: 'the accounts of arson and destruction by the military at Mallow...must fill English readers with a sense of shame'.

Right: the Cleeves condensed milk factory (employing 300 people) was destroyed.

Below: Liam Lynch, O/C, No. 2 Cork Brigade, one of the outstanding IRA commanders of the war.

Left: Major George Osbert Smyth, one of the officers killed in Drumcondra (see below). He was the brother of Lieutenant-Colonel Gerald Smyth, assassinated in the Cork County Club on 17 July 1920. He had requested a transfer from Egypt to Ireland, to work in intelligence, to avenge his brother's death.

Seán Treacy and Dan Breen, veterans of Soloheadbeg, Knocklong and the Lord French ambushes, were on the run in Dublin, and carrying out operations with the Squad. Early on 12 October 1920, a raiding party was guided to their Drumcondra safe house, home of Professor John Carolan, by an informer. In the ensuing gunfight Major Smyth and a captain were mortally wounded. Professor Carolan was shot in the neck, afterwards stating that he was lined up and shot by the raiders – he died weeks later. The IRA pair had escaped out the back, crashing through the conservatory. Breen was severely wounded and brought to the Mater Hospital where he was hidden by the nuns.

Left: Seán Treacy, 3rd South Tipperary Brigade.

Right: Auxiliaries hurry towards the scene of the shooting on Talbot Street.

On 14 October 1920 Seán Treacy headed to a Squad meeting at the 'Republican Outfitters', 94 Talbot Street. However, he was trailed by a tout. The meeting was concluding when Treacy reached the shop. An armoured car and lorry raced up the street. Treacy emerged and made to escape down the street. A plain-clothes agent grappled with Treacy who drew his Parabellum. In an exchange of fire Treacy was shot in the head, dying immediately. The agent, Lieutenant Price, was killed, as were two civilian bystanders.

Right: plaque at the Talbot Street location where Treacy was shot.

Below: memorial. The Wexford IRA were manufacturing bombs in a remote house at St Kearn's Quay, Saltmills. On the night of 12 October 1920 a detonator was accidentally sparked and there was an explosion, killing five men.

Left: the Greville Arms, Granard, Co. Longford. At around 8 pm, on 31 October 1920, District Inspector Philip Kelleher was in the bar of the Greville Arms (owned by the family of Kitty Kiernan, Michael Collins's girlfriend). Two masked Volunteers of the North Longford Brigade burst in and shot him at point-blank range. Kelleher, aged 23, had won the Military Cross in WWI and had only recently arrived in Granard. He was from Macroom, Co. Cork. Coincidentally, his father was the doctor who conducted the autopsies on the bodies of the Auxiliaries after the Kilmichael ambush some weeks later. He controversially testified that some of the bodies had been mutilated (page 166).

On the night of 3 November 1920, Crown forces looted and burnt Granard, and then headed for Ballinalee. Seán Mac Eoin, anticipating a reprisal, had positioned volunteers at the approaches to the town. As around ten lorries charged in, they were met with a heavy fusillade. Sometime later the Crown forces withdrew, leaving behind some of the loot they had seized at Granard.

Left: locals inspect the damage at Granard.

Above: this film still depicts a typical IRA ambush. Well-concealed men lie in wait at a commanding point above a bend in a road.

Right: dead bodies lie around as the IRA move in to disarm the 'Tans'.

Given that this is guerilla warfare, there are no photographs of actual IRA ambushes. However these film stills evoke a sense of how it might have been. They are from the first full-length Irish feature film with sound, 'The Dawn' (1936) shot around Killarney, using extras, many of whom were IRA veterans.

THE ILLUSTRATED LONDON NEWS

No. 4258 VOL. CLVII   SATURDAY, NOVEMBER 27, 1920.   ONE SHILLING.

THE REIGN OF ASSASSINATION IN IRELAND: AFTER A STREET BATTLE—DEAD AND WOUNDED; AND SINN FEINERS "HELD UP."

The condition of affairs in Ireland has grown worse and worse. Terrible events took place in Dublin on Sunday, November 21, when fourteen British Army officers and ex-officers were murdered in their homes by gangs of assassins, and a fight between troops and a football crowd resulted in twelve deaths and the wounding of over fifty people. The above photograph is typical of the state of things in the country. It was taken during the "battle of Tralee," where a convoy of R.I.C. Cadets was ambushed by Republicans. Three Sinn Feiners were killed and one cadet was wounded. The cadet and two of the dead Sinn Feiners are seen lying in the road. The cadet is in the foreground. In the background, cadets are taking Sinn Feiners prisoners.

PHOTOGRAPH BY TOPICAL.

An ADRIC engagement at Ballymacelligot (Tralee) on 12 November 1920 left two men dead. Coincidentally, a press party (with a Captain Pollard) showed up that afternoon. ADRIC burned the creamery (above) the next day.

Left: a depiction of 'the Battle of Tralee'. Three dead lie in the foreground while cadets take 'Sinn Féiners' prisoner.

Right: the caption in the 'Graphic' ran: 'Searching a rebel prisoner taken... in a fight at Tralee'.

However, this was 'fake' news'. Trying to show that they were winning, Dublin Castle press officers, principally Captain Pollard, staged the event, supposed to be near Tralee, using Auxiliaries, some dressed as civilians, at Vico Road, Killiney. Pathé also filmed the fictional encounter. On 2 December an MP asked in the Commons about the faked photograph. 'I know nothing as to the circumstances in which the picture...was taken.' was the official reply.

Right: with more tree growth – the scene at Vico Road today.

139

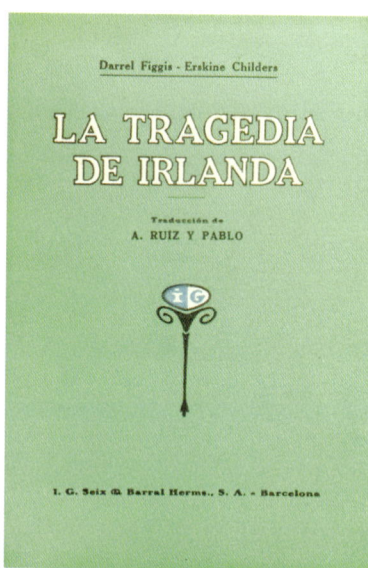

The Dáil Propaganda Department spread the republican message in Europe, North America, Australia and South Africa.

Near left: a Spanish book is titled 'La Tragedia de Irlanda', as written by Darrel Figgis and Erskine Childers.

Far left: a poster issued by 'Les amis de la liberté irlandaise' tells of English terror in Ireland.

The news-sheet 'Irish Bulletin' was produced by the Dáil Propaganda Department from November 1919. It was published several times a week and circulated internationally, presenting the Republican view of events. For journalists in Britain and on the Continent, it provided a source of information (an alternative to the Dublin Castle-fed British news agencies). With just a typewriter and a duplicator, the staff (initially Frank Gallagher and a doughty typist, Kathleen McKenna) had to move frequently from hide-out to hide-out.

On 26 March 1921, the office of the Bulletin was raided by Auxiliaries, who seized the typewriter and duplicator as well as the circulation list.

Left: an 'Irish Bulletin' of early December 1920.

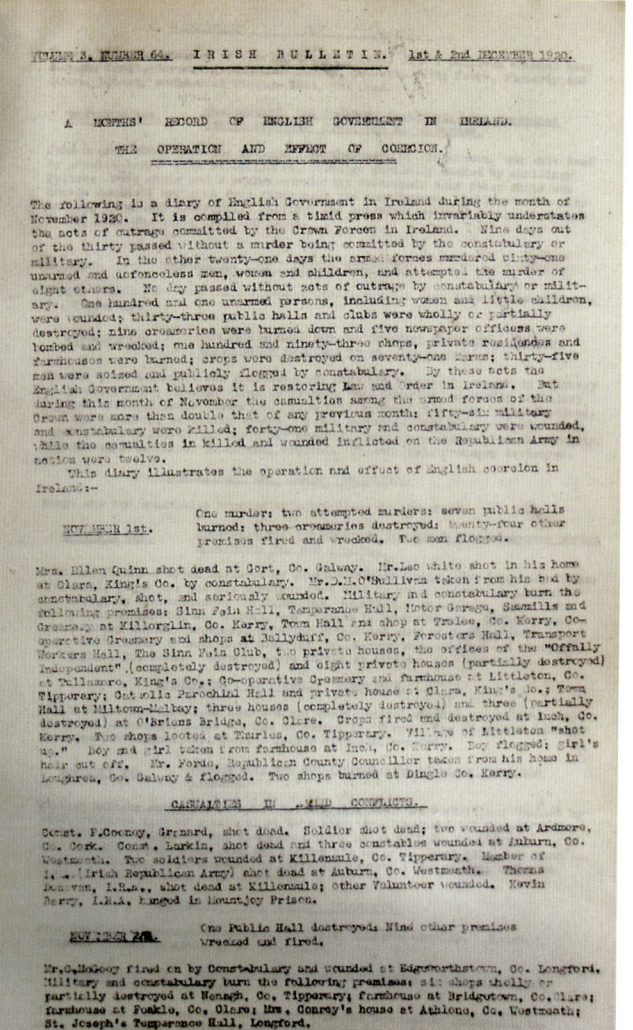

The Castle press officers, Captains Pollard and Darling, produced the official 'Weekly Summary'. It gained a poor reputation due to its crude falsehoods. Pollard (who, in 1936, travelled on the plane that transported General Franco to Tetuan to start the Spanish Civil War) had staged the faked event at Vico Road in 1920. After the March 1921 raid on the 'Irish Bulletin', the pair decided to produce fake issues, using the captured equipment. However, the deception was soon discovered. An MP in the Commons requested the Chief Secretary 'not to waste their money in sending me any more of their forgeries'.

Right: pages of the fake 'Irish Bulletin' of 30 March 1921. The top page states that the RIC 'held the respect of the whole community'. The lower page presents evident nonsense: '18,321 enemy strongholds were taken by the Republican Forces in the month of February.'

Below: later, genuine copies of the Bulletin were stamped 'official copy' in green ink.

VOLUME 4. NUMBER 56.   IRISH BULLETIN.   WEDNESDAY 30th March 1921.

LYING INSULTS OFFERED TO IRELAND.

SIR HAMAR GREENWOOD'S WEEKLY.

"The Weekly Summary" is a paper issued by the Chief Secretary in Ireland to the Police Forces. It has been described as "infamous" and its object is to hound the mercenaries of the English Government on with "the job of making Ireland a hell." How well it has served its devilish purpose all the world knows. The thousands of murdered men, women and children, the millions of ruined houses, the blackened and devastated country, these have been testified to by hundreds of eye-witnesses. Ireland today is a desert, and her exports of agricultural produce, which at one time went in boat loads are now so dwindled that practically all the export trade of Ireland is done by the English parcel post.

"THE WEEKLY SUMMARY".

The latest issue of this pernicious murder sheet has fallen into Republican hands. It consists of twelve columns, the first of which is devoted to a "leaderette." Sir Hamar Greenwood has said that this sheet is written "by policemen for policemen". He might with greater truth have said that it is written "by perjurers for perjurers". The first of the two leaderettes is called "Propaganda against the Police", and begins as follows:-

"Propaganda is always against the Police in Ireland."

This is a gross falsehood. The writer of this lie hopes to persuade the English public that the Irish nation make false statements against the Police. It is on a par with the statements so frequently made in the English press and by the heads of the English Government regarding the so-called murder of police. There is no single authenticated case of a policeman being murdered in Ireland. These vile lies are the creation of enemy hacks whose business it is to defame Ireland with their pens. There is no propaganda against the police in Ireland. The Royal Irish Constabulary - as long as it was a purely Irish force - held the respect of the whole community.

THE POLICE HAVE NO POLITICS.

"The Police have no politics.
"The Police want only public peace.
"All their interests lie that way.
"They would rather find the country law-abiding than rebellious.
"They don't want assassinations.
"They don't want ambushes.
"They don't want arson, though from what one reads, one would suppose "they delighted in it.
"Yet such is the subtlety of the propaganda of the Murder Gang, that it "is made to appear that the Police have provoked - and still seek - "disorder in the land."

"The Police have no politics." The Republican Government in Ireland is not so misinformed. The English Government can not trust its servants. It is well known that the Police have politics. They have politics all day long and, such are the activities of the undefeated Republican armies, that in many cases they have politics all night. On more than one occasion the heroic levies of the Republic have kept up the fight for "Ireland a nation" long after the mercenary police have fled the country. No less than 18,321 enemy strongholds were taken by the Republican Forces in the month of February.

ARE THE POLICE AGGRESSIVE?

"The exact opposite is true, and so true that it is astounding that anyone can believe the extravagant charges made against the Police. Over two hundred and fifty policemen have been murdered, and not one single murderer of policemen has been hanged.
Does that suggest that the Police exceed their duty or are violently aggressive?
Hundreds of carefully-prepared ambushes have taken place all over the country, but the Police have never once ambushed their enemies.
Does that suggest that the Police are the murderous marauders they are usually depicted in the news for foreign circulation?"

The lying statement about policemen being murdered is again repeated. It must be as emphatically contradicted. There have been no murders of police in Ireland and even the hack who pens this piffle has to admit the truth that the police have never once ambushed their enemies. All ambushes have been carried out by the Republican forces. Such action take place daily and the gibe that the Republican forces are ignorant of the art of war is answered by their unvarying success. Irishmen have shown Europe - aye and the whole world - that, although their principles prevented them from fighting for other small nations, they can fight for Ireland.

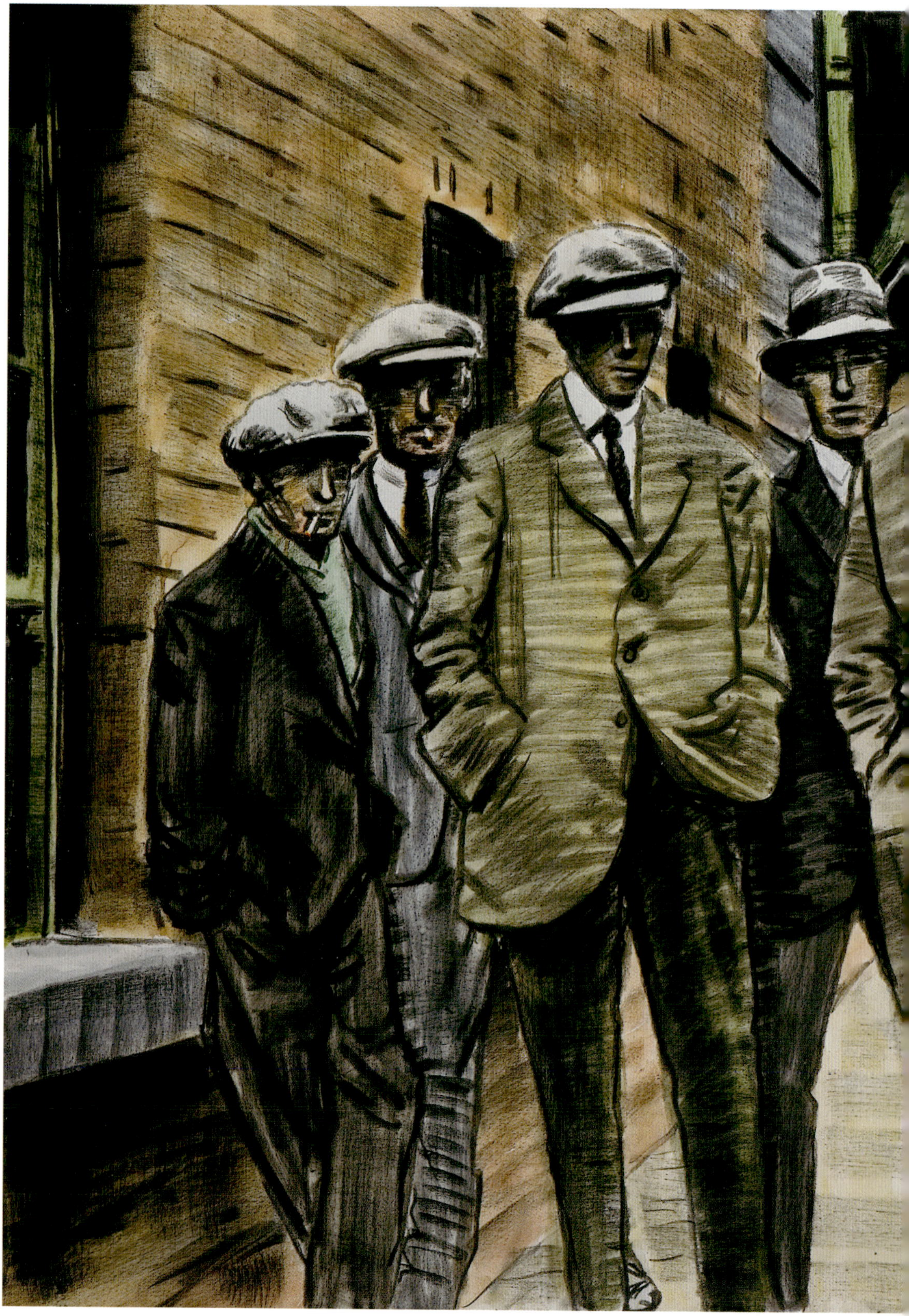

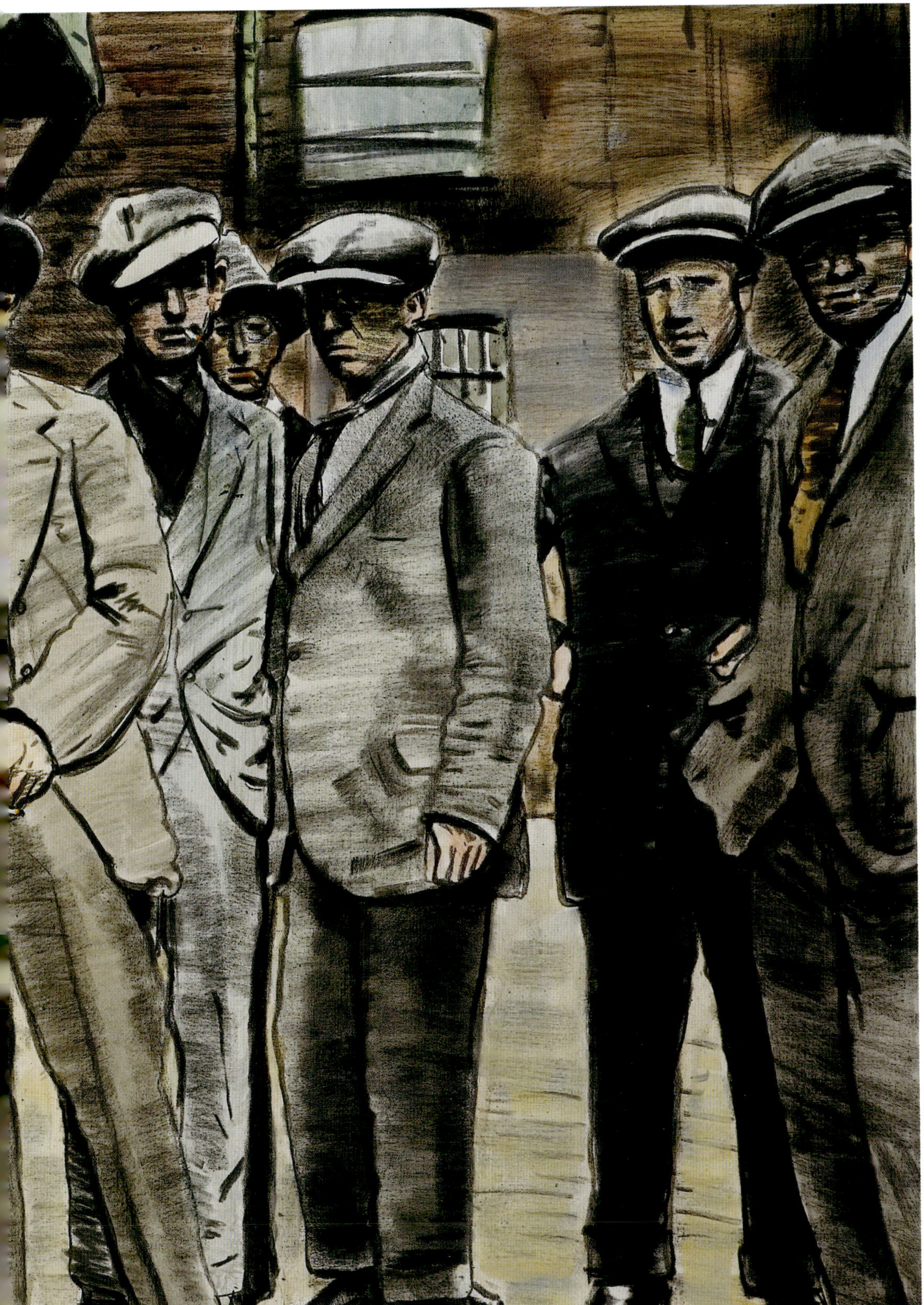

Preceding page: the 'Cairo Gang' as painted by Mick O'Dea.

Left: a page from an IRA intelligence ledger (now in the Military Archives, Dublin), with an original photograph of the group. The present-day name 'Cairo Gang' was not in use at the time. This latter-day term possibly derives from the Café Cairo (on Grafton Street) or from officer-spies drafted from imperial service in Cairo. The ledger denotes them as the 'Special Gang', of the 'F' Company, Auxiliaries, with an identification key.

Below left: the photograph of the 'Special Gang' was taken in this lane inside the Palace Street entrance to Dublin Castle.

The most violent day of the War of Independence was 21 November 1920, when it truly earned the epithet 'Bloody Sunday'. Thirty people died that day, with several others dying later of their wounds. On that morning, the IRA set out to assassinate suspected British spies. Later that day, the Crown forces fired on the crowd at a football match at Croke Park. That night, also, three men in custody in Dublin Castle were 'shot trying to escape'.

Right: shock and awe in Georgian Dublin – some of the British officers and cadets killed.

Collins's intelligence network had gleaned a great amount of information from a wide array of sources, including housemaids and hotel porters, and importantly, from his spies in Dublin Castle. Collins and senior IRA staff devised the target list but there were some local amendments by the IRA Dublin Brigade. Most of the attackers were from the Dublin Brigade, and were usually led by members of the Squad. With large backup groups of lookouts and protection in place, the selected hit teams fanned out to strike at the most effective time, 9:00 am on Sunday morning, 21 November 1920.

Right: the news of the killings flashed around the world – the front page of the 'New York Tribune' of 22 November. The sub-headlines 'British troops in Ireland to be heavily reinforced' and 'Fear of assassination spreads to England' reflect the alarmed British reaction.

145

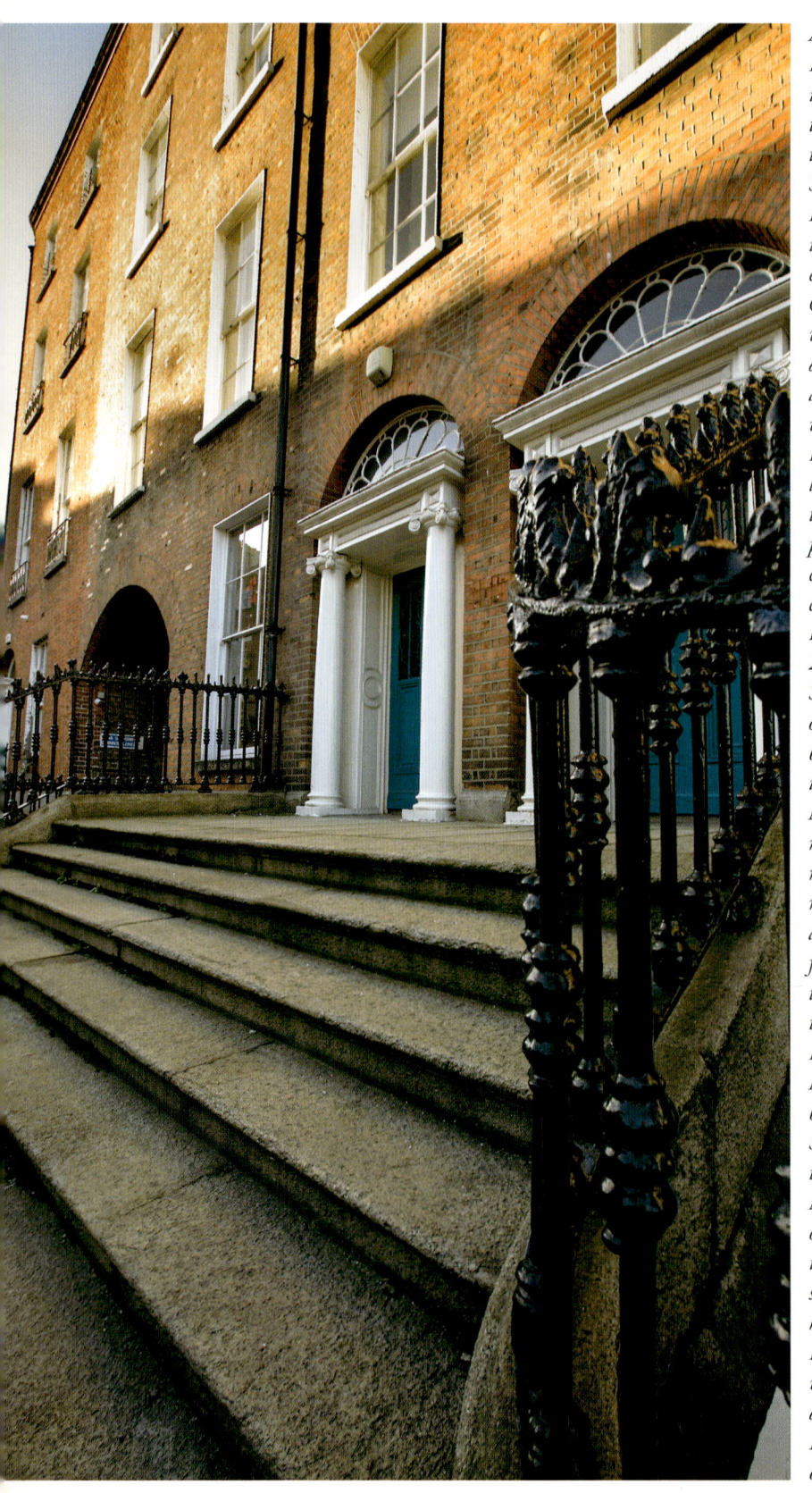

As the 'G' Division of the DMP had been rendered ineffective by the Squad, the British had set out to build up their Secret Service and Military Intelligence network in Ireland. It has been estimated that around 60 men, mostly young veteran officers, had been drafted in from Britain and the Empire and were lodged across central Dublin. Some had Irish links and, such being the vagaries of the secret profession, some enjoyed chequered and colourful careers.

Left: a nest of spies? No. 28 Upper Pembroke Street is a terraced house of three storeys over basement. In 1920, it contained ten flats. Most of the tenants were military officers. The raiders entered via the rear garden (accessible by a side lane) and by the front door. They raced up to a third-floor flat where they shot dead Captain Leonard Price, as well as Major Charles Dowling, both intelligence officers. Senior staff officer Lieutenant-Colonel Hugh Montgomery (a cousin of Bernard Montgomery, the future General) was shot at the entrance to his ground-floor flat. His wife was slightly wounded. Montgomery died of his wounds on 10 December. Three other officers were wounded.

Right: Earlsfort Terrace and below, Lower Mount Street. Years of property development have made these streets unrecognisablle.

Captain John Fitzgerald was lodging at a boarding house at 28 Earlsfort Terrace. He was shot dead in bed. A 'Blackrock College boy', he was from Co. Tipperary. He had had a colourful war career: wounded in the trenches, then transferred to train as a pilot in the Royal Flying Corps, and finally shot down and captured. One account says that he was in Dublin awaiting transfer to the Auxiliaries.

An agent using the alias 'Mahon' was registered as a guest at 22 Lower Mount Street. He was Lt. Henry Angliss. IRA reports said that Angliss had been responsible for the murder of John Lynch, and that he had drunkenly revealed this to a fellow lady guest. Armed men burst in and shot Angliss – his other intelligence colleagues lodging there escaped.

Right: 22, Lower Mount Street as it was in 1920.

A party of Auxiliaries heard the disturbance at Mount Street. Two were dispatched to Beggar's Bush to get reinforcements. They were seized by the IRA at Northumberland Road and shot.

WHERE LIEUTENANT MAHON, ONE OF THE MURDERED OFFICERS, WAS KILLED: NO. 22, LOWER MOUNT STREET, DUBLIN—SHOWING BULLET-HOLES IN THE WINDOW.

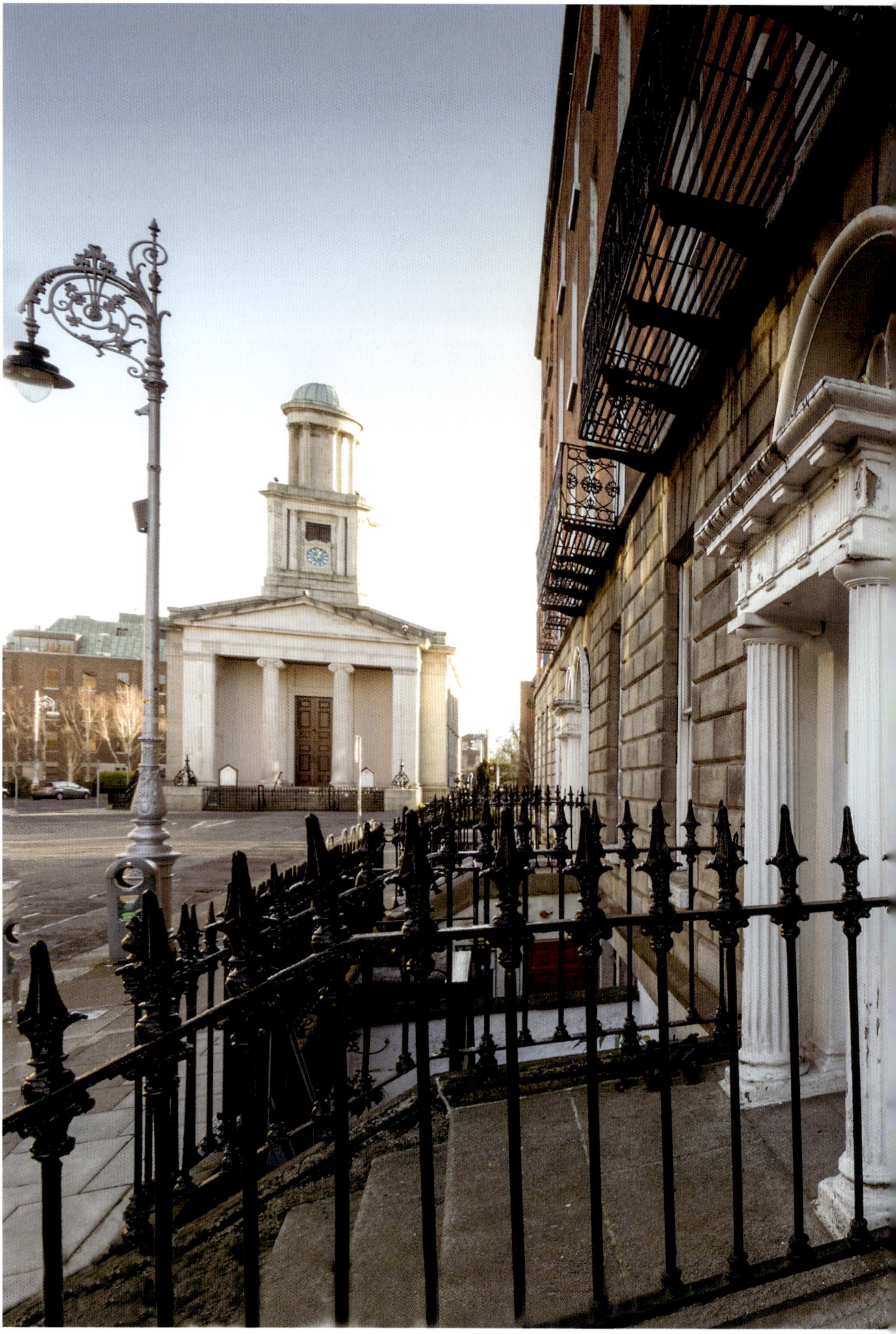

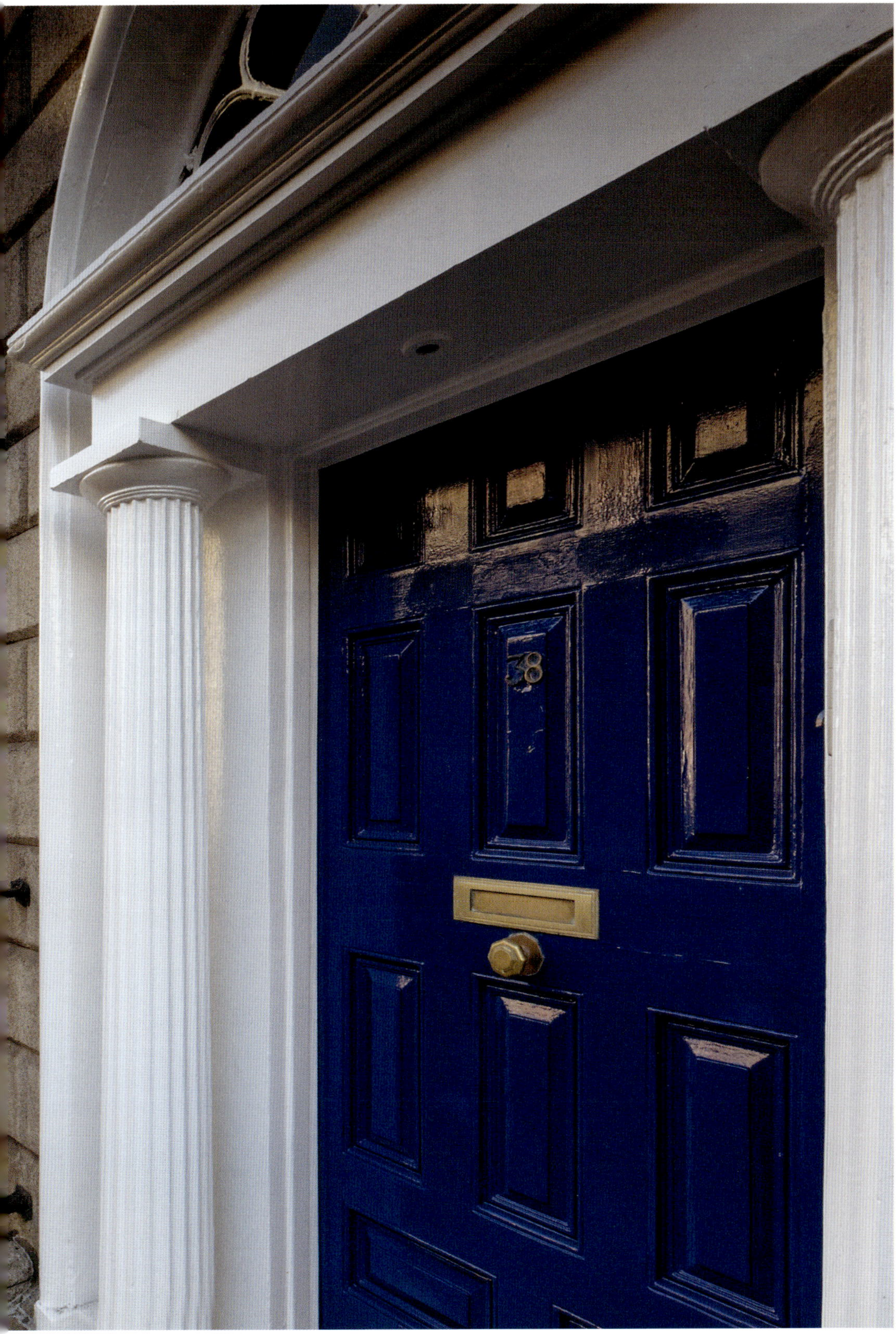
38

Preceding page: with the 'Peppercannister' Church in the background, 38 Upper Mount Street is set in the heart of Georgian Dublin. Lieutenants George Bennett and Peter 'Ashmun' Ames (born in Pennsylvania) were lodgers here. Both had intelligence backgrounds and were in Dublin on 'special service'. Squad member Vinnie Byrne shot both.

Left: still a guest house, 92 Lower Baggot Street with its red door. In 1920, an officer, listed as a courts martial officer, was lodging here. Captain William Newberry was shot dead as he attempted to climb out his ground-floor bedroom window. His wife, who was there, had tried to shield him.

An intelligence officer, Captain Donald Maclean, was boarding with his wife at 117 Morehampton Road. The gunmen burst into his bedroom and took him out to a different room. He was lined up along with the landlord, Thomas Smith, who was also living in the house. Both were shot dead.

Left: map showing locations of assassinations.

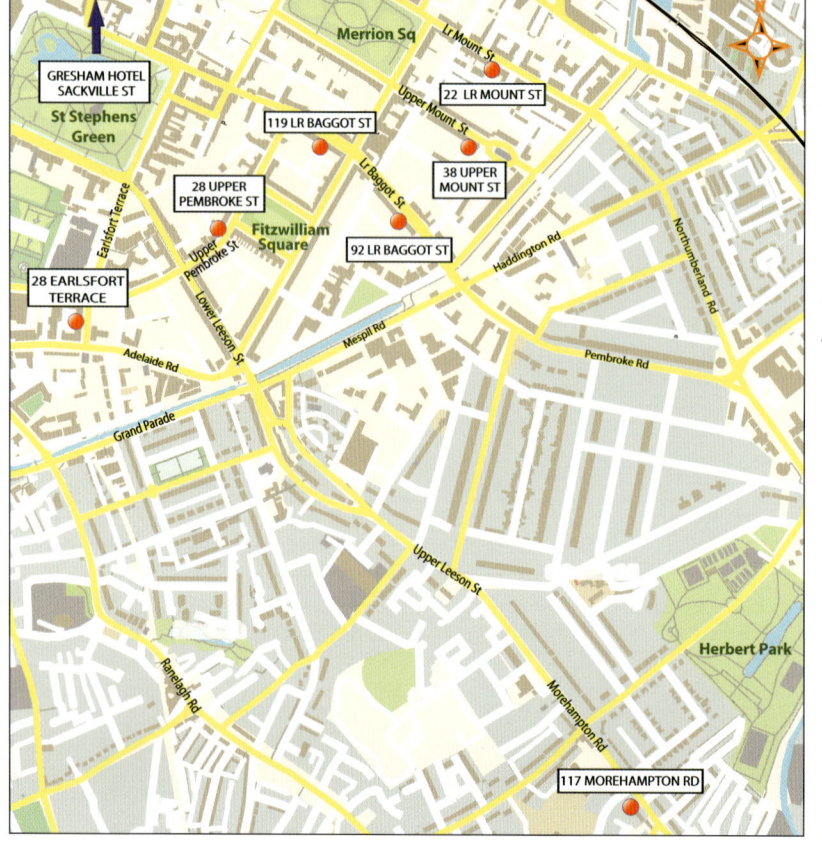

Right: 119 Lower Baggot Street. Captain Geoffrey Baggallay had been lodging here on 21 November 1920. That morning, callers knocked on the door and said they had a letter for him from Dublin Castle. They were directed to his bedroom, where they shot him. One of the gunmen is said to have been Seán Lemass (future Taoiseach). Baggallay was listed as a courts martial officer. He had lost a leg in WWI. It was claimed that two months previously he had directed reinforcements to the Royal Exchange Hotel in Parliament Street where officers, including Lieutenant Angliss (see page 147), had murdered John Lynch, a Limerick lawyer and County Councillor, mistaking him for Liam Lynch, the Cork IRA commander.

Above: 'Murder Most Foul' depicted in the 'Illustrated London News'. *Left:* the only assassinations north of the Liffey occurred at the Gresham Hotel. Lieutenant Leonard Wilde was registered here as a commercial traveller – he was shot at his bedroom door. A veterinary officer and ex-captain, Patrick MacCormack, was also shot. He was reported to be in Dublin to purchase horses for Egyptian turf clubs. MacCormack's mother vehemently declared that he was innocent. Collins later accepted that it was a case of mistaken identity.

Right: ticket for the football match at Croke Park on 21 November. The match, attended by a large crowd, began late, at 3:15 pm. The Crown forces, in a state of high agitation after the morning's events, set out to surround and search the crowd. As a convoy of troops arrived along Clonliffe Road, Auxiliaries approached from the southern (canal) direction. The cadets began firing at ticket sellers (mistaking them for IRA pickets). As these ran away, the Auxiliaries entered the grounds. Fire was directed on the panicked and fleeing crowd. Seven were shot dead, five more died later and two were trampled to death.

Right: relatives of the victims at Jervis Street Hospital, where a military enquiry was held.

Michael Hogan, a Volunteer and one of the Tipperary team, was shot dead on the pitch. The Hogan Stand at Croke Park is named after him.

Right: prayers at the spot where Hogan was killed.

Below; memorial at Grangemockler Co. Tipperary.

Left: the former detective offices (later a guardroom) attached to Dublin Castle, in Exchange Court, a cul-de-sac beside City Hall.

On 20 November, McKee and Clancy (see below) had attended a meeting of GHQ staff with Michael Collins, where the plans for the following day were finalised. In the early hours of the following day, Clancy and McKee were arrested at a house on Gloucester Street, betrayed by a tout, a former British serviceman, who was later shot by the Squad.

Below left: Brigadier Dick McKee, O/C Dublin Brigade, after his arrest following a raid at the Sinn Féin offices, Harcourt Street, in 1919. A 1916 and Frongoch veteran, he was also attached to GHQ as Director of Training. McKee (formerly Marlborough) Barracks in Dublin is named after him.

Below: plaque recording the killings.

Right: mugshot of Vice-Brigadier Peadar Clancy, a 1916 veteran, a Squad leader, and GHQ Director of Munitions. He was the owner of the 'Republican Outfitters' on Talbot Street, near where Seán Treacy was shot.

Clancy and McKee were brought to a guardroom in the Castle. Also there was Conor Clune, an Irish-language enthusiast (but not a Volunteer), rounded up at Vaughan's Hotel. Brigadier-General Winter, head of the Secret Service in the Castle, led the interrogation. The authorities later announced that the three had been shot while 'trying to escape'.

It was widely believed that they had been tortured to extort the names of the assassins of earlier that day and summarily shot. There was extensive bruising on the bodies, with multiple bullet wounds.

Right: in another exercise of 'fake news' these photos were staged by the Castle press office re-enacting the purported events: the prisoners got hold of grenades supposedly stored there, threw these, but they did not detonate. Next they grabbed rifles (and a shovel) and fired at their guards who killed them in the 'exchange of fire'.

155

Reflecting the shock at this ruthless attack at the heart of the British presence in Ireland, there was a large funeral procession in Dublin and then grand processions and elaborate funeral services in London.

Left: the funeral procession of the slain officers on 25 November, watched by large crowds in Dublin. It was patrolled by Auxiliaries checking that businesses stayed closed and that men removed their hats.

Left: coffins are loaded at Dublin docks onto HMS 'Sea-Wolf' en route for Holyhead.

Near right: Captain Price's sister follows his coffin.

Far right: memorial programme at the Westminster Abbey service.

Below: gun-carriages carrying the coffins, en route to Whitehall.

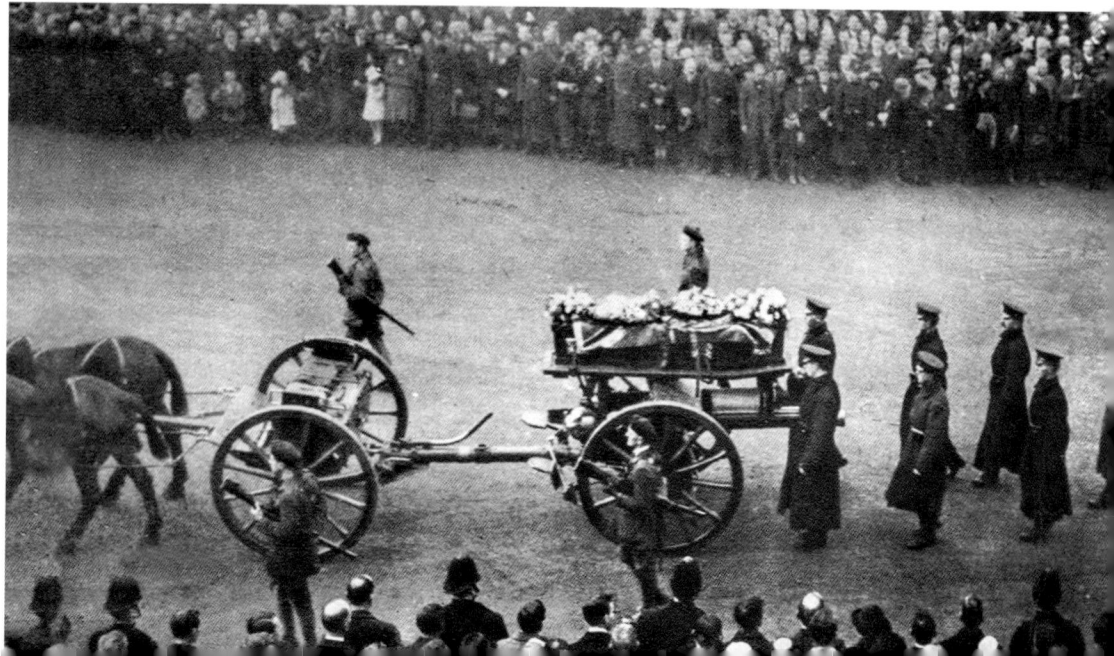

WESTMINSTER ABBEY.

✝

THE FUNERAL SERVICE

OF

The Officers of H.M.'s Army
and Cadets of the R.I.C.

MURDERED IN DUBLIN ON
SUNDAY, NOVEMBER 21ST.

NOVEMBER 26TH, 1920.

11 A.M.

In the aftermath of Bloody Sunday there was a massive crackdown. Senior British officials moved into a crowded Dublin Castle and their wives were sent back to Britain. In Dublin, there were roadblocks and widespread raids, and a curfew was imposed.

Left: in a raid on Liberty Hall on 24 November, Thomas Johnson, Secretary of the Labour Party (left), and other union leaders were arrested.

Below: a patrol by 'I' Company ADRIC, posing in their Crossley Tenders in front of Amiens Street (now Connolly) Station.

Above: No. 1 Camp, Ballykinlar, sketched by Aodh Mac Néill.

Over 500 arrests were made in the roundup at the end of November 1920. Ballykinlar camp in Co. Down was opened to house the internees. By December, Ballykinlar was getting full. The Admiralty was asked to provide vessels to carry prisoners. 'Rebels' were interned at various places including Spike Island, Bere Island, Sligo Prison and the Cork Detention Barracks.

Right: a hut at Ballykinlar. The crosses remember two Volunteers, shot by a sentry in January 1921.

Left: Father Michael Griffin, curate at Rahoon in Galway city, who was known to be sympathetic to the Republican cause. On the night of 14 November 1920, he was arrested and taken to the 'D' Company ADRIC HQ at Lenaboy Castle. On 20 November, his body was found buried in a bog near Barna. He had been shot in the head.

On 26 November a large force, made up of RIC and ADRIC, made a sweep through south Galway. As Patrick and Harry Loughnane (both Volunteers) were threshing at their farm at Shanaglish, they were picked up and arrested. After torture they were dragged by ropes attached to the back of a lorry, and brought to an Auxiliaries' base. On 5 December their charred and mutilated bodies were found in a pond near Ardrahan.

Right: in an open coffin – the body of Patrick Loughnane alongside the coffin of his brother, Harry.

Left: Lenaboy Castle, Galway, the HQ of 'D' Company, who earned a reputation for brutality. In early November they shot dead a pregnant woman sitting on her lawn near Gort, as they drove by.

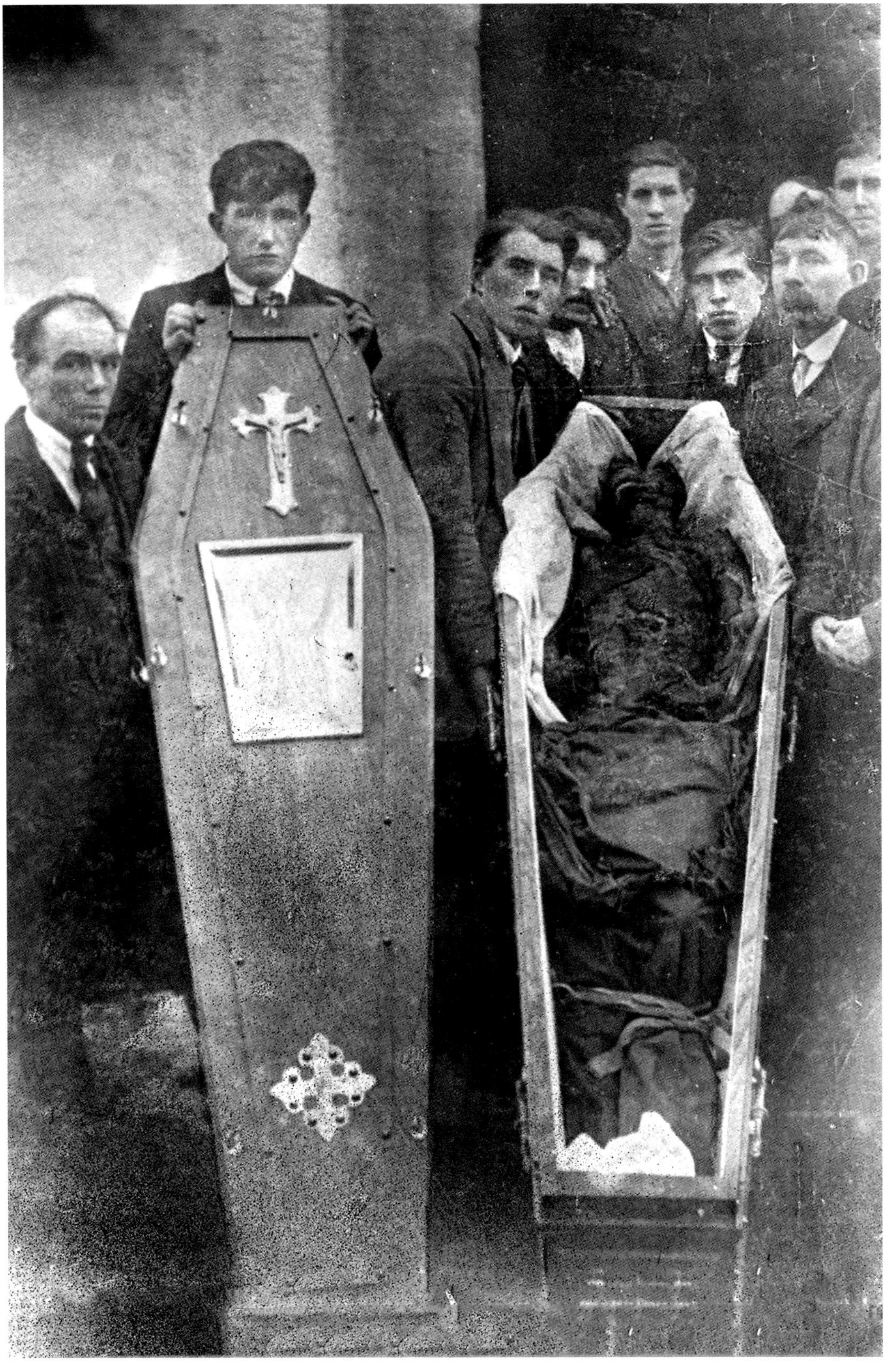

Above: looking south, a fish-eye view at Kilmichael, Co. Cork where on 28 November, an Auxiliary patrol was ambushed. This place of rock, bog and heather now has some trees, but in 1920, it was barren, with little cover. With rising ground at either side and sited at an 'S' bend, it was an ideal ambush location.

Left: the entrance to Macroom Castle, base of 'C' Company, ADRIC. At around 4 pm on the fatal day, 18 Auxiliaries in two Crossley Tenders headed out for Dunmanway.

As they approached Kilmichael, Tom Barry and the 3rd West Cork Brigade flying column lay in wait.

Commandant Barry was in charge of 40 men of his flying column, as well as several scouts from local units. He established his command post (and positioned three marksmen) at a point, fronted by a low stone wall, on the eastern (Dunmanway) end of the road. Barry placed three sections in commanding positions on higher ground: No. 1 (ten men) around 15m to his west; No. 2 (ten men) about 150m further west; and No. 3 divided into seven men south of the road, with others as a reserve north of the road.

Right: map of the Kilmichael ambush.

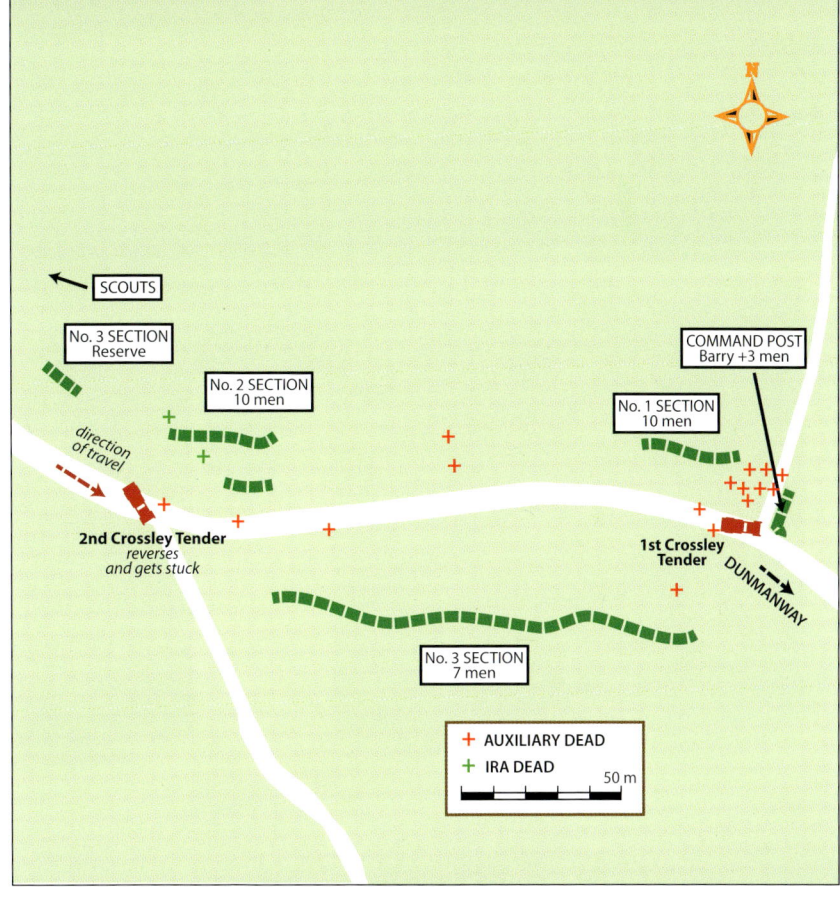

Left and below: damaged Crossley Tenders at the ambush site.

Barry stepped out wearing a Volunteer's tunic. As the leading Crossley Tender stopped, he threw a Mills bomb which killed the driver and the commander, D/I Colonel Crake. Fire was poured on the tender from both sides of the road. The driver of the second tender, about 150m behind, tried to turn around but got stuck. The Auxiliaries jumped out and took cover. No. 2 Section, ideally placed, opened fire on them. With the cadets in the first tender vanquished after fierce hand-to-hand combat, Barry and his men headed west to deal with the second tender.

By the end of the action 16 Auxiliaries were dead. Another, Cadet Forde, suffering a head wound, was left for dead, but survived. Another wounded Auxiliary escaped and reached within three km of Macroom, but was captured by the IRA and shot. His body was dumped in a bog. Two of the IRA were killed and another later died of his wounds.

Left: marker of the IRA command post. It states unambiguously that on this road died 'seventeen terrorist officers of the British forces'.

Right: crossed rifles, carved in stone, the memorial at Kilmichael.

The ambush here has suffered, if anything, from over-analysis, based on tendentious or false evidence. The controversy hinges on why all the Auxiliaries had been shot. Barry stated that some of the Auxiliaries made a false surrender, resulting in his men being shot by other Auxiliaries, who fired as his men advanced – thus he ordered that they be killed.

The American military historian WH Kautt concluded that the most likely scenario was that some Auxiliaries did indeed call out a surrender, but that others, out of sight or hearing, may have been reloading and fired when they saw the Volunteers move out of cover. He concludes that while there is no way to prove that this suggested scenario occurred, the evidence fits this supposition better than any other. He adds: 'Further, there is no reason to presume that this was deliberate murder or deliberate perfidy on either side'.

Right: stern of mien – the bust of Commandant-General Tom Barry, by Séamus Murphy at Fitzgerald Park, Cork.

Left: a burnt-out farmhouse near Kilmichael. The next day, when other Auxiliaries saw the bodies, they burnt two nearby farmhouses.

It was alleged that the dead bodies had been mutilated. The autopsy by Dr Jeremiah Kelleher (whose son Philip, an RIC D/I, had been shot at Granard just weeks before) stated that, as well as the general range of bullet wounds and bomb injuries, two bodies had sustained head injuries inflicted after death. Cadet Forde claimed afterwards that as he lay feigning death, an IRA man hit him on the head with a rifle butt.

The history of the war, written afterwards by the British Army, referring to the post-Bloody Sunday round-ups, said: 'from this time, the initiative may be said to have passed to the Crown forces'. This egregious statement was disproved by the Kilmichael ambush and events over the following months. Being an IRA victory over an elite force, Kilmichael undermined the confidence of the British Government in their prosecution of the war.

Left: coffins of the cadets, wrapped in Union flags, en route to Britain.

Right: a view eastwards to Dillon's Cross. This crossroads on the northern heights of Cork City is around 500m from Collins (previously Victoria) Barracks.

At around 8 pm on 11 December 1920, six Volunteers of the 1st Battalion, Cork No. 1 Brigade, lay in wait behind this wall. The location had been chosen as regular Auxiliary patrols from Victoria Barracks slowed down while making a sharp turn at the crossroads heading towards the city centre.

On that bright frosty night, two tenders, with around 20 Auxiliaries, came into sight. As they slowed, the IRA opened fire using rifles and revolvers. Mills bombs were hurled into the tenders. Hearing the noise, reinforcements rapidly arrived from the nearby barracks. Searchlights were brought into play and the Volunteers withdrew. Bloodhounds were used in the chase. One Auxiliary had been killed and 11 wounded in the ambush. The Auxiliaries' blood was up – as Cork city centre was now to discover.

Right: a Mark IV tank demolishes a butcher's shop, as part of reprisals at Dillon's Cross a few days after the ambush.

Left: the night sky glows as Cork burns.

The Auxiliaries had been on edge – it was less than two weeks since their colleagues had been killed at Kilmichael. The Dillon's Cross ambush proved to be the tipping point.

The Auxiliaries immediately headed to the city centre. They began an orgy of burning, drunkenness and looting. Auxiliaries and soldiers roamed along St Patrick Street, Cork's main thoroughfare. Some were uniformed, others in plain clothes. Civilians were beaten up, while others fled. Bombs were thrown in stores. As the streets emptied the burnings began. The Crown forces poured petrol into buildings. (Some 300 gallons of petrol had been taken from the stores at Victoria Barracks.) The mayhem continued and by 4 am the City Hall was ablaze.

Left: ruined buildings on St Patrick's Street, Cork after the reprisal.

Right: 'fake news' from Italy. The caption accepts the official British spin that troops were defending the city. It says that in the: '...historic northern (sic) city – the troops had to...disperse looters'.

La Tribuna Illustrata

La caccia alle jene fra le rovine di Cork

Durante l'incendio di Cork, in Irlanda, — incendio che ha distrutto in breve ora oltre trecento case della storica città nordica — la truppa ha dovuto affrontare e disperdere numerose bande di saccheggiatori che attorno all'immenso braciere depredavano i cadaveri e frugavano fra le rovine che le fiamme avevano abbandonato.

(Disegno di E. Abbo)

'K' Company ADRIC, (who wore burnt corks on their caps, celebrating the burnings) were moved to Dunmanway. En route to the funeral of their colleague, killed at Dillon's Cross, they shot a priest and a farmer. Left: letter (captured by the IRA) to his mother from Charles Schultze of "K" Company, dated 16 December: '...I have never experienced such orgies of murder, arson and looting as I have witnessed during the past 16 days...On our arrival here...one of our heroes held up a car with a priest and civilian in it and shot them both...without cause or provocation...The burning and sacking of Cork followed immediately on the ambush of our men...Many who witnessed similar scenes in France...say that nothing they experienced was comparable to the punishment meted out in Cork...General Higginson arrived this morning to have a "straight talk" with us about discipline, etc., as he put it. I am afraid we struck terror into him for the "straight talk" never materialised. He was most amiable...' In another letter, he wrote to his girlfriend, regarding Cork: 'We took a sweet revenge...'

Left: the ruins of Cork's largest drapery store.

Above: fire brigades at work – a steam pump and the Dublin Leyland fire engine pumping water from the river Lee. As Cork Fire Brigade struggled to put out the fires, they were intimidated by Crown forces. Hoses were cut by bayonets and were deliberately run over by lorries. They were shot at and two firemen were wounded.

Limerick Fire Brigade came by road to Cork's assistance. Dublin Fire Brigade, under the command of Chief Officer Jack Myers, travelled to Cork by a special train.

Right: this photograph of a Cork scene from the American Commission Report is captioned 'Soldiers and members of the RIC sampling the contents of a shop before it was blown up.'

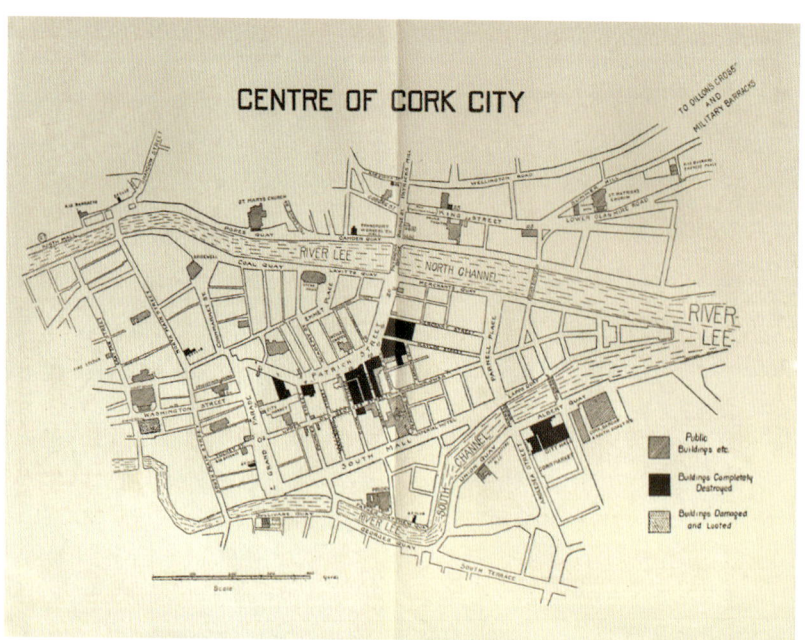

Left: map of damage. Cork's centre was devastated. There were 20 burned stores on Patrick Street, with 35 wrecked premises in the side streets. Hundreds of residences were destroyed. The City Hall and the Carnegie Library were in ruins. Damage amounted to over €160 million in today's values.

In the aftermath, Sir Hamar Greenwood informed the Commons that '…he did not believe …that forces of the Crown were responsible…(they) ..had actually saved Cork because when the Fire Brigade was exhausted the police and military took over their work…'

A military court of enquiry was ordered by (the 'amiable' – see page 170) Brigadier-General Higginson, Cork garrison commander, which concluded that the Auxiliaries were responsible. In light of this, a second, more wide-ranging, military enquiry was held, reporting in February 1921. Known as the Strickland Report, it determined that, while the Army and the RIC did their job efficiently that night, the Auxiliaries were to blame (mentioning 'K' Company in particular). The British Government refused to publish the report.

Left: cartoon by Shemus.

Right: in Co. Clare, Crown forces, with a Rolls-Royce armoured car, pose, simulating a response to an ambush. As 1920 ended, the number of attacks by the IRA continued apace.

Right: proclamation of martial law, 27 December 1920, by Major-General Strickland. It covered most of the Munster counties: Cork, Tipperary, Kerry and Limerick.
In the Martial Law areas the British initiated a system of carrying what they termed 'IRA leaders' in every lorry convoy, in effect as hostages against attack – with mixed results.

Below: Major-General Peter Strickland (Commanding 6th Division), who was based at Victoria Barracks, Cork.

DIVISIONAL PROCLAMATION

By the General Officer Commanding 6th Division, and Military Governor.

WHEREAS, Martial Law has been declared in the Counties of Cork, Tipperary, Kerry and Limerick. And whereas the Generals, or other Officers commanding 6th Division, 16th, 17th, 18th and Kerry Infantry Brigades, have been appointed Military Governors for the Administration of Martial Law in the above Counties, and all persons ordered to render obedience to their Orders in all matters whatsoever.

Now I, MAJOR-GENERAL SIR E. P. STRICKLAND, K.C.B., C.M.G., D.S.O., Commanding 6th Division and Military Governor, do hereby give Notice and Order that:

1. Any person found committing any crime punishable under the ordinary law (including the Restoration of Order in Ireland Regulations), any person disobeying any Order or contravening any Regulation duly given or issued by any lawful authority, or doing any Act prejudicial to the safety, efficiency, or well being of any of His Majesty's Naval, Military, Air or Police Forces, and any person who is guilty of any act, conduct, or neglect to the prejudice of good order, or the Restoration of Order in Ireland commits an offence against Martial Law, and may be apprehended and tried under and suffer such punishment as is in accordance with Martial Law.

2. Any person found defacing, or otherwise tampering with Martial Law Proclamations or Notices will be rigorously dealt with.

3. The Owner, lessee or responsible occupier of every occupied building shall have on the inside of the outer door of each inhabited building a list stating the name, sex, age, and occupation of every person residing in such building.

Such owner, &c., will be held responsible for fixing such a list of the members of his household, and for the accuracy of the list and for making all alterations necessary owing to the departure or arrival of members of the household.

In the case of an inhabited building containing several flats or tenements, a separate list shall be made out for each flat or tenement and fixed on the inside both of the outer door of the flat or tenement and of the outer door of the main building. The head of each separate household will be responsible for the list of persons forming his household.

Any alterations in a list necessary owing to changes in the members of a household shall be made by the head of the household within three hours of the change occurring.

This Order shall come into force on the 4th day of JANUARY, 1921.

4. (1) Every Hotel or Boarding House-keeper is responsible for the conduct of persons in his house or hotel.

(2) Every Hotel or Boarding House-keeper shall keep a Book (open to the inspection of any officer or non-commissioned officer or police constable) wherein he shall cause to be entered the names, occupations and addresses of all persons arriving in or departing from the Hotel or Boarding House. Such Book shall also shew the places from, or to which, such persons have come or gone.

(3). A daily written report setting forth such particulars must be furnished to the District Inspector Royal Irish Constabulary of the district by every Hotel or Boarding House-keeper.

(4) Every Hotel or Boarding House-keeper will be made liable for any arms, ammunition or explosives found on his premises.

This Order shall come into force on the 4th day of JANUARY, 1921.

Signed this 27th day of December, 1920.

E. P. STRICKLAND,

Major-General Commanding 6th Division, Military Governor.

Above: in late March, 1920, Ian MacPherson, then Irish Chief Secretary, presents the second reading of the 'Government of Ireland' Bill. Lloyd George sits behind him. After a slow passage it finally became law on 23 December 1920 (Inset: the Act.). Nationalist MPs and the few southern Unionists voted against it. By this bill the British parliament now imposed partition on Ireland.

Left: a view by Punch in March 1920 of Lloyd George's partition trickery. His decision to 'kick the can down the road' and give the Unionists what they wanted, still reverberates today.

This, Britain's fourth attempt at Home Rule, divided Ireland into two parts. To placate the northern Unionists, the carve-out of the north was subsequently restricted to the six north-eastern counties ('Northern Ireland') of Ulster where they had a majority. The remaining 26 counties constituted 'Southern Ireland'. Each entity had a bicameral parliament with limited powers. A Council of Ireland was to coordinate, with (as a sop to nationalists) the implication that it might evolve into an all-Ireland parliament in the future.

Right: demographics – why the six counties, not all of Ulster, were chosen.

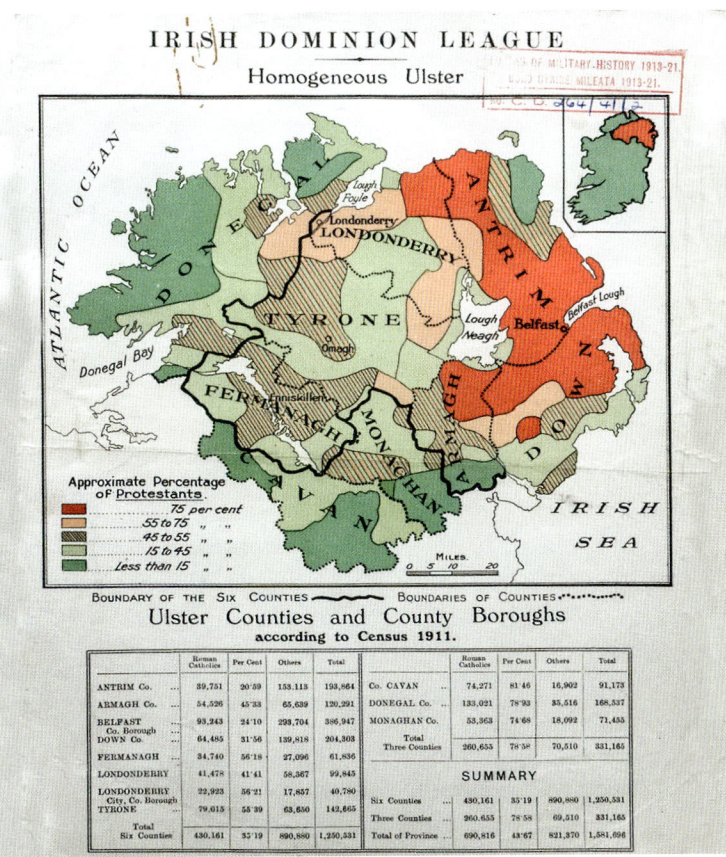

IRISH DOMINION LEAGUE
Homogeneous Ulster

Approximate Percentage of Protestants
- 75 per cent
- 55 to 75
- 45 to 55
- 15 to 45
- Less than 15

Ulster Counties and County Boroughs according to Census 1911.

	Roman Catholics	Per Cent	Others	Total		Roman Catholics	Per Cent	Others	Total
ANTRIM Co.	39,751	20.59	153,113	193,864	Co. CAVAN	74,271	81.46	16,902	91,173
ARMAGH Co.	54,526	45.33	65,639	120,291	DONEGAL Co.	133,021	78.93	35,516	168,537
BELFAST Co. Borough	93,243	24.10	293,704	386,947	MONAGHAN Co.	53,363	74.68	18,092	71,455
DOWN Co.	64,485	31.56	139,818	204,303	Total Three Counties	260,655	78.58	70,510	331,165
FERMANAGH	34,740	56.18	27,096	61,836					
LONDONDERRY	41,478	41.41	58,367	99,845	**SUMMARY**				
LONDONDERRY City, Co. Borough	22,923	56.21	17,857	40,780					
TYRONE	79,015	55.39	63,650	142,665	Six Counties	430,161	35.19	890,880	1,250,531
					Three Counties	260,655	78.58	69,510	331,165
Total Six Counties	430,161	35.19	890,880	1,250,531	Total of Province	690,816	43.67	821,370	1,581,696

Above: the impossibly tall men of the DMP search an American ship, docked in Dublin, for Éamon de Valera (left). On 23 December, he arrived back in Dublin smuggled aboard a ship from Liverpool, where he had transferred from an American ship.

It was a change for de Valera, to have to operate clandestinely in Ireland, in contrast to the adulation and rallies of America. Tensions developed with Collins and Mulcahy. De Valera began to criticise their guerrilla warfare approach.

Above: members of the Dublin Brigade Active Service Unit (ASU).

The ASU was established a few days before Christmas 1920. It comprised 50 Volunteers, in four companies, each assigned to one of the city Battalions. Each man was full-time and paid £4 10s per week. Attacks on Crown forces in Dublin soon intensified.

Right: Gardiner Row, from where the ASU operated.

Below: plaque.

REMOVING THE BLACK BOX WHICH CONTAINED THE NOTORIOUS TYPHOID PLOT PAPERS: SOLDIERS AT A HOUSE IN DUBLIN.

Above and left: the press reported 'a raid on Professor Hayes's house in Dublin', although the accompanying photos show a different location. The British claimed that proposals for a 'Typhoid Plot' had been among papers of the IRA Chief of Staff, Richard Mulcahy, seized in the raid. It shocked the spymaster Brig.-General Winter so much that he sent the documents by plane to London poste-haste. Hamar Greenwood read out the captured document in parliament on 18 November 1920. Joseph Devlin MP responded that this was concocted by Dublin Castle.

Right: the captured document. It muses on spreading glanders amongst British horses, as well as using milk to infect troops with typhoid. It concludes with a hearty 'God bless all'.

Middle right: international press reaction. The British indeed had form with black propaganda in Ireland (see pages 138 to 141).

However, the document was genuine. Thought had previously been given to germ warfare – James O'Donovan, Director of Chemicals, IRA, recalled later in his Witness Statement (extract below right), referring to the conscription crisis of 1918, that he had considered glanders and botulism.

In 1962 Richard Mulcahy recalled that Dr Pat McCartan had sent the typhoid paper to Michael Collins – but 'this was a joke as far as Mick and myself were concerned' – and had been destined for the wastepaper basket, when captured.

Below: such was the nervousness that an outbreak of typhoid in West Cork was investigated to see if it was part of the alleged plot.

Typhoid Spread Alarming.
Dublin, Nov. 25.—There is an alarming outbreak of typhoid fever in the Skibbereen district. Several deaths are being investigated by the authorities, but no evidence has been uncovered to connect the outbreak with the alleged plot by the Sinn Fein to spread typhoid germs.

Sinn Fein Plot to Spread Typhoid Among Troops

By Associated Press.

London, Nov. 18.—Sir Hammar Greenwood, chief secretary for Ireland, said in the house of commons today that during a recent raid in Ireland troops captured a document sent by the commander-in-chief of the Irish republican army to his chief of staff containing a "series of remarkable and horrifying statements regarding the spreading of typhoid among the troops and glanders among the cavalry horses."

SINN FEIN METHODS
TYPHOID GERMS IN MILK
Remarkable Letter
PEACE DEPUTATION DECLINED

Consideration was also given to the possibility of infecting the horses in the various cavalry barracks with glanders or some similar infectious disease. Another aspect of bacteriological warfare was the possibility under consideration of spreading disease, e.g. botulism, on which I wrote a couple of articles about 1918. The whole thing arose out of the conscription scare because in the highest circles, even in the Castle, it was definitely expected that conscription would be applied here. It was the nearest miss that this country ever experienced.

Left: the Co. Roscommon IRA Roll of Honour memorial at Elphin.

As 1920 ended, the war had reached a new intensity. The number of casualties among the Crown forces for that year had spiralled – a total of 231 killed (178 police and 53 military).

Guerrilla warfare has been called the method of the weak versus the strong. The Boers had demonstrated the value of this decades before, as did the Volunteers' action at Ashbourne in 1916. Over the course of the conflict, the IRA adopted guerrilla warfare in an ad-hoc way, responding to circumstances. Units across the country empirically crafted their tactics to suit the local situation. A major development was the setting up of flying columns from late Summer 1920. Generally operating in groups of around 25, these were full-time and were better armed. The flying columns generally proved very effective. They had local knowledge and operated with flexibility (enjoying much independence from GHQ in Dublin).

The 28 December 1920 edition of 'Hue-and-Cry' (left), the internal bulletin of the RIC, sets out its priority list of 'Sinn Féiners', whose apprehension is sought.

Chapter 4
Ambushes, Truce and Treaty
1921

As the British increased their forces and roamed the country, IRA ambushes and raids escalated. Both sides improved their tactics. These included the IRA gaining mastery of road mines. The British Army developed cross-country sweeps; the RAF was newly empowered to use machine guns and drop bombs. A Government of Ireland bill enacted in the British parliament established partition, with 'Northern' and 'Southern' parliaments. In an election for these in May, Sinn Féin, unopposed, won practically all the seats in the 'South'. Unionists won a majority in the 'North' and King George V opened the parliament there in June. The British government ended a period of confused direction of the war, by inviting Éamon de Valera to talks in London. A Truce was agreed for 11 July. As the shooting stopped, de Valera met Lloyd George in London but there was no meeting of minds. Plenipotentiaries were sent to London in October. The negotiations hit against the rock of British intransigence over allegiance to the King and membership of the British Empire – a Republic was not on offer. On 6 December, the delegates signed a treaty, without consulting Dublin. The British agreed to Dominion status for the twenty-six counties and the die was cast for a Civil War in Ireland, which broke out six months later.

WHERE THERE IS NO PEACE AND GOOD-WILL
THE FIRST OFFICIAL REPRISALS IN IRELAND

RUINS OF A SHOP AND HOUSE at Midleton occupied by Mr. J. O'Shea.

ALL THAT NOW REMAINS OF THE HOUSE AT MIDLETON OCCUPIED BY MR. COTTER. Miss Cotter in the midst of the debris of the old home.

Miss Cotter and two of the farm servants.

NOTICE. "B".

To:- PAUL McCARTHY.
    MIDLETON.

WHEREAS attacks by unknown rebels were made on the Forces of the Crown on the 29th December 1920 at MIDLETON and near GLEBE HOUSE, MIDLETON, in the County of CORK, and whereas it is considered that you being in the vicinity of the outrages were bound to have known of the ambushes and attacks and that you neglected to give any information to the Military or Police Authorities, now therefore I, Brigadier General. H.W.HIGGINSON, C.B., D.S.O. Commanding 17th Infantry Brigade and Military Governor have ordered the destruction of your property.

Signed at CORK this first day of January 1921.

H. W. Higginson.
Brigadier General.
Military Governor......

Left: the 'Graphic' reports on reprisals at Midleton.

On 29 December 1920 a flying column ambushed an RIC patrol on the main street at Midleton. Three constables died as a result. A reprisal followed – seven houses were destroyed. There had been many reprisals but this was the first 'official' reprisal, allowed for under martial law. In the following months, official reprisals across Munster became commonplace.

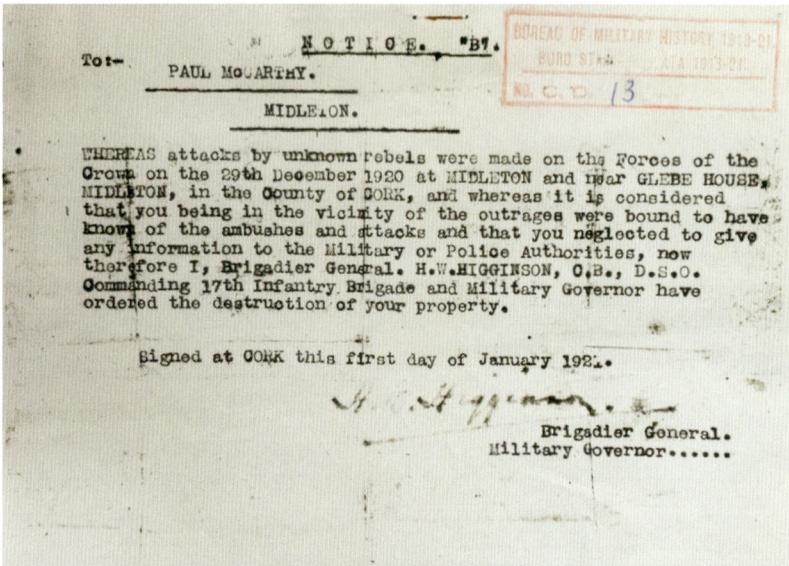

Left: Brigadier-General Higginson informs Paul McCarthy that his property is about to be demolished. A Volunteer had sheltered in McCarthy's doorway during the ambush.

A reprisal at Meelin, Co. Cork, followed soon after Midleton. Six houses were burnt and a teenager killed in retaliation for an ambush there (led by Seán Moylan) on 4 January 1921.

Left: this photograph from Meelin is captioned: 'Widow Brown's daughter in charge of the furniture after the destruction of their home'.

On 5 January 1921 martial law was extended to cover the counties of Clare, Waterford, Kilkenny and Wexford.

Right: the Labour Commission sitting in the Shelbourne Hotel, Dublin, December 1920.

The British Labour Party had opposed the partition of Ireland, but also opposed the concept of a republic – it wanted to maintain the connection between the two islands. The party wished to preserve its British patriotic 'brand' and concentrated more on social improvements in Britain. Amidst the uproar in Ireland, however, the leadership was assailed for its timidity. As a sop, a commission of enquiry on Ireland was proposed in November 1921. After duly making investigations it published a report which detailed reprisals and atrocities. It concluded: 'Things are being done in the name of Britain which must make her name stink in the nostrils of the whole world...a nation is being held in subjection by an empire which has proudly boasted that it is a friend of small nations'.

Right: Punch opines that the Sinn Féiners duped the 'Labour Bhoys'. Reverting to form and continuing its anti-Irish racist trope (which appeared regularly during the Victorian era), it depicts one of the men in simian form.

PUNCH, OR THE LONDON CHARIVARI.—January 5, 1921.

THE GLAD EAR.

First Sinn Feiner. "SURE 'TWAS A FINE TALE WE GAVE THIM LABOUR BHOYS TO SWALLOW."
Second Ditto. "AN' 'TWAS A FINE APPETITE THEY HAD FOR UT."

Left: Tolka Bridge at Drumcondra, Dublin.

On 21 January 1921, eight ASU members of the 1st Battalion, Dublin Brigade headed to Tolka Bridge and opened fire on two approaching RIC tenders. However, the IRA position had been given away (the alleged informer was executed five months later). The Auxiliaries of 'F' Company were alerted and attacked the ASU as they were dispersing. Two Volunteers escaped. One died of his wounds and the remaining five were captured – four of whom were later executed in Mountjoy.

Below: an IRA intelligence book depicts 'F' Company, ADRIC.

```
                    "F" Coy. Aux.
   1. Dore 2. Halper 3. Palmer 4. Herrott (London). 5. Reynolds (L'pool).
   6. - .7. Lewis (wounded at Custom Ho.) 8. Huntingford 3rd D.I.
   15. Shelton. 10. Cassmaker Sec Ldr. 12. Thompson (Intelligence) 16.
   McClean 17. Axminster (bad pill). Fletcher(18). 19. Gorman. 20. Hughes
   21. Florry 3rd D.I. 22. Derrick (Tortures prisoners) 23. Igoe (Mur'er)
   26. Webb. 27. Bennett. 29. Frail Lt. Tony. 30. Coaker. 31. Costigan
   35. Beckett. 36. Carew. 39. Lamb. 40. Sparron. 41. Capain (O/C "F").
   42. Barrett. 43. Downes. 44. Cutting. 46. Webber (Lt. Tank Corps.)
```

Right: the view from Milan in January 1921 – 'after searches made by English soldiers and police in the homes of Sinn Féiners, they burned in the (Dublin) streets the revolutionary brochures and books...' In reality this refers to a search of Liberty Hall after Bloody Sunday at the end of November 1920 where the troops burn the 'revolutionary literature' found there.

Right: a large-scale sweep in Dublin by Crown forces. The British Army official history of the war relates: 'In February 1921 some extensive operations were carried out by troops and police in Dublin. Areas of the city were surrounded by cordons and troops and systematically searched'.

Above: site of the Dripsey ambush.

The IRA planned an ambush here at Dripsey, to intercept a regular army patrol from Macroom to Cork. On the night of 27 January 1921, Captain Frank Busteed and 68 men set up on the high ground here. Trees were prepared ready to fall to trap the army lorries. The next morning, Mrs Mary Lindsay (left), a loyalist, heard of the ambush and ordered her driver to bring her to Ballincollig Barracks, where she informed the military. A strong force of soldiers accompanied by two armoured cars set out and at around 4:15 pm encircled the ambushers. Most escaped, save eight who were captured.

Right: Victoria (now Collins) Barracks, Cork. A court martial was held here in early February 1921 and five of those captured at Dripsey were sentenced to death.

On the night of 17 February Mrs Lindsay and her chauffeur were taken hostage by the IRA. Mrs Lindsay was forced to write a letter to General Strickland saying she would be shot if the prisoners were executed. This was disregarded and the five prisoners were executed by firing squad on 28 February. On 11 March, Mrs Lindsay and her driver were shot and their bodies buried. The next night her house was burnt down.

Right: applying for a military service pension, Frank Busteed in his evidence explains how: '... we arrested Mrs Lindsay and driver as spies. Both were executed later'.

Below: memorial to the executed Volunteers at UCC (the former Cork County Gaol where they had been buried.)

> In March 1921 we held up train for mails at Blarney, and some useful information from same. We also got information Gen Strickland was coming by train. We held up the train, but Strickland wasn't on, we also had a party holding traffic on the Main Road to Cork. In March 1921 we arrested Mrs Lindsay and Driver as being Spies. Both were executed later. We burned Mrs Lindsay House; at this period Military came in thousands into our area in search of the Spies. The result was it gave our column all they could do to keep out of the Rings around us.
>
> *Frank Busteed*

Left: extracts from a GS&WR memo on the events at Mallow.

```
GREAT SOUTHERN AND WESTERN RAILWAY.
            District Superintendent'S Office,
0078.                    CORK.
                                   February 1st, 1921.

Dear Sir,
        Attack on Mallow Station by armed men - 31/1/21.
        ------------------------------------------

        I wired you to-day as follows :-

        "I am at Mallow inquiring into serious attack made on
        Station Staff and premises by armed men last night
        one Loco Cleaner Bennett killed, and Drivers Maher,
        Howe, Martin, Cleaner Cronin, Train Examiner Morrissey
        Steam Riser Mahoney, also Traffic Signalman Devitt
        wounded several Traffic and Loco men arrested.    All
        trains delayed but all now cleared except following
        Goods trains 8.10p.m., 10.30pm., 11.45 p.m., 4.0a.m.
        and 5.30 a.m. ex Cork.    Some wrecking done at Station
        contents of both 1st and 3rd Class Refreshment Rooms
        looted.   No material damage done to Company's property.
        Full report follows."
```

```
            The armed forces first entered Mallow Station about
10.15 p.m. last night following the shooting of County Inspector
King and his Wife, who it would appear were walking on the
Public road crossed overhead by the Railway at Annabella Bridge
which is adjacent to, and immediately south of the South Signal
box at Mallow Station, and from which point the Police appear to
think the shots came and that it could not have taken place without
the cognizance of our Staff.
```

On the night of 31 January 1921, Volunteers lay in wait by a road near the entrance to Mallow station, intending to ambush 'Black and Tans'. In the darkness they fired at RIC County Inspector William King and his wife, Alice, who were walking back to their lodgings in the west end of the town. King was wounded but his wife died soon afterwards. Infuriated RIC and Auxiliaries arrived from nearby barracks and charged into Mallow station. They shot up a train, then ordered railway staff to run for their lives. These were fired on – many were hit. Two men died and another later died of his wounds. Brigadier-General Cumming presided at the military court of enquiry. He was killed at Clonbanin (see page 198) before the enquiry was completed. The eventual findings concluded: 'there is no evidence to show who is guilty of the alleged heavy depredations'.

Left: the South signal box at Mallow station, referred to in the GS&WR memo.

Above: the ambush site at Clonfin, Co. Longford

Right: Seán Mac Eoin, popularly known as 'the Blacksmith of Ballinalee'.

On 2 February 1921, 17 members of 'M' Company, ADRIC, were returning in two Crossley Tenders from Granard to Longford. At Clonfin, as the road dipped down approaching a small bridge, a mine exploded under the leading tender, throwing it across the road, and injuring the occupants. In a well-planned ambush, the North Longford flying column, led by Seán Mac Eoin, opened fire on the second tender. After 20 minutes four Auxiliaries lay dead and eight were wounded. Mac Eoin prevented the survivors from being executed and chivalrously ensured that the wounded were cared for.

Right: the North Longford flying column in May 1921.

Above: ambush site at Dromkeen.

The flying columns of the East and Mid-Limerick Brigades, IRA (under Donncha O'Hannigan) ambushed an RIC patrol here, (returning to Pallasgreen) on 3 February 1921. It was a bloody encounter for the Crown forces, resulting in 11 dead. The first tender came under heavy fire and crashed into a wall. The second was fired on from the cemetery and the opposite side of the road. Eight RIC died immediately. A column member, Maurice Meade (a veteran of Casement's Irish Brigade), stated that O'Hannigan held a court martial on the spot – the officers voted three to two to execute the remaining Black and Tans. Meade said that he then shot them.

Left: memorial

Above: near the Drishanbeg ambush site.

On 11 February, two Volunteers entered the locomotive driving cab of the 6:30 pm Mallow to Tralee train as it stopped at Rathcoole station. The train was carrying a party of soldiers, en route to Killarney. The Volunteers ordered the driver to give a warning whistle blast as they approached Drishanbeg, about two km beyond Millstreet, and then stop. As the train stopped in a cutting at a lighted cycle lamp placed on the track, the IRA commander shouted out for the soldiers to surrender. There was a volley of shots in reply. In the darkness, the North Cork Brigade poured fire at the military in the train, lit up with oil torches thrown down the embankment at the start of the engagement. The British party surrendered and the attackers gathered up their rifles and ammunition, and then withdrew. Two soldiers died as a result of the exchange of fire in the ambush.

Right: troops search under a carriage of a train on the Mallow-Tralee line.

Above left: Upton station (on the Cork-Bandon section of the West Cork Railway), closed in 1961.

Another (but disastrous for the IRA) train ambush occurred at Upton, near Inishannon, on 15 February 1921. Led by Charlie Hurley, O/C 3rd Cork Brigade, 13 Volunteers with seven rifles lay in wait at the station. They had been expecting just 20 soldiers of the Essex Regiment, but another 30 had joined at Kinsale. After Drishanbeg, the British had ordered that troops were not to be concentrated but to spread out along trains. As the train to Bandon arrived the IRA opened fire at the centre carriage where they thought the British party were located. The soldiers replied with heavy fire from all along the train. The death toll after the ten-minute battle was eight civilians, and three IRA. Charlie Hurley was wounded.

Left: a dramatic Italian depiction of the ambush.

Right: Shemus's view of Sir Hamar Greenwood, the Chief Secretary, in 1921. He waves his Union flag, as troops charge into the inferno that Ireland was becoming for the British.

Below right: bust of Ernie O'Malley, one of the most senior commanders of the IRA. He had travelled to Kilkenny in December 1920 to shake it up because, as he later wrote: 'Kilkenny was slack'. Arrested by Auxiliaries at Inistiogue, he was brought to Kilmainham Gaol, and placed in a cell in the corridor of condemned cells known colloquially as 'Murderers' Gallery'. The next cell contained Patrick Moran, awaiting trial for a Bloody Sunday shooting. Another prisoner was Frank Teeling (who had been wounded in the leg and captured at the back gate of 22 Lower Mount Street on Bloody Sunday. His execution date was drawing near). On the night of 14 February 1921 O'Malley, Teeling and Simon Donnelly (Vice Commandant 3rd Battalion, Dublin Brigade) escaped from the Gaol.

Far right: Simon Donnelly years later points out the gate at Kilmainham, through which he and his companions escaped.

Left: the Limerick landscape as seen from Italy. 'La Tribuna Illustrata' breathlessly states: 'There are no longer any limits in the daring of the "Sinn Féiners"...the assault of a train in Co. Limerick.'

On the morning of 17 February 1921, the IRA lay in wait for a train at Barragone, Co. Limerick, midway on the line between Foynes and Askeaton. It was expected to be carrying RIC to testify at a court martial of a Volunteer that day in Limerick. As the train approached, a red flag was waved and the train stopped. As fire was poured on the train, a Black and Tan crawled under the train to the locomotive. At the point of a revolver he ordered the driver to move the train, which stopped after a bend. The RIC constables replied to the attacker's fire. The Volunteers withdrew with one wounded.

Left: a combined military and police patrol in Co. Limerick. Two Crossley Tenders jammed full of RIC are followed by a lorry-load of soldiers, with a Peerless armoured car taking up the rear.

194

Above: memorial at Clonmult (near Midleton) Co. Cork, where the one-story farmhouse once stood.

The 4th Battalion of the 1st Cork Brigade, after several successful actions, including the December ambush at Midleton, were billeted in the farmhouse at Clonmult where they were training and planning further attacks. Unwisely, they had spent five weeks there.

An informer told the British of their location. On 20 February 1921, two tenders carrying soldiers of the Hampshire Regiment headed from Midleton towards Clonmult.

Right: even though it depicts an earlier event at the end of 1920, this 'Petit Journal' cover eerily presages the attack by Crown forces on the cottage at Clonmult.

195

Left: the burnt-out farmhouse at Clonmult.

The military halted about a kilometre from the cottage and split into two groups. On the way they shot two Volunteers who were outside, then surrounded the cottage and opened fire. The Volunteers within were trapped, with no back door and only a few windows at the front to return fire. After an hour of shooting, five men made an attempt to escape. Three were shot dead, one retreated back inside and Captain O'Connell managed to cut through the British cordon. Two truckloads of ADRIC now arrived. The thatched roof was set on fire. As the smoke swirled, the remaining occupants decided to surrender. Throwing their weapons into the fire, nine men exited the house. One was clubbed to the ground. The Auxiliaries began to shoot the rest. By the end of the action, 12 IRA men lay dead. The British later contended that there was a false surrender (claiming firing continued as the IRA exited to surrender). It has been called 'Kilmichael in reverse', but oddly has not garnered the same exhaustive analysis.

Left: memorial at Clonmult church.

As the munitions crisis faded away at the end of 1920, British troops were able to resume travel by railway. In turn, the IRA ramped up their attacks on the railway: holding up trains and destroying signalling, track and bridges.

Right: torn up track and boulders resulted in a derailment near Glenties (where the train 'precipitated down the embankment into the lake...'). The traffic manager of the County Donegal Railways threatens that if there is any further interference with the Stranorlar and Glenties Line, it will be closed for all traffic.

Right: IRA Volunteers working for the railway were in danger of impromptu revenge by Crown forces. This GS&WR memo recounts the fate of Charles Daly. At midnight on the night of 28 February, 1921, Daly, a young GS&WR parcels porter and Volunteer with Cork No. 1 Brigade, was seized from an office in Glanmire railway station, Cork, by masked men. He was dragged to the mouth of Cork tunnel, beaten up and shot dead.

Above: ambush site at Clonbanin (near Banteer), North Cork.

On 5 March 1921, Brigadier-General HR Cumming was returning to Brigade HQ from an inspection tour in Kerry. His touring car was escorted by three Crossley Tenders and a Rolls-Royce armoured car.

Left: on the day before he was killed, Cumming awards medals to the Royal Fusiliers at Killarney.

Below: Cumming's funeral in London.

Right: Brigadier-General Cumming.

Around 100 Volunteers from the Cork and Kerry brigades lay in wait at Clonbanin – Seán Moylan was one of the commanders. An earlier attempt to detonate a mine as an westbound convoy passed, had failed. Cumming's convoy, spaced out along 800m, approached from the west. The IRA opened fire. A bullet (from a Hotchkiss machine gun, previously captured by the IRA) entered the drivers slit of the armoured car and wounded the driver. The armoured car crashed, but continued firing with its Vickers. Cumming was shot as he ran for cover. After three hours of battle, the IRA withdrew. Cumming and three soldiers were killed.

On 11 March, a large force of Auxiliaries and military (acting on information from an informer), surrounded and attacked a training camp of the Leitrim Brigade, IRA, at Selton Hill (near Mohill, Co. Leitrim). Seán Connolly, organiser for Leitrim and Longford, and five Volunteers were killed. The informer, a doctor, fled to London after an attempt on his life.

Right: memorial at Selton Hill.

DATE of death	No.	NAMES.		Age.	Medical Opinion of the Cause of Death.
1921 March 14	1	Thomas	Whelan 422	22	✗
" " "	2	Patrick	Moran 439	26 (33)	✗
" " "	3	Patrick	Doyle 453	29	✗
" " "	4	Bernard	Ryan 455	20	✗
" " "	5	Thomas	Bryan 454	22	✗
" " "	6	Frank	Flood 456	19	✗
" April 25	7	Thomas	Traynor 654	40	✗
" June 7	8	Patrick	Maher 906	32	✗
" " "	9	Edmund	Foley 907	23	✗
" " "	10	William	Mitchell 908	33	

Above: the Mountjoy Jail record of executions in 1921.

Captain Patrick Moran, a 1916 veteran, had led the assassinations at the Gresham Hotel on Bloody Sunday. He was arrested five days later and wrongly convicted for the shootings at Upper Mount Street.

Left: the day before they were hanged on 14 March, in an unaccountably jolly mood, Patrick Moran and Thomas Whelan. Whelan had been sentenced to death for the Bloody Sunday killing of Captain Baggallay at Baggot Street.

	REGISTRY OF DEATHS.	1921.	
...nce to ...ittal.	Whether Inquest was held.	Verdict of Jury.	OBSERVATIONS.
3 21	Military Inquiry held	-	Hanged at 6am. 14.3.21 Buried within the Prison
3 21	Do	-	Do
3 21	Do	-	Hanged at 7am. 14.3.21 Buried within the Prison
3 21	Do	-	Do
3 21	Do	-	Hanged at 8am 14.3.21 Buried within the Prison
3 21	Do	-	Do
4 21	Do	-	Hanged at 8am 25.4.21
5 21	Do	-	Hanged at 7am 7.6.21
5 21	Do	-	Do
5 21	Do	-	Hanged at 8am 7.6.21

The Volunteers seized at the Drumcondra ambush on 21 January – Patrick Doyle, Bernard Ryan, Thomas Bryan and Frank Flood were also executed on 14 March.

The English executioner, John Ellis (who had hanged Roger Casement and Kevin Barry), and his three assistants were smuggled into the jail in an armoured vehicle. The Squad had planned to kill him at his hotel, but he had already reached Mountjoy.

Right: reflecting the outrage at the six executions on 14 March, a postcard from Germany.

A GERMAN VIEW OF THINGS.
ENGLAND
HANG-LAND
"ZUM GEDÄCHTNIS FÜR IRLANDS FREIHEITSKÄMPFER"
REMEMBER IRELAND'S GALLOWS.
(THE ORIGINAL WAS PUBLISHED IN BERLIN, BY THE GERMAN-IRISH SOCIETY ON THE OCCASION OF THE SIX EXECUTIONS IN MOUNTJOY.)

THE WAY OF THE WORLD

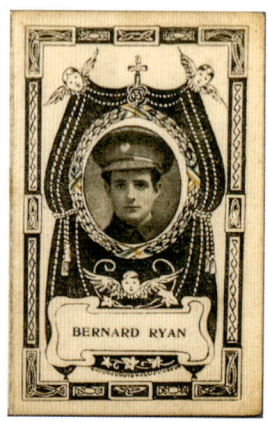

Remarkable Scenes at the Execution of Six Irish Rebels in Dublin: 1. Reciting the Rosary outside the gaol; 2. Fixing religious pictures to the prison gate; 3. An armoured car arriving.

Above: the 'Graphic' records the thousands who knelt in prayer outside Mountjoy on the day of execution. The ITGWU called for a general work stoppage that morning.
Left: memorial cards for some of the executed.

At 6:00 am on 14 March, Patrick Moran and Thomas Whelan were led from their cells, bound and hooded, placed on the trap door, and simultaneously hanged. The other four were hanged in pairs in the following two hours.

The executed were buried next to Kevin Barry, in a corner of Mountjoy Jail. Three others were hanged in 1921 (Thomas Traynor for killing an Auxiliary in Dublin, as well as Edmond Foley and Patrick Maher for the Knocklong rescue of 1919). In 2001 the remains of the executed ten were transferred to Glasnevin Cemetery in a state ceremony.
Left: the ten graves.

Above: the funerals of Clancy and O'Callaghan.

Early in the morning of 7 March 1921, during the hours of curfew, men in civilian dress burst into the homes of the Mayor of Limerick, Seoirse Clancy, and his predecessor, Michael O'Callaghan, and shot them dead. Mrs Clancy had attempted to save her husband but was wounded. The assassins had collars turned up, caps over faces and wore goggles. Suspicion immediately fell on the Auxiliaries.

MURDERED: ALDERMAN GEORGE CLANCY, MAYOR OF LIMERICK.

MURDERED: MR M. O'CALLAGHAN, EX-MAYOR OF LIMERICK.

Above: memorial at Crossbarry, around 18 kilometres south-west of Cork city.

Tom Barry, with 104 men of his 3rd West Cork flying column had spent a miserable St Patrick's Day in 1921 lying in wait along the Bandon-Kinsale road, awaiting a British patrol which never showed up. By the night of 18 March they had reached their HQ north of Crossbarry village and were billeted in several houses. However, the Crown forces had just extracted information on their location from a Volunteer captured at the Upton ambush some weeks before, and planned a vast sweep to capture Barry's column. At around 1:00 am on 19 March, the Crown forces set out with around 1,000 men to encircle a large area.
Left: Tom Barry.

Soldiers were drafted in from Cork, Ballincollig, Bandon and Kinsale as well as 120 Auxiliaries from Macroom. Barry was wakened at 2:30 am – the lookouts had noticed the lights and sounds of lorries. At 3:00 am he paraded the men. With his customary decisiveness, he decided to attack one side of the encirclement. This was at the Crossbarry road, which, as luck had it, turned out to be a weak part of the cordon. His Volunteers were in place by 5:30 am.

Right: monument to Charlie Hurley, O/C 3rd Cork Brigade, near where he was killed. At around 6:30 am a raiding party rushed into a farmhouse near Crossbarry where Hurley (wounded at Upton) was staying. He was killed in an exchange of fire.

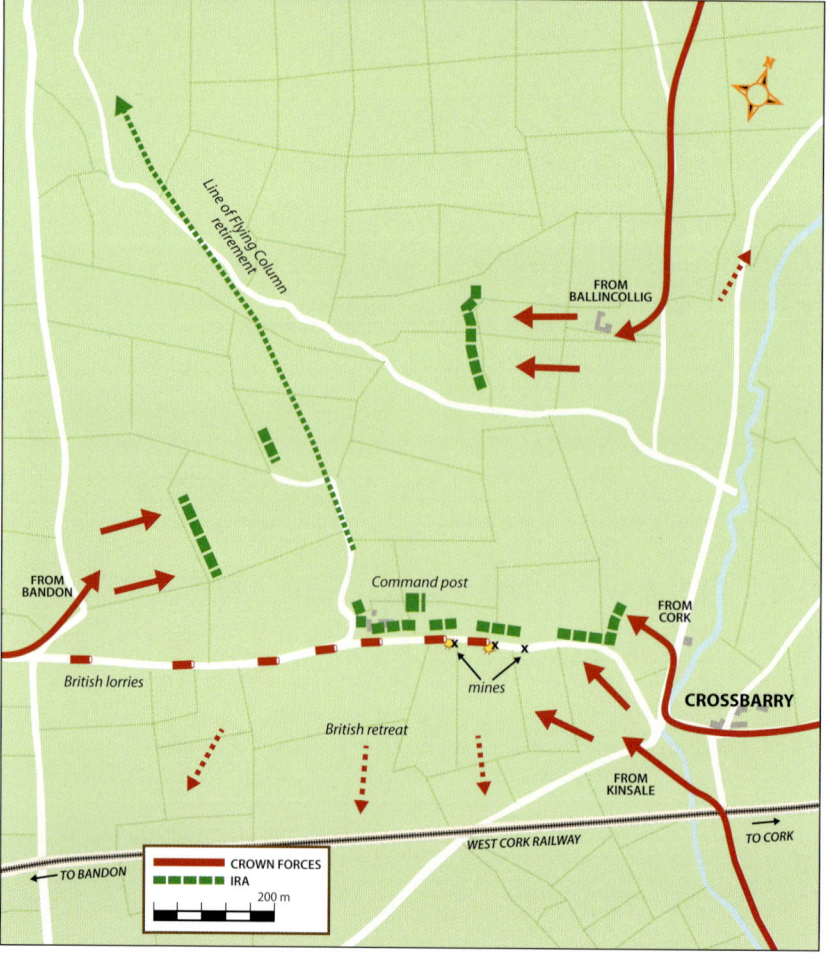

Above: the military barracks at Bandon. The Essex Regiment, based here and at Kinsale, fought at Crossbarry.

At around 8:00 am as lorryloads of troops slowly crept along the road at Crossbarry, a mine exploded and IRA rifles opened up. The British took heavy casualties and many soldiers fled, with Volunteers in pursuit. There were several fierce exchanges, as waves of military arrived. The IRA then withdrew to the northwest. Three Volunteers (plus Charlie Hurley) were dead – the British declared ten killed. This large-scale battle was the most successful carried out by the IRA.

Left: map of the battle at Crossbarry.

The British Army was well equipped with combat-proven weapons. Above is the general-issue British infantry rifle of WWI, the Lee Enfield bolt-action SMLE Mk III. A soldier could fire off the ten .303 rounds in the magazine in 15 seconds.

Near right: the standard officer's sidearm – a Webley Mk 6 .455 calibre revolver (with belt and holster).

Above far right: a Mills bomb, or grenade.

Right: a Vickers heavy machine gun. Water-cooled, it could fire .303 bullets at 500 rounds per minute.

Below: the American-designed Lewis machine gun, of .303 calibre. With a pan magazine, it was air-cooled using an aluminium barrel radiator. It was light, but could pump out 550 rounds per minute.

Above: Royal Fusiliers in Kerry, with a Vickers machine-gun truck in front of a locomotive.

At Headford Junction the branch line to Kenmare diverges from the Mallow-Tralee line. On 21 March 1921, the 2nd Kerry Brigade assembled to ambush a party of 28 men of the Royal Fusiliers travelling by train from Kenmare, who planned to detrain at Headford to catch a later train from Mallow to Killarney. At 3:00 pm the train, with a Vickers in the first carriage, pulled in at Headford.

Left: the train after the ambush.

Above: burial party for the Royal Fusiliers killed at Headford Junction.

The Kenmare train was early and the 30 Volunteers, spreading out on either side of the tracks, opened fire. The Vickers in the front carriage was put out of action. Shooting continued for about 50 minutes. When the connecting train from Mallow pulled in (which also had troops aboard, and a machine-gun truck in front), the IRA withdrew. Lying dead were: eight British soldiers; two civilians (another died later) and two IRA men.

Right: a GS&WR memo succinctly reports the events at Headford Junction

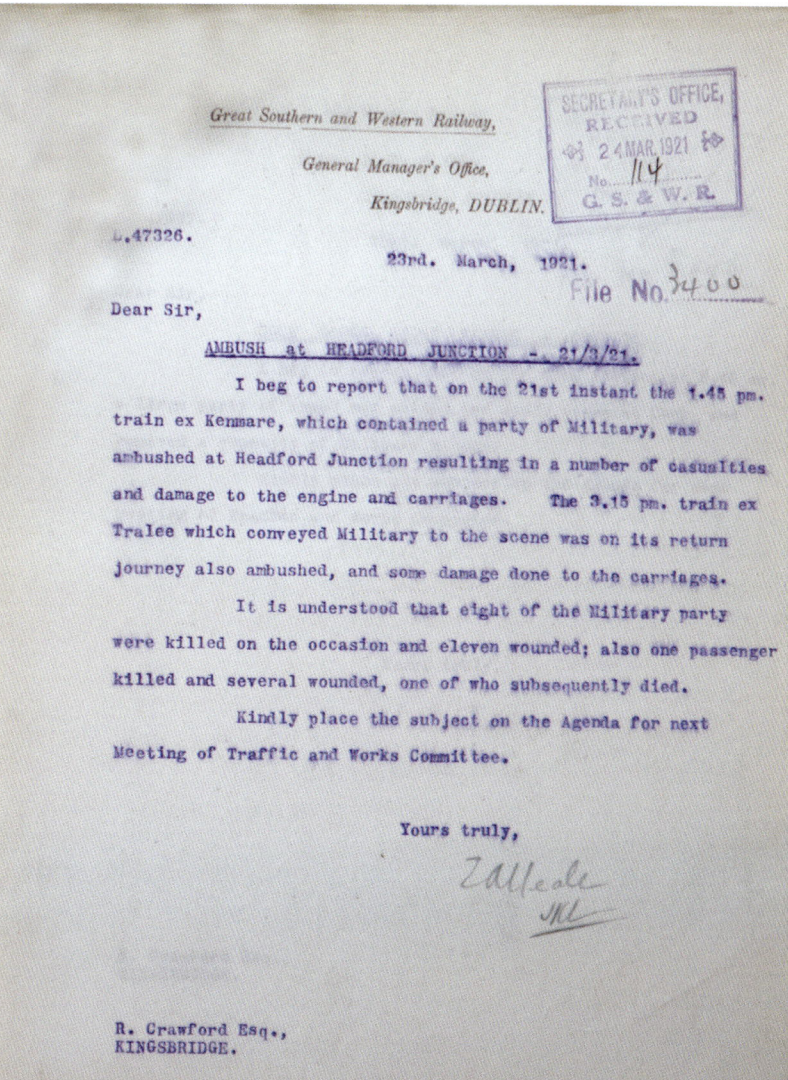

Great Southern and Western Railway,

General Manager's Office,

Kingsbridge, DUBLIN.

SECRETARY'S OFFICE, RECEIVED 24 MAR. 1921 No. 114 G.S. & W.R.

L.47326.

23rd. March, 1921.

File No. 3400

Dear Sir,

AMBUSH at HEADFORD JUNCTION - 21/3/21.

I beg to report that on the 21st instant the 1.45 pm. train ex Kenmare, which contained a party of Military, was ambushed at Headford Junction resulting in a number of casualties and damage to the engine and carriages. The 3.15 pm. train ex Tralee which conveyed Military to the scene was on its return journey also ambushed, and some damage done to the carriages.

It is understood that eight of the Military party were killed on the occasion and eleven wounded; also one passenger killed and several wounded, one of who subsequently died.

Kindly place the subject on the Agenda for next Meeting of Traffic and Works Committee.

Yours truly,

[signature]

R. Crawford Esq.,
KINGSBRIDGE.

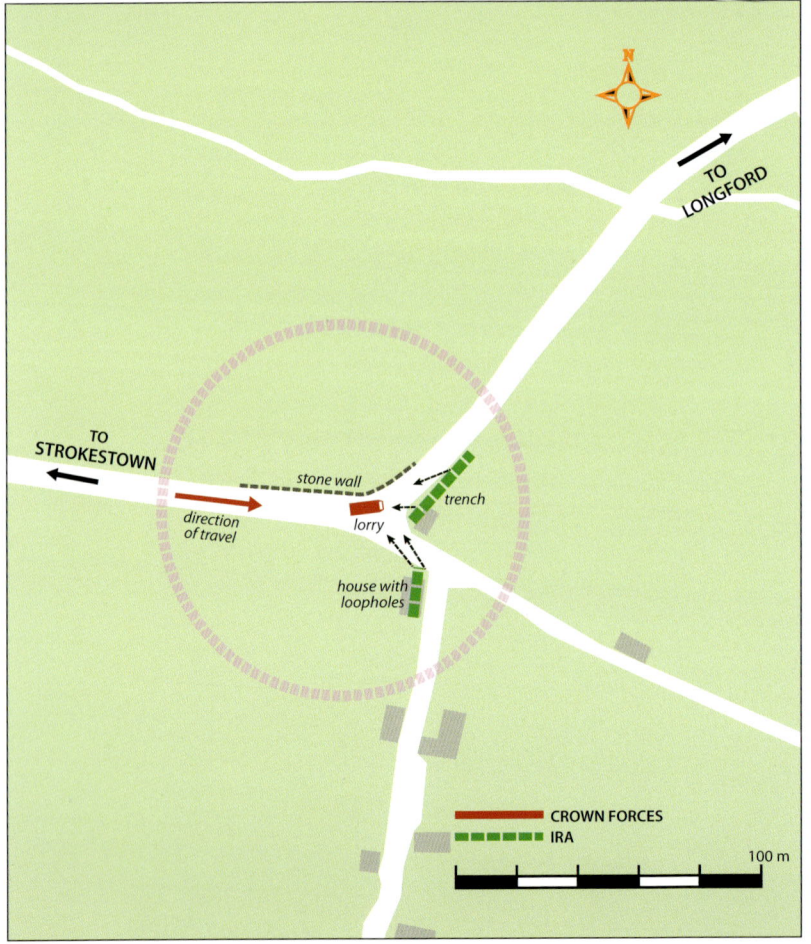

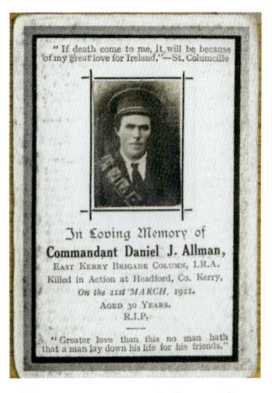

Above: memorial card for Commandant Dan Allman, leader of the Headford ambush, killed on the platform ramp.

Left: monument to IRA dead at Headford.

On 23 March the combined Roscommon brigades had dug in for an ambush at Scramogue, Co. Roscommon. One of their aims was to avenge their organiser, Seán Connolly, and his comrades who had been killed at Selton Hill 12 days before (Connolly had previously chosen Scramogue as an ambush site). As a lorry with RIC and soldiers drove up, the attackers opened fire, stopping the lorry. The occupants took cover behind a stone wall. The survivors soon surrendered. Four (including two army officers) lay dead. Two RIC constables (Black and Tans) were taken prisoner and later killed.

Map, left: the ambush site on a bend of the Strokestown-Longford road.

Above: this painting by Mick O'Dea depicts Michael Kilroy, and Volunteers, one with a Lewis machine gun (probably the one captured at the Carrowkennedy ambush), and the other with a Thompson submachine gun.

In early 1921, Kilroy (described by historian Michael Hopkinson as a 'puritanical and ascetic blacksmith') was appointed O/C West Mayo Brigade. In the Spring of 1921 there was increased activity against Crown forces.

Right: a map of the Castlebar Battalion area, West Mayo Brigade.

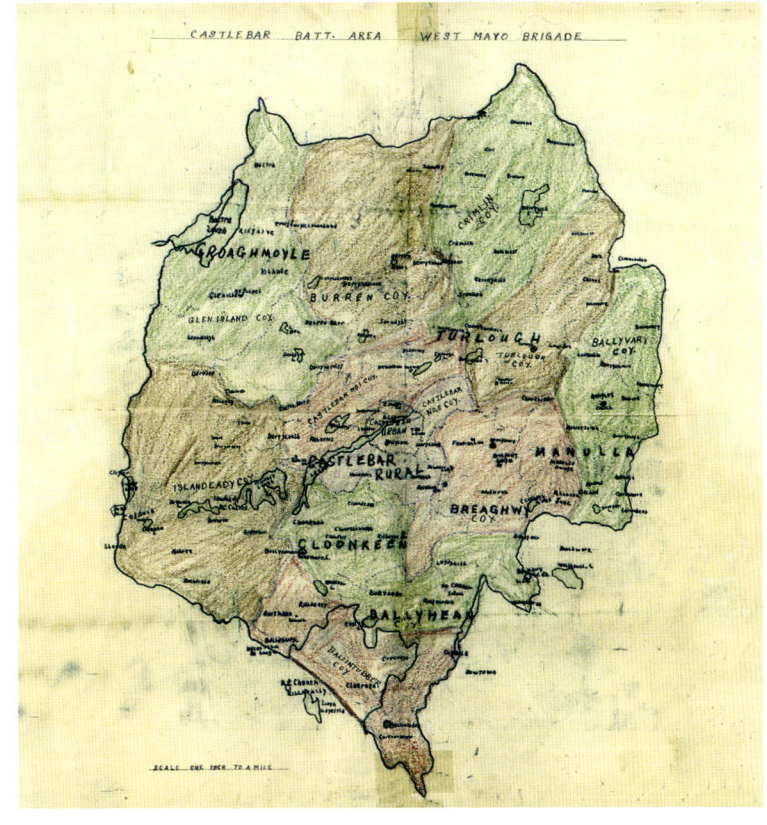

Left: the London & North Western Railway Hotel (built 1884) at North Wall, Dublin. From March 1920 it was used as a HQ and barracks by 'Q' Company, ADRIC. Made up mostly of former naval and merchant navy men, their mission was to control port security and particularly to interdict IRA arms imports.

On 11 April, the IRA, under Tom Ennis, attacked just after 8:00 am, opening fire at the front and sides of the hotel. A mine placed at the front door failed to explode. Grenades were thrown through the windows. These included gas grenades (phosphorus in carbon bisulphide in a small bottle). The Auxiliaries, suffering from the noxious fumes, burst out of the building, firing at the attackers. A whistle blew and the IRA withdrew, having suffered one dead.

Left: cadets in celebratory mood after the attack.

Below: an officer shows unexploded grenades.

Above: pleased to pose for the cameras after the attack – a simulated search.

Right: The Scherzer bascule lifting bridge at Spencer Dock (seen here against the backdrop of the present-day Convention Centre.) Volunteer Garry Houlihan was detailed to lift the bridge to deny passage to reinforcements coming to the aid of the beleaguered Auxiliaries. He tried to lift the electrically-operated bridge but was unsuccessful. However, he managed to close the road gates, which delayed the Crown forces.

Left: the genealogist Sir Arthur Vicars. In 1893 he had been appointed Ulster King of Arms. He was also Registrar for the Order of St Patrick. In 1907, the insignia of the order, also known as the 'Irish Crown Jewels' (then under his custody) were stolen from Dublin Castle. Vicars resigned in some disgrace. He moved from Dublin to Kilmorna House, near Listowel, Co. Kerry. As the military frequently visited his house, a local IRA unit decided he was a spy. On 14 April 1921 Vickers was executed and, for good measure, Kilmorna House was burned down, to 'prevent it being used by the military'.

Another assassination occurred the following day, around 20km to the south-west. Major MacKinnon, commander of the Auxiliaries, was playing golf at Tralee. As he reached the third green, he was shot twice in the head. The usual reprisals ensued in the district. The 'Kerryman' works were blown up after a refusal to print with a black border.

Left: Major MacKinnon. During his time in Tralee, this tall war hero had earned notoriety, burning houses with great zeal and personally killing two Volunteers.

Above: memorial at Clogheen (around 5km north-west of Cork City).

Early in the morning of 23 April 1921, the RIC encircled a barn near Clogheen, where six Volunteers (all from Blarney Street) of 1st Battalion, Cork No 1 Brigade, were asleep. All were shot dead – the bodies were badly mutilated. They had been betrayed by an informer, who fled to New York. In April 1922, he was shot four times near Central Park by Cork IRA men, and later died of his wounds.

Right: an armoured car and troop lorries shadow the Volunteers' funeral at Cork Cathedral.

Map of IRA divisions in Ireland:

- 1st Northern
- 2nd Northern
- 3rd Northern
- 4th Northern
- 5th Northern
- 3rd Western
- 4th Western
- 2nd Western
- 1st Western
- 1st Midland
- 1st Eastern
- 2nd Eastern
- 3rd Eastern
- 1st Southern
- 2nd Southern
- 3rd Southern

Left: the eventual IRA divisional structure.

In Spring 1921, GHQ decided to introduce a decentralised divisional structure The idea was that this would result in better cooperation across boundaries and simpler management. First was the 1st Southern. The map, right, shows the brigades in mid-1920.

Below: officers of the 1st Southern Division meet at the Mansion House in April 1922. Senior figures in the front include Divisional Commander Liam Lynch (1), with Liam Deasy (2) Seán Moylan (3) and Florrie O'Donoghue (4).

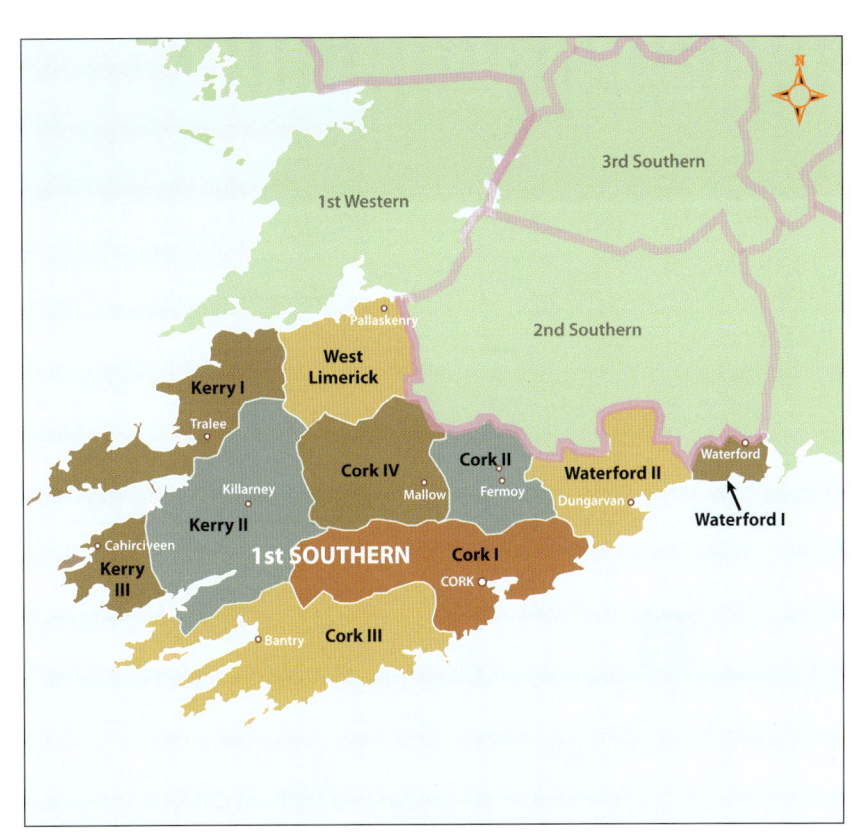

RESIGNED OWING TO THE REINSTATEMENT OF R.I.C. CADETS: BRIG.-GEN. CROZIER.

THE REINSTATEMENT OF DISMISSED R.I.C. CADETS: MAJOR-GENERAL TUDOR.

Left: Brigadier-General Frank Crozier, commander of the ADRIC, resigned at the end of February 1921, in protest at the reinstatement by Major-General Tudor of 21 Auxiliaries. Crozier had earlier dismissed these for looting and indiscipline during a raid on a shop and public house in Trim, Co. Meath on 9 February.

Crozier's replacement was his deputy, Brigadier-General EA Wood. Wood had experience of being on the other side of the law. At New Year 1896, as a lieutenant he had ridden with the Bechuanaland Border Police in the Jameson Raid to Johannesburg, which failed – the raiders were captured by the Boers. This was an illegal attempt (supported by Cecil Rhodes and other British colonists) to overthrow the Boer Transvaal republic.

Left: On 27 April 1921 Viscount Fitzalan replaced Viscount French as Lord Lieutenant (Viceroy) of Ireland. This high Tory was a Catholic, the first ever such to hold that office since 1685. However, being of that religion did not result in any particular initiative and he is solely remembered for being the last Lord Lieutenant.

Right: No. 2 Battalion, Cork No. 1 Brigade.

A world away from the gilded halls of the Viceregal Lodge, all over Ireland young men were inspired to take up the fight for Irish freedom. There was a strong sense of nationality and they were propelled by the pervasive folk memory of English injustice to Ireland over the centuries. In urban areas many were lower middle class, or artisans and shop assistants. In the country many were small farmers. It was a dangerous and difficult life, with no prospect of gain. Some fought part-time, others were on the run in flying columns.

Right: No. 2 Flying Column, 3rd Tipperary Brigade.

Below right: a rifle section of 3rd Battalion, Waterford Brigade.

Memorials to fallen Volunteers are to be seen throughout Ireland. Below: plaque to John Cummins, killed by the British military at Ballyvoyle, Co. Waterford in June 1921.

219

Above: at Clonakilty in West Cork, a joint patrol of the RIC and the 1st Battalion, Essex Regiment, about to set off on their bicycles. The naval rating in the background is most likely a wireless operator assigned to the army.

On 2 May 1921 the East- and Mid-Limerick flying column were surprised, on a road at Lackelly, Co. Limerick, by a joint bicycle patrol of 11 men of the Green Howard Regiment (based at Galbally) and three members of the RIC. After a fierce exchange of fire, four Volunteers lay dead.

Left: a 1912 model Raleigh military bicycle.

Right: the back page of 'La Domenica de Corriere' depicts what they term as an official reprisal in Dublin – 'soldiers demolish a house in the area that was the recent scene of an ambush by Sinn Féiners'. As the troops energetically flail with their picks, the armoured car looks like a Peerless which has metamorphosed into having only one turret.

La lotta in Irlanda: rappresaglie ufficiali a Dublino. Protetti da un'autoblindata, parecchi soldati demoliscono una casa nella zona che fu teatro, recentemente, di un'imboscata da parte dei Sinn Feiners.

Right: In a not-so-subtle demonstration of military might, soldiers use a Mark IV tank to punch in the door of a premises in Capel Street during a large sweep in Dublin in 1921.

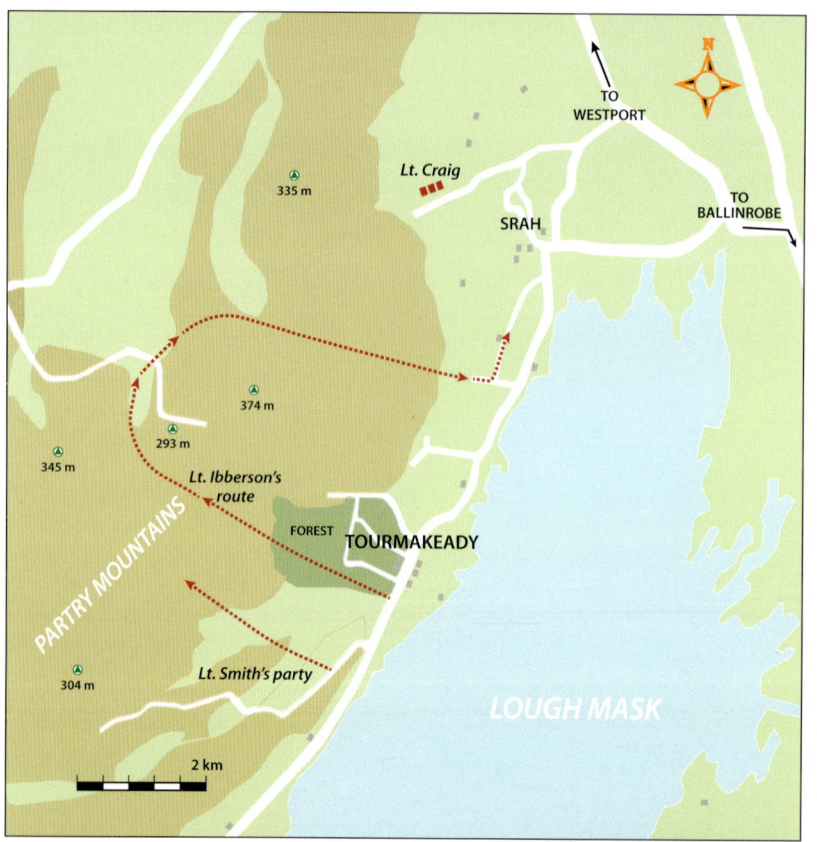

Left: map of the Tourmakeady area (after Donal Buckley).

In the early afternoon of 3 May 1921, the South Mayo Brigade flying column, under Tom Maguire, ambushed an RIC supply column at Tourmakeady. Four RIC were shot dead. The local IRA disbanded and the remaining 30 withdrew west into the Partry Mountains. News of the ambush was phoned to Ballinrobe and the Border Regiment, based there, set out. Arriving at Tourmakeady around 3:15 pm, the leader of the company, Lieutenant Ibberson, deployed his men. Lieutenant Craig and a party with a Lewis gun, were assigned to go north by Srah to encircle the mountain. Ibberson led a unit west into a forest, while another group under Lieutenant Smith advanced to the south. By the time Ibberson emerged from the dense wood only two of his party were with him.

Left: Commandant Tom Maguire, wounded on the mountain.

Below: bare terrain – the Partry Mountains.

Right: a 1956 letter, from Ibberson to Craig, discussing Tourmakeady.

Ibberson noticed some armed men on a ridge, around 300m away, and fired at them. Then he saw a larger group ahead.

Ibberson was an experienced runner, and, telling his men to catch up, he sprinted after the IRA column – Ibberson wanted to turn them towards Craig's position. Having reached a point ahead of the IRA column's line of advance, Ibberson fired several rounds at the leader of the column, who fell wounded. The column was next fired on by Craig's Lewis gun. Ibberson ran on, shouting to his imaginary troops: 'Come on my Borders', then 'Hands up, surrender'. Adjutant Michael O'Brien, who had been helping the wounded Maguire, shot at Ibberson, who returned fire, killing O'Brien. Volunteers blazed at Ibberson, who sustained several wounds (including a pellet lodged near his heart). With difficulty he made his way down the mountain and eventually reached his men. The IRA had dispersed. A search party the next day found O'Brien's body and discarded weapons.

Right: Lieutenant Craig's award for gallantry.

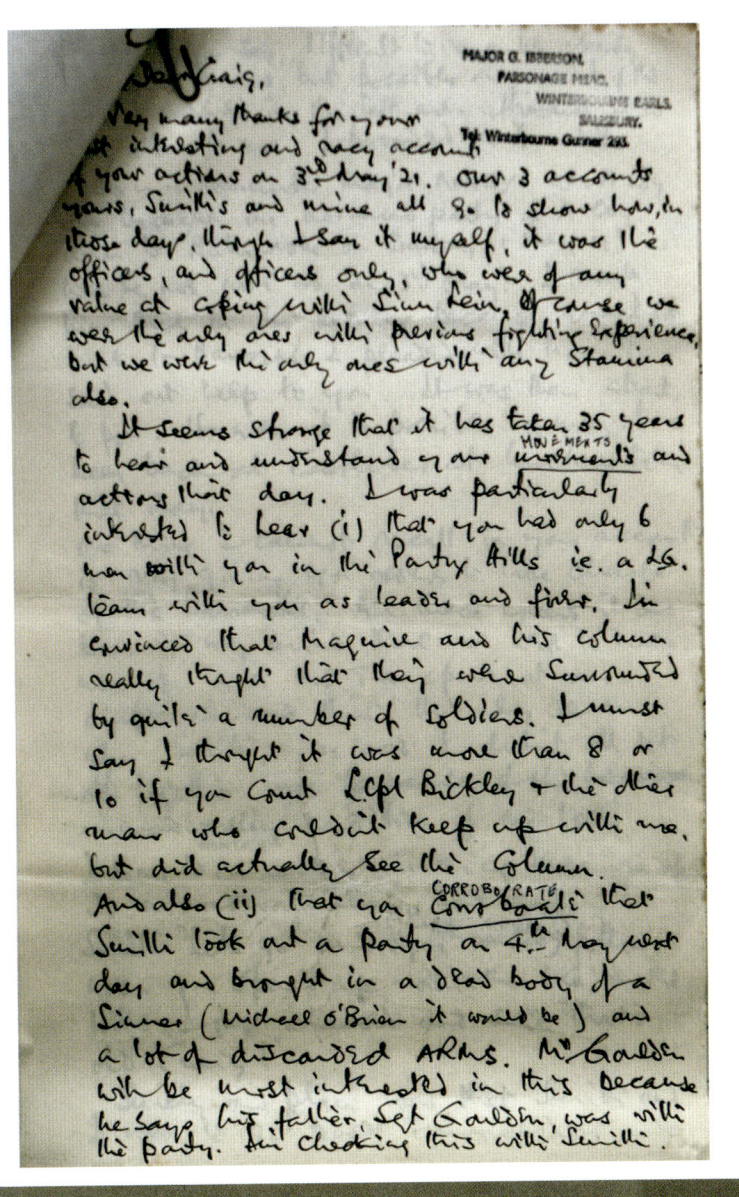

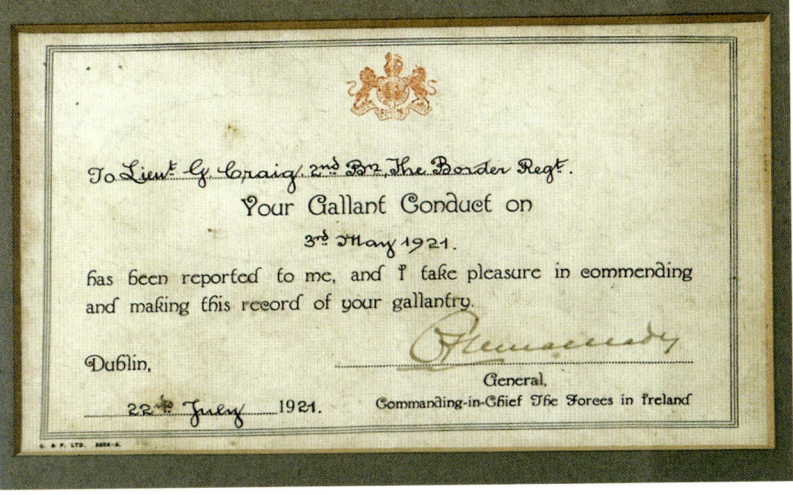

Left: the cattle markets, North Circular Road near the Dublin city abattoir.

Michael Collins had planned a rescue of Seán Mac Eoin (under death sentence) from Mountjoy Jail – it was to take place when Mac Eoin was scheduled to be in the governor's office at a given date and time. On 14 May, Volunteers seized a Peerless armoured car at the city abattoir – part of an escort for rations lorries calling there. They then drove to the jail, with Emmet Dalton and Joe Leonard dressed as British officers

Below: a Peerless.

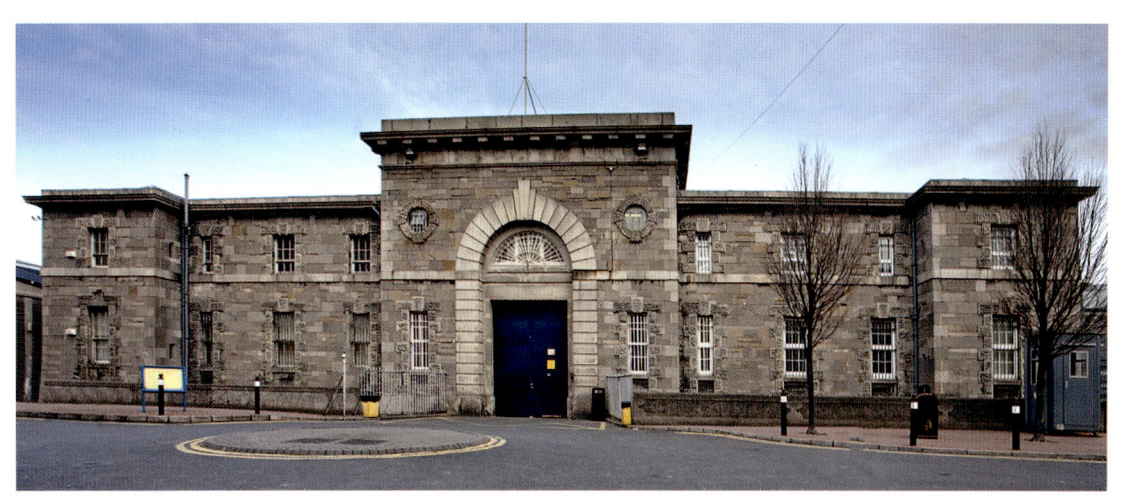

Above: the entrance to Mountjoy Jail.

Right: the driving seat of a Peerless – the captured one reportedly behaved like an 'old tub'.

On arrival at the gates, Dalton waved an official paper and they were allowed drive in. They deliberately parked so the gate remained jammed open. They were brought to the governor's office, but Mac Eoin wasn't there. Dalton presented a prisoner removal order – but the governor proceeded to ring Dublin Castle for confirmation. Smashing the phone, the 'officers' drew their revolvers. They heard firing outside. A soldier on the roof had opened fire, but had been shot by one of the men in the Peerless. The 'officers' withdrew as Auxiliaries and soldiers closed in. The Peerless and occupants made off safely at speed.

Right: Joe Leonard, Seán Mac Eoin and Emmett Dalton.

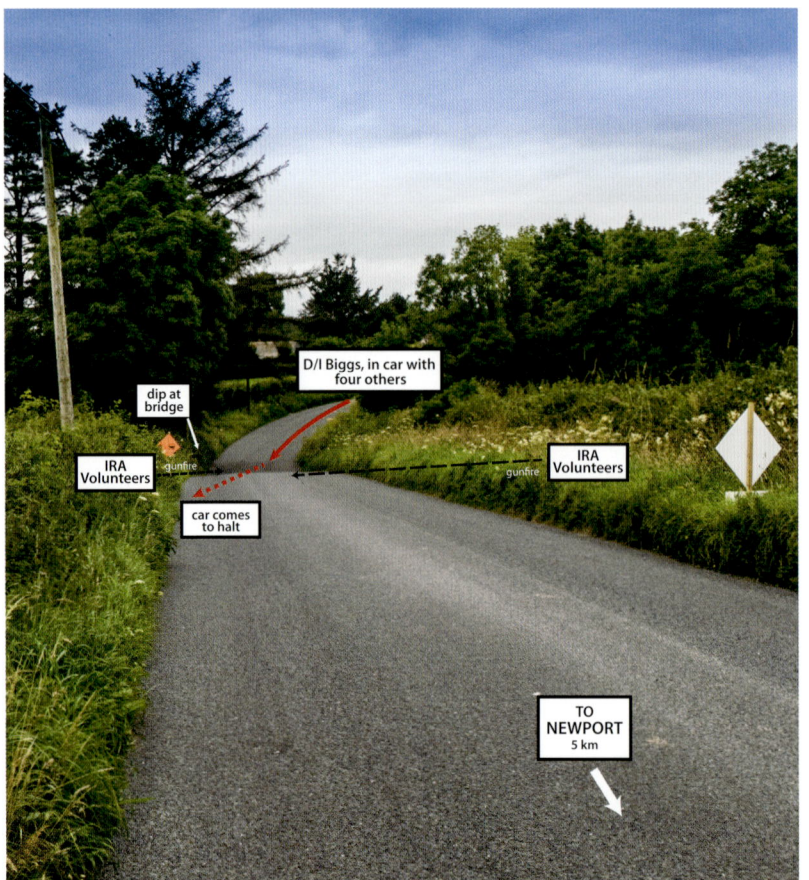

Left: RIC in front of a burnt-out barracks.

On 4 May, a mixed party of Kerry No. 2 and Cork No. 2 Brigades lay in wait at the Bog Road, near Rathmore. 'Old Tom', a tramp, considered an informer, had just been executed and his body left on the road, as 'bait' for an ambush. Eventually a party of RIC left the barracks at Rathmore and came to investigate. The IRA opened fire, resulting in eight police dead.

On Sunday 15 May, District Inspector Major Biggs was returning from a fishing trip with some companions, in the direction of Newport, Co. Tipperary. Biggs had won a reputation for brutal behaviour and the IRA determined to get him. As the party drove down a dip at a small bridge by a bend, at Coolboreen, the IRA opened up. Biggs was killed as was Winifrid Barrington, of a prominent Limerick family.

Left: ambush site.

Below: Winifrid Barrington.

Above: another District Inspector was shot on the same day, ambushed at Ballyturin House, near Gort, Co. Galway.

On 15 May, District Inspector Captain Blake and a party, including his wife, had been playing tennis at Ballyturin House. As they left in the evening, they approached the exit gate. There was a shout: 'hands up!' The IRA opened fire. Captain Blake and his wife were killed, as were two other officers.

Right: Captain Blake and his wife.

MURDERED, WITH HER HUSBAND, IN THE BALLYTURIN AMBUSH: THE LATE MRS. BLAKE.

MURDERED, WITH HIS WIFE, IN THE BALLYTURIN AMBUSH: CAPTAIN AND DISTRICT INSPECTOR BLAKE.

Above: a Hucks starter (a device to start the engine) is being attached to a DH9A at the RAF aerodrome at Baldonnell.

After WWI the RAF shrunk to less than one-sixth of its wartime strength. Most squadrons were based in India, Egypt and Iraq. With just two squadrons in Ireland in 1919, the RAF had a minimal role – reconnaissance and delivery of mails. However, as the war intensified in Ireland, there was an increased demand for the services of the RAF.

Left: in November 1920, a plane, delivering mails to the military barracks at Waterford, crashed onto the roof of houses opposite the barracks. The crew were badly injured.

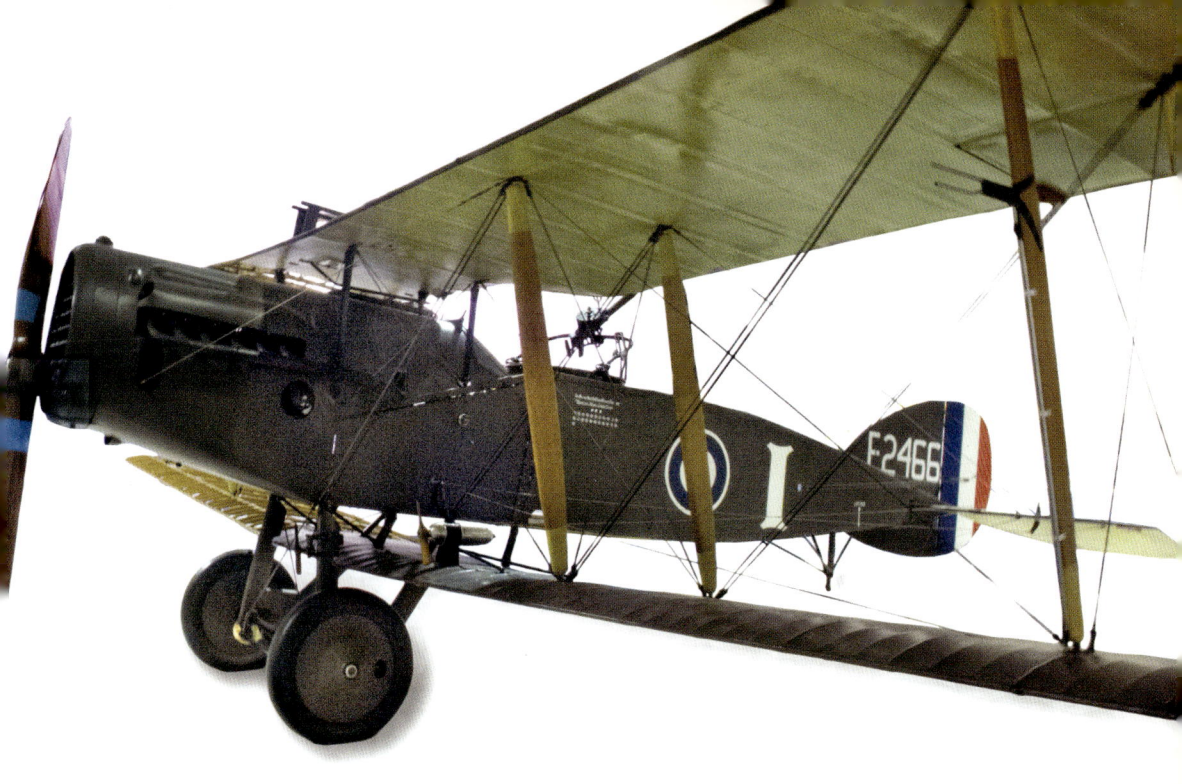

Above: a Bristol F.2b fighter. This agile two-seater was one of the most successful fighters of WWI. As part of a build-up of RAF resources in response to increased IRA attacks it was decided to standardise on the Bristol fighter in Ireland. Over the first half of 1921 the DH9As were replaced by Bristols.

On 10 February 1921 a BF.2b on a mail delivery flight made a forced landing at Kilfinnane Co. Limerick, due to engine trouble. Flying Officer Mackey was captured by the IRA and the plane was burned. Mackey was released several days later, unharmed.

Right: letter written by Mackey attesting that he had been well-treated.

COPY.

13.2.'21.

I have pleasure in stating that, from the time of my being taken prisoner on the 10.2.'21 until the eve of my release, (i.e. when I write this) I have been treated by the I.R.A. as well as could possibly be wished for under the conditions prevailing. I have been treated with every possible consideration and respect, and have no complaints whatever, in fact feel gratitude in the way that they have done everything in their power to make me comfortable.

The inhabitants, who were forced to house me, by the I.R.A., made me very comfortable and I do not consider that they could be held responsible.

(Signed)   L. O MACKEY, F.O.
R.A.F.

LA DOMENICA DEL CORRIERE

Anno XXIII. — Num. 12. — 20-27 Marzo 1921. — Centesimi 20 il numero.

Uno spettacolo di guerra, nell'Isola senza pace. In Irlanda, gli aviatori sventano un'imboscata di ribelli contro autocarri carichi di truppe, e uccidono cinque degli assalitori.

(Disegno di A. Beltrame).

Right: a BF.2b at Baldonnell. Disruptive camouflage was used in some British squadrons during WWI.

Left: 'La Domenica del Corriere' of March 1921 relates: 'the airmen foil an ambush by rebels... killing five assailants'.

The reality was quite different. RAF planes, up to early 1921, were not allowed to fire at rebels. Planes diligently transported mail and senior officers between barracks. Escorts and reconnaissance were also carried out. The British cabinet had been worried about the difficulty of distinguishing innocent from guilty from such speed and height (even though they had no such qualms about allowing aerial attacks on the tribesmen of the North-West Frontier and in Iraq). As the war escalated in 1921, approval for armed attack by RAF planes was given on 24 March. Senior army officers could now ask for the immediate assistance of armed aeroplanes.

Right: principal wireless stations (based on an RAF map, August 1920) of the military services. It was to take until November 1922 for a test of planes (in Northern Ireland) communicating directly by radio with sets in an armoured car and lorry.

231

AEROPLANE PHOTOGRAPHS II.

The best means the English have at their disposal for locating our standing positions, strong points and dumps in the country is the aeroplane photographer. In order to overcome this difficulty it is therefore necessary to understand what an aeroplane photograph records.

A photograph records colours, accident of ground such as bare earth, vegetation, woods, etc., in terms of light and shade, and is a patchwork or pattern of black and white meeting in varying intensities of grey. An agricultural district presents a regular chess board pattern, with large rectangular expanses of monotone, the only accidents to break the monotony being hedges, houses with their attendant deep shadows. Broken ground such as patchy vegetation presents a highly complex pattern, full of merging lights and shades.

Photographically, the effect of colour is not so marked or important as the effect of light and shade. Earth is towards the white end of the scale, and grass and vegetation towards the black—not because of their respective colours, but on account of the amount of contained shadow or texture.

A billiard table or top hat illustrates this quality. Brush them the wrong way, against the nap, and their tone is lowered to dark green or dead black; brushed the right way, with the nap, they appear much lighter in tone. They absorb light in the former case and reflect it in the latter. Nap is constituted of millions of slender hairs, each one throwing a shadow when erect, but casting none when "laid." Grass, or vegetation, possesses this same property to a marked degree. The longer it is, the darker it appears on a photograph: but when it has been pressed down the amount of shadow thrown is lessened and consequently it appears lighter. Hence the obviousness in a photograph of a slightly worn track in grass which is quite inconspicuous from the ground.

Earth, on the contrary, contains little texture, and the longer it has been turned up and exposed to rain and sun the less it has. A beaten track is, however, noticeable, as it contains no texture at all, and will therefore reflect more light.

The reason for mottled effect in a photograph of a patchy mixture of grass and earth, which blend imperceptibly into each other is therefore evident.

A field of young corn, viewed from the ground, appears green, but from above, probably the earth only is seen, darker in tone than the normal owing to the shadows cast by young blades of corn.

It is of first importance to grasp this principle of regarding any locality purely from the point of view of the pattern it will present on a photograph. Once understood, the problem of choosing and erecting a cover which will reproduce that pattern, or will fit naturally into it, is rendered far simpler. This is the basis of successful camouflage.

DESTROYING WAR MATERIAL

Latterly we have been able to greatly increase the number of attacks on Enemy War Material in various parts of the country. Previously some of our units were slow to realise the importance of this; an attack on a barrack, a well-planned ambush etc. these took the public eye. But the mere burning of a lorry or shooting of a horse did not seem anything And yet, what are the actual facts? The enemy is hit far harder by losses of material in a war of this kind than by losses of men-unless on a unusually big scale.

Attacks on War Material have three results: (a) They inflict loss on the enemy, (b) They weaken his fighting strength by making him split up his forces to provide numerous escorts, (c) They often help to provide ourselves with warlike stores. We have latterly in this way secured many motors, bicycles, instruments, tools, clothes etc. And if the matter were placed on a more systematic basis we would have still more useful captures to record.

The amount of direct loss inflicted on the enemy recently has been very great: in some of his big centres great quantities of valuable stores have been destroyed. The most recent example was the burning of lorry tyres worth many thousand of pounds at the North Wall under the noses of Auxiliaries. One day in April a train rumbled into Waterford with six disabled Crossleys on trucks—and a Crossley is worth nearly £1,000.

Again consider the value of a mule—the difficulty of breeding good mules, of transporting them across the Atlantic, of training them—in all these hundreds of pounds are involved. The mule can work harder, stand climates better, and resist disease better than the horse. The enemy can replace the full of a Crossley of Black-and-Tans more easily than a single mule. Even a horse shot is far more serious loss than a couple of soldiers. These things are not evident at first—we must point them out.

Finally by compelling the enemy to split up his forces to provide escorts we make him offer opportunities for attack. Some of his escorts will be weak, and some will be carelessly commanded. All such as these must be pounced upon speedily and vigorously. We preserve the Initiative by energetically attacking all points that the enemy must protect.—War Material of all kinds gives us abundant opportunities.

Frequent Road-cutting, wire-cutting and the seizure of tools and telephone apparatus are reported from all the Battalion areas of the West Limerick Brigade for the month of April.

Left: the 3 June 1921 'An tÓglach' gives rather wordy advice on deceiving the aerial photographer. The RAF did indeed have six BF.2bs fitted with cameras, based at Baldonnell. Over the second half of June 1921 they had taken 258 exposures in counties Galway, Cavan, Dublin, Mayo and Wexford. There was much mapping of the Wicklow mountains, probably because it was close to base. Little was achieved – an end-of-June report on photography said a dugout was identified (and raided) but adds that the other chief value 'has been in the mapping of footpaths on the hills and in yielding information as to the non-existence of works…'.

SUGGESTION FOR "GROUND DEFENCE TACTICS".

(1). GENERAL PRINCIPLE.-

The governing principle in all matters of disguise "avoid suspicion" is equally applicable to the work of defeating observation from the air.

To accomplish this there are two main points to be considered:-

(1). The perception and utilisation of all weakness in the enemy's men, methods or materials.
(2). The full employment of all the natural advantages we enjoy. This results chiefly in concealment of the unusual by the usual.

All Ground Defence Tactics to be sound must be based on one or the other, or on both of the above principles.

(2). INTELLIGENCE.-
(a). SCOUTS.- The visibility and engine-hum of the enemy's machines should be taken full advantage of as affording a warning to our troops. For this purpose a scout, or scouts, according to the number of viewpoints and subject to the discretion of the O/C operations, should be posted.

These men ought to possess excellent hearing and good sight and where possible, should be allotted the task on each occasion so that they might become accustomed to rapidly associating the direction of the machine, as indicated by its engine-hum, with its exact position in the air.

This picking up of Aeroplanes is not, at first, an easy matter especially when they are high and at a distance, and it is made still more difficult by the presence of brilliant sunshine or clouds. However, with a little practice it becomes fairly easy to a man with good organs of sight and hearing.

This type of Scout should also endeavour to become skilful in recognising the direction in which a particular machine is travelling. Accuracy on this point will prevent a number of false alarms and annoying interruptions of the work in hand.

It is too much to expect, nor is it needful, that he should be able to distinguish particular types of machines, but he ought, in time, be able to say whether it is a single-seater or a double-seater carrying an Observer.

The comparative length of the fuselage or distance from wings to tail, making due allowance for the foreshortening effect of the angle of the machine in the air, ought to help him in making the decision. Familiarity with the difference in engine-hum will also assist him, while field-glasses will be found very useful in detecting the nature and extent of the activities of the Aeroplane and its occupants.

It is suggested that this work ought not to be given in rotation to all, as a duty, but, rather, confined to specially chosen men.

(b). DETECTORS.- Enemy messages from the Air may provide very valuable information if detected, and, where necessary, decoded. Such knowledge as they convey may be even turned against the enemy themselves.

For this purpose each detachment or Flying Column should possess a simple form of W.T. Receiver tunable to the Aeroplane's wave length, with a man able to

---

Left: an extract from IRA instructions on dealing with planes. In reality, up to the Truce, RAF activity was a lesser strand of the British war effort in Ireland. (It is likely that the RAF might have achieved better results using the aggressive tactics applied on India's North-West Frontier and better radio communication with troops.) However, the IRA recognised the potential danger of the aeroplane, and, as seen in this document, tried to mitigate the danger.

Above: a Lewis fitted to a BF.2b.

Right: schematic of a Lewis machine gun Model 1918, aeroplane version.

From April 1921, there were frequent requests from the army to the RAF for armed support. On 4 May, after the ambush at Rathmore, Co. Kerry, the RAF were called there for priority assistance. The pilot flying over observed the eight dead bodies of the RIC on the ground but received the signal that no help was needed. RAF records of June list a few instances of Lewis fire from planes at ground targets: Gort (11th – bombs also dropped); Woodford (15th) and during a major drive in Kerry. No casualties were recorded.

Right: hundreds of thousands of propaganda leaflets were dropped by the RAF. In what appears to be a pointless waste of effort, this leaflet informs the IRA that they are being duped by their leaders, then adds a complex bit of moral theology.

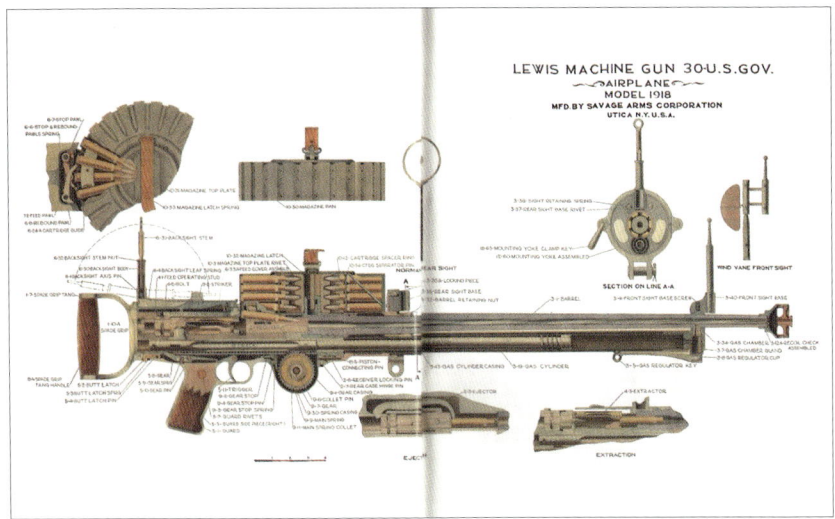

TO THE IRISH REPUBLICAN ARMY.

Your leaders are trying to make you believe that you are being kept in complete ignorance of the true state of affairs in this country through the terrorisation of the Press.

It is true that you are kept in ignorance: but it is because a large section of the Irish press does not dare to publish opinions which are unfavourable to the policy of the Sinn Fein extremists; and you are being completely misled by a constant distortion of the facts, and by mis-representations and innuendo which amount practically to open rebel propaganda and the encouragement of crime.

The Government attitude towards the Press is one of the utmost toleration, and extremist newspapers have been permitted a licence which would not be allowed for a single day by any other nation engaged in the suppression of murder and rebellion.

For example, a paragraph appeared a short time ago reporting "a daring seizure of arms" at Queenstown, and imputing cowardice to a party of soldiers under an officer.

The news was entirely false; and although the correspondent responsible for it was arrested, he was merely warned that if he repeated this type of offence he would be expelled from the Martial Law area.

Again, what is the object of your leaders in stating that the opinions of the Archbishop of Tuam are "known to spring from a lack of political understanding;" and that Cardinal Logue's "great age prevents him from mixing with his people."?

These disparaging remarks are made to weaken the influence of the Church over you, because its Heads, although they may be in full sympathy with your political aims, have emphatically denounced the Sinn Fein murder campaign.

Cardinal Logue has said "it is an act of murder—no one need tell me to the contrary—to lie behind a wall, and if a policeman goes for an ounce of tobacco to shoot him;" and he "warned the young people to keep away from organisers who are going about the country, getting them under control and advocating violence."

Do you know that most of the Roman Catholic Bishops have spoken in a similar strain? And that the Bishop of Cork has said (what all reasonable men know) that the resolution of DAIL EIREANN is not sufficient to constitute Ireland a Republic according to the teaching of the Church; and that such a claim strikes at the stability of all States?

Do you know that he also published the following Decree of Ex-communication?— "Besides the guilt involved in these acts by reason of their opposition to the Law of God, anyone who shall, within the diocese of Cork, organise to take part in an ambush or in kidnapping, or otherwise shall be guilty of murder, or attempted murder, shall incur, by the very fact, the censure of Ex-communication."

In contradiction to all this, you are told in "An t-Oglac" that "it is the *moral duty* of the Volunteers to wage war against the forces of England; and of the people of Ireland to give them every assistance and encouragement in their power. It is the duty of every Irish citizen to aid and abet us in this holy work. All who preach a different doctrine, all who endeavour by word or deed to weaken or impede the soldiers of Ireland in their duty to their country are acting the part of traitors."

P.T.O.

Left: weapons of the IRA – Volunteers pose for the camera. Over the course of the War of Independence the IRA was woefully short of arms. Seán MacMahon, the Quartermaster-General, spent most of his time fending off demands for weapons and ammunition.

Managing weapon and ammunition stocks posed a nightmare for the quartermasters. There was a great variety of rifles, some from raids on RIC or military barracks, some purchased from British soldiers – or captured in ambushes. There were many shotguns, but these were only of worth in close-quarter exchanges.

Left: a December 1921 memo on munitions from the Quartermaster to Cathal Brugha, Minister for Defence. In the context of the requirements to fight a nationwide guerilla war, the amount of arms imported over the 11 months up to the Truce on 11 July 1920 was minimal – a mere 96 rifles and 522 pistols. (The pace of imports radically accelerated in the six months after the Truce.) In reality most IRA units had to depend on their own resources – weapons that they captured themselves.

Above: a .303 calibre Lee Enfield SMLE Mk III – most were captured or purloined from Crown forces. In comparison to the miscellany of other rifles used by Volunteers this was the most reliable and effective.

Above right: a .303 calibre Lewis light machine gun, with ammunition pan. The IRA captured a small quantity of these.

Right: popular with Volunteers (if they could get them), a 9 mm Luger Parabellum semi-automatic pistol, with an eight-round magazine.

After Detective-Sergeant Smyth was shot (he was able to flee, but died later from wounds) by the Squad using .38 calibre revolvers on 30 July 1919, Jim Slattery noted: 'We never used .38 guns again, we used .45 guns after that lesson'. The Squad commonly used .455 Webleys or .45 Colts, but also Parabellums.

Right: weapons training at an IRA camp. Matt Fitzpatrick, commandant of the 1st Battalion, 5th Northern Division (centre) demonstrates how to operate a pistol.

Above: the Mauser C96 semi-automatic pistol with detachable wooden stock, which gave it the stability of a short-barrelled rifle. It was called the 'Broomhandle' due to its round wooden handle. Used to good effect during 1916, it was a prized possession of IRA units during the War of Independence. Volunteers referred to it as 'Peter the Painter' (named after a Latvian anarchist who reportedly used one in the Sidney Street Siege in London in 1911).

Left: IRA training instructions for the Mauser pistol.

Right: the .45 calibre Thompson submachine gun. Designed for close-quarter trench work, it was inaccurate over 50m. It had a legendary reputation, but in reality was not very effective and did not make much difference by the end of the War of Independence, nor during the subsequent Civil War.

Right: a tunnel at the Casino, Marino. Three Thompsons arrived in early May 1921 and one was test fired here by the Squad and others, including Tom Barry.

Harry Boland and his comrades had purchased 653 Thompsons in the US. On 13 June 1921 Customs seized 495 of these on a ship at Hoboken, New Jersey, as they were about to be shipped to Ireland The rest were smuggled to the IRA after the Truce.

Right: captured Thompsons at Hoboken.

A Thompson was used in action for the first time on 8 July 1921, when Pádraig O'Connor (below) led an attack on a troop train from a Ballyfermot bridge. Several soldiers were wounded.

Left: grenade production at Rogers Brothers foundry at Bailieboro, Co. Cavan. The men sit behind their output of cast grenade cases and some wooden moulds. Grenade cases were filled with gelignite and fused with detonators (usually stolen from quarries).

Below left: the Director of Munitions, Seán Russell, reports on 1921 grenade production from the improvised factories spread around the country. From March to the Truce in July total output was a mere 1,408. However, in the period from the Truce to end October 1921, output soared to 9,602, with the 1st Southern and Dublin city being neck and neck for highest production.

Below: in Dublin, an IRA Volunteer, dubbed 'TNT Mick', poses at his lathe, where he is producing components for grenades. The photograph is by Joseph Cripps, who had also taken the iconic images in the GPO in 1916.

Above: grenades, fuses and firing components captured at Parnell Street.

Right: the aftermath of a November 1920 raid on a grenade factory in the cellar of a bicycle shop at Parnell Street in Dublin.

As the war progressed, IRA engineers gained more expertise in the use of mines. Their efficacy was demonstrated during the Rathcoole, Co. Cork ambush (see page 255) where mines were successfully exploded under an armoured Lancia and two lorries.

Right: an experimental mortar. It was made by Captain Matt Furlong (in charge of grenade manufacture at Parnell Street). Black powder was used to fire a mortar bomb from the tube. In October 1920, trials were conducted in Co. Meath. Furlong first experimented using dummy shells. Then he fired a live round which exploded in the tube, severely injuring him – he later died.

Left: quenching the conflagration. On the night of 27 November 1920, the IRA set fire to 41 cotton warehouses and timber yards in Liverpool and Bootle, causing huge damage.

The Volunteers in Britain could effortlessly swim within the large Irish community. They acted as a valuable auxiliary to the IRA in Ireland and supplied many weapons and explosives, transhipped from ports like Liverpool – sourced from Britain, the Continent and the USA. The IRA in Britain carried out sporadic attacks on infrastructure across Britain, which resulted in economic damage but nothing of military value. Nevertheless, the existential danger of IRA attack was a source of anxiety for the British authorities and public.

Left: 'Police News' depicts the supposed scene when the IRA attacked signal boxes in the Manchester area in June 1921.

Below: the nervousness continues. In December 1920, barricades are placed at the end of Downing Street to guard against 'Sinn Féin' disturbances.

PLUCKY SIGNALMAN ROUTS SINN FEIN ATTACKERS.

Right: the 'Illustrated London News' records the low-key 'Irish elections' in Dublin, sandwiching a report of a roundup in the Wicklow mountains.

The elections were a curious construct: while necessary under the Government of Ireland Act, but the British cabinet were reluctant to hold elections as they knew it would result in a clean sweep for Sinn Féin in the 'South'. However they proceeded with them as they principally wanted to establish a northern parliament for the Unionists.

Right: a Unionist election rally in Co. Down. Polling took place for the 'Northern Ireland House of Commons' on 24 May 1921. Of the 52 seats, 40 were won by Unionists, Sinn Féin won six with another six for Joe Devlin's nationalists. In the six counties, carved out to ensure permanent Unionist dominance, the seal was now set for Unionist rule.

For the 'Southern Ireland House of Commons', no polling took place – all candidates were returned unopposed. Of the 128 seats, Sinn Féin won 124, with Trinity College, Dublin returning four independent Unionists.

Right: southern results with maverick loyalists amidst a sea of green.

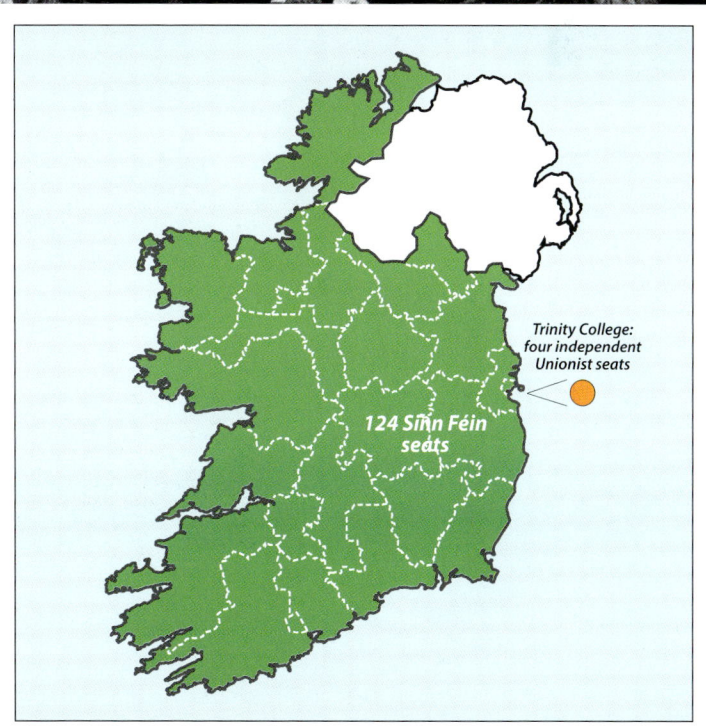

241

Custom House, Dublin.

Above: the great bulk of the Custom House. Éamon de Valera returned to Ireland in December 1920. Aware of the power of propaganda from an international perspective (but somewhat detached from practical military strategy), he failed to see all the advantages of the guerrilla war as it had actually evolved.

Left: in 1921, the Custom House was at the heart of the civil administration of Ireland and contained all local government records and tax files.

De Valera was dismissive of current minor actions and demanded a 'good battle about once a month'. Early in 1921 two possible targets were considered by the Army Council: an attack on Beggar's Bush Barracks, or the destruction of the Custom House (previously considered for attacks by the Dublin Brigade). Unsurprisingly, attacking Beggar's Bush, the ADRIC HQ, was seen as not feasible.

Right: who ruled Ireland? On high at the Custom House – the crown over the harp.

Left: the Custom House from the south quays.

The Dublin Brigade of the IRA began detailed preparations for the Custom House operation. Plans were obtained of the huge building – a 110m long by 65m wide complex with three floors, a basement and hundreds of offices.

On Wednesday 25 May, 270 Volunteers of the Dublin Brigade mustered. At 12:55 pm, 120 men of the 2nd Battalion (including some Squad members) under the command of O/C Tom Ennis, entered the building. At the same time, the 1st Battalion had spread out in the surrounding area to protect the operation. Units took over fire stations across Dublin. Inside the Custom House, the staff were rounded up. Volunteers went upstairs, poured paraffin on piles of files and set them on fire. It took far longer to lay the fires in the labyrinthine building than had been planned.

A DMP constable cycling by at 1:10 pm alerted Dublin Castle. 'F' Company of the Auxiliaries, and two armoured cars, were immediately deployed.

Left: an Auxiliary with Lewis gun in Dublin, painted by Mick O'Dea.

Above: a British officer, Mauser pistol in hand, stands next to a Peerless armoured car, in front of the Custom House.

As the Auxiliaries drove into Beresford Place, Volunteers outside opened fire and threw grenades. Minutes later, 'Q' Company raced up from their L&NWR base down the quays The Auxiliaries began to surround the Custom House and exchanged fire with the IRA units outside. Later in the battle, truck loads of military also arrived.

Right: map of the Custom House area.

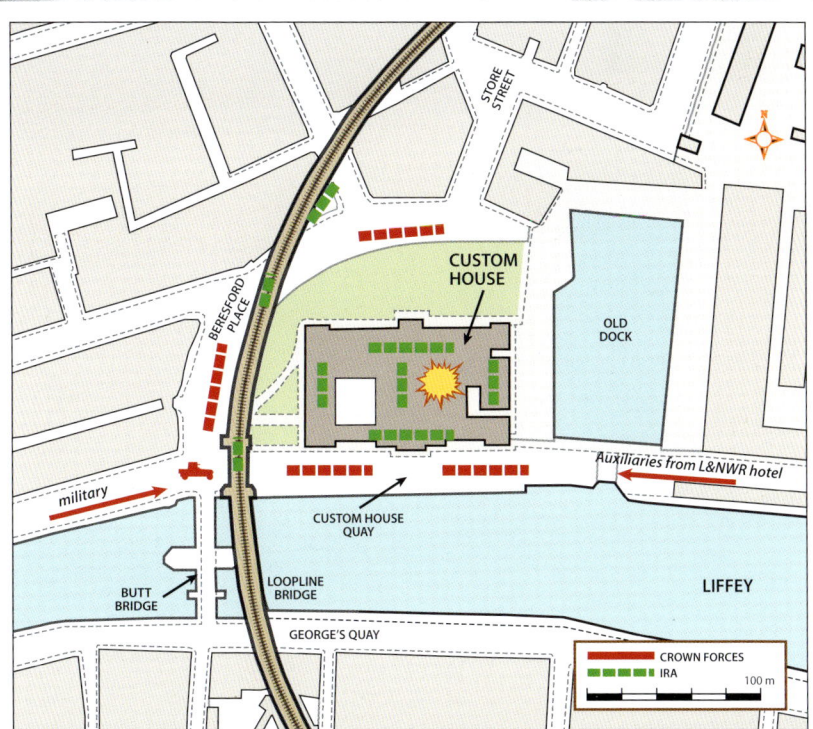

Above: an imaginative, if fanciful, French depiction of the scene inside the Custom House, with guns blazing and women on fire.

As the Custom House went on fire, the battle raged outside between the Volunteers and the Crown forces. The Volunteers inside the building fired from the windows. As the IRA outside ran out of ammunition, they began to withdraw. Some managed to escape from the building. Others tried to blend in with the civil service staff.

Left: British troops round up civilians.

Above: in the lee of the Loop Line bridge, prisoners under detention.

Right: civilians corralled for interrogation.

The Auxiliaries began to enter the building. Mistaking some staff for IRA they opened fire, resulting in one death. All within were ordered to leave the building with their hands up. They were lined up outside to be identified, with officials from the Custom House picking out their staff. With the building in flames in the background the remainder were closely questioned. A few Volunteers managed to bluff their way out, but the majority were detained and herded onto trucks.

Above: the caption in the 'Illustrated London News' reads: 'Said to have been shot by Auxiliaries after he had thrown a bomb from a bridge...the body of a Sinn Féiner...'

Left: prisoners sit in an Auxiliary tender, awaiting the drive to captivity. An estimated 107 Volunteers were captured. Most were brought to Arbour Hill Prison, others to Mountjoy.

Above: the Custom House burned for ten days.

Right: a horse lies dead on the quays after the battle.

Below: Auxiliaries help a comrade – five were wounded in the action. Four Volunteers died (plus one later of wounds) and four civilians were dead.

Above: ambulances and an armoured Lancia are parked on the quayside by the stricken building. A fire engine refills with water from the Liffey.

Early in the action, the IRA had taken control of the fire stations. Many of the firemen were Volunteers or sympathisers. Callers on the phone were assured that help was on the way – but no firemen showed up. Eventually the Fire Brigade arrived and when it was safe, they entered the burning building. However, as one fireman recalled: 'many parts of (the building) that were not on fire when we entered were blazing nicely in a short while'.

Left: the Fire Brigade arrives.

Above: 'Sir George Vanston's room'. Legal advisor to the Local Government Board, he continued working in his office until the very end. Quite deaf, he had been unaware of the attack.

Right: the dome with melted copper sheeting.

This, the biggest IRA operation in the war, resulted in nine dead. The capture of over a hundred experienced Volunteers was also a blow. However this must be seen against Dublin Brigade's nominal strength of 4,500. More were immediately recruited in the ASU – and the IRA deliberately intensified their Dublin activities in the aftermath.
Despite the (temporary – it was rebuilt) loss of Gandon's masterpiece, the objective of destroying this administrative centre was achieved, another big step in making Ireland ungovernable. This 'spectacular' added to the pressure on the British to begin truce negotiations.

Right: a ruined corridor.

251

Hunter and hunted.

Left: Lieutenant Grazebrook, intelligence officer of the Gloucestershire Regiment, deployed in north Cork. Through raids he began to build up intelligence on the local IRA, whose leader Seán Moylan was high on Grazebrook's list. On 15 May, in a well planned raid, Grazebrook with around 60 troops captured Moylan and others at a farm near Kiskeam, north-west Cork. In a court martial, Moylan (now an MP after the recent election) was acquitted of levying war. He escaped the death penalty, receiving 15 years penal servitude, and was sent to Spike Island.

Moylan had been arrested for sedition in February 1919 but escaped several months afterwards. He led at the Clonbanin ambush where Brigadier-General Cumming was killed on 6 March 1921. The 1st Southern Division of the IRA was set up at the end of April 1921, Moylan's chivalry, dedication and astuteness were recognised when he was appointed O/C of Cork No. 2 Brigade.

Left: Seán Moylan after capture. The strains of living on the run, as well as bouts of ill-health, can be seen.

Above: the 2nd Battalion Royal Hampshire Band.

In May 1921, the 2nd Battalion of the Hampshires, with band, was in Youghal for musketry practice. On the morning of 31 May a company was being played by the men and boys of the band down to the range for Lewis gun practice. Less than a kilometre from the range, the road passes through a glen, with rising ground to the left and a low masonry wall on the right. A mine (an empty shell case, discarded from Fort Carlisle and packed with explosives) had been hidden near the road. Two local Volunteers electrically detonated the mine as the band passed. Seven bandsmen were killed and around 20 wounded.

Right: curiously jolly, bandsmen display broken instruments recovered after the explosion.

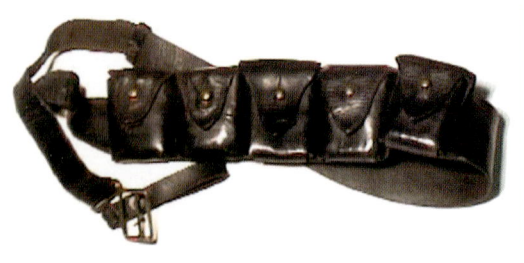

Above: the West Mayo Brigade flying column, painted by Mick O'Dea (after a JJ Leonard photo, taken just after Carrowkennedy.). O/C Michael Kilroy is at the back on the left.

Left: Carrowkennedy site. On 2 June 1921 Kilroy and his men ambushed an RIC patrol, in two Crossley Tenders, on the Leenane-Westport road at Carrowkennedy. The battle raged for several hours. Eight RIC (including D/I Stevenson, killed as he drove the first tender) died as a result and 16 surrendered – these were later released.

Far left: bandoleer captured at the ambush.

Near left: D/I Stevenson's Silver War Badge.

Above: memorial at the Rathcoole ambush site.

Right: pictured on a remote road, an armoured Lancia at a road crater after a mine was exploded.

Below right: the ambush road, looking east.

As the IRA had cut the railway line to Millstreet, the Auxiliaries based there regularly drove to Banteer station for supplies. The Cork Brigade IRA planned a large and elaborate ambush. Just after dawn on 16 June, around 130 Volunteers assembled in woods near the Millstreet-Banteer road at Rathcoole. Barricades were readied and six mines laid along a section of road one kilometre long. As an Auxiliary convoy of three Crossley Tenders, with a Lancia leading, returned from Banteer around 7:30 pm, the well-armed Volunteers attacked. Mines were precisely detonated under the Lancia and two tenders. After a two-hour firefight, the IRA withdrew, leaving two Auxiliaries dead and several wounded.

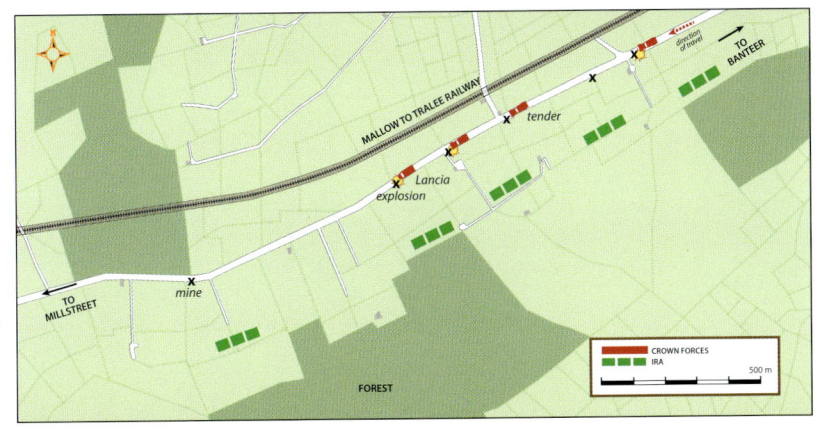

Right: map of ambush.

255

On 3 June the 'Gentlemen of Ireland' were playing cricket with the 'Military of Ireland' at the Trinity College Park. There was a strong military presence including a band. At around 5.30 pm, Volunteers Pádraig O'Connor and Jim McGuinness opened fire from the railings at Nassau Street. Down below Miss Wright, a Trinity student, stood up from her seat and died from a stray bullet.

Left: Kathleen Wright.

On the afternoon of Sunday 19 June, 2nd Lieutenant Donald Breeze, based at Dublin Castle, was motoring with some female friends. They were stopped near Carrickmines by the local company of the 6th Battalion, Dublin Brigade, who were felling trees to block roads. There was an altercation, where Breeze was wounded. Two Volunteers set off in the car with Breeze (and one woman companion) taking him to Leopardstown as a prisoner. It appears that Breeze tried to grab a revolver en route. The IRA stopped the car, put him against a low wall and shot him.

Left: a dramatic depiction of the killing of Lieutenant Breeze, who was aged 20, having been commissioned a year earlier.

Above: As painted by Mick O'Dea – cadets outside Hynes's public house in Dublin, well armed with revolvers and a pump-action shotgun.

By mid-1921, Dublin was flooded with the forces of the Crown. Searchlights pierced the sky as night raids and round-ups continued.

Right: a ring of steel. On Kildare Street, in front of the National Museum: soldiers with bayonets; a truck with mounted searchlight; two armoured Lancias.

Left: the Fastnet lighthouse, scene of a daring raid in 1921.

The IRA needed explosives for mines. In June, aware that gun-cotton was stored on the Fastnet, Volunteers of the Schull Battalion set out in a motor boat for the lighthouse. As there was a high swell, they put ashore at Cape Clear island. There, they commandeered the local mail boat, the 'Máire Cáit' and headed again to the Fastnet. One Volunteer leaped onto the rock, revolver in pocket and a rope around his waist. He entered the lighthouse and held up the three keepers. Three boxes of detonators and 17 boxes of gun-cotton were swung by derrick down to the 'Máire Cáit.' As they headed back to Schull harbour, HMS 'Truro', a minesweeper (on patrol along the West Cork coast) passed astern, but did not stop. The gun-cotton was landed and distributed among the Cork brigades.

Below: insignia of HMS 'Truro'.

Above: the ruins of the large Schull Union Workhouse, (scene of much misery after the Famine) built on an 11-acre site in 1849-50.

On 24 June, the Schull Battalion burnt down the workhouse, to prevent it being used as a barracks by Crown forces. At the same time, the Royal Marines stationed at Schull were attacked.

In early December 1920, the IRA attacked an RIC patrol on the Clonakilty-Bandon road. Michael McLean, Lieutenant of the Leamcon Company (Schull Battalion), was subsequently captured in a house opposite the ambush site. He was brought down the road and shot dead.

Right: memorial to Michael McLean at Lowertown, near Schull.

Left: Head Constable Eugene Igoe, who was born in Co. Mayo.

In one of the initiatives to counter the successes of the Collins intelligence system, Igoe was drafted in from Galway to Dublin where he led the 'Intelligence Company', a group of RIC men from the country, known to the IRA as the 'Igoe Gang'. Igoe reported to Brigadier-General Winter, the spymaster in Dublin Castle. The group's mission was to travel around Dublin and identify Republicans. They frequented railway stations to spot arrivals from the provinces. They shadowed suspects and arrested or on occasion shot them. It was, to some degree, a mirror-image of the Squad. The IRA struggled to get to grips with this new element. A Volunteer was brought from Galway to identify Igoe, who was spotted in early January 1921. It was a matter of frustration for Collins – his intelligence men spent much time trying to catch the Igoe Gang. It was a constant irritant and danger for the Dublin Brigade. There were reports of failed ambushes on vehicles carrying the Igoe Gang. In any event, Igoe and his men successfully survived the war.

Right: Brigadier-General Ormonde Winter, at the centre of the British spy web in Ireland.

As part of the big shake-up of the Irish administration in May 1920, Brig.-General Winter (a friend of Major-General Tudor) was appointed head of the Combined Intelligence Service in Ireland. Slight and dapper, he exuded energy and cleverness. One senior administrator in Dublin Castle was not impressed, calling him 'a wicked little white snake'. Like many other senior British officers, he brought a racist and colonial attitude to Ireland, writing: 'The Irishman, without any insult being intended, strongly resembles a dog, and understands firm treatment...'.

Winter methodically reorganised intelligence. Filing and coordination were improved. There was a flood of secret service men. New types of operatives (like Igoe's men) were appointed to track down the 'Sinn Féiners'.

Right: Dublin Castle, heart of English rule for seven centuries. As well as being the civil administrative hub, it was Winter's spy HQ. After Bloody Sunday, it was packed to capacity with intelligence officers obliged to lodge there.

261

Left: Michael Collins and bicycle. Dressed in a suit, he posed as a respectable businessman and journeyed around Dublin, under the noses of the military and police.

As IRA Director of Intelligence, Collins established a GHQ Intelligence staff based at Crowe Street.

He had all the qualities to set up an IRA intelligence system: he was tireless, efficient, shrewd, quick-witted, cunning, ruthless, charming and more. He gathered an astute and equally ruthless group including Liam Tobin, Frank Thornton and Tom Cullen.

At an early stage, he cultivated a string of valuable informers. These included Ned Broy, a confidential clerk of 'G' Division; David Neligan, a detective working on political crime and Lily Mernin, a typist working for the British Army chief intelligence officer.

Far left: the view from the atmospheric lane connecting the Stag's Head public house on Dame Court (where he met informants from Dublin Castle) across to Crowe Street.

Near left: the main Department of Intelligence office was located on the second floor of No. 3, Crowe Street.

Right: forbidding in granite, the police station on Great Brunswick (now Pearse) Street. When Ned Broy (his DMP informant) smuggled Collins in here late on 7 April 1919, it was the HQ of G' Division of the DMP. Collins spent the night inspecting the intelligence files, by candlelight, in an office in the circular gable. He was particularly amused to see that in his own file he was noted as 'coming from a particularly brainy West Cork family'.

Collins set up a system of safe houses, pubs and hotels (complete with many hidden places to hide material) across Dublin, where he and his shadowy operatives functioned.

Collins had phenomenal energy: his portfolio included intelligence, being Minister of Finance and President of the IRB. There was an excellent working relationship between the boisterous Collins and the more introspective and precise Richard Mulcahy, IRA Chief of Staff. It was a good mix: Collins's pro-activism and brilliance and Mulcahy's methodical organisational skills.

Right: under the bridge – Cleary's bar on Amiens Street was another haunt where Collins held meetings.

263

Collins's intelligence service maintained records on the important aspects of the British military and civil grasp on Ireland. Here are extracts from an IRA intelligence photo book (1919-1921) held by Frank Thornton, Deputy Assistant Director of Intelligence. The contents of the book ranged from newspaper clippings to stolen or captured photographs. The indexed pages included 'spies', British military, Auxiliaries, RIC, DMP as well as judges and even a typist.

Above left: helpfully identified, the ermined senior judges administering British justice in Ireland.

Left: the photo book includes the wedding in Monkstown in late 1920 of Captain Lorraine King (commander of 'F' Company ADRIC), to the daughter of a British colonel. His Auxiliaries form a guard of honour. King earned a reputation for ruthlessness in Dublin. He had participated in the brutal interrogation of Clancy and McKee at Dublin Castle on the fatal night of Bloody Sunday. King was arrested in February 1921 for shooting two IRA prisoners. He was acquitted, as a statement by a dying man was not admissible.

Right: this photograph from a hospital ward labels three men as 'Secret Service, Dublin Castle'.

1. Rodgers. 2. Jones. 3. Hyde.
Secret Service, Dublin Castle.

Right: some Auxiliaries from 'F' Company are named. On the far right, Olive Cox, a typist at Dublin Castle, is noted.

Below right: the photo book included this image of Inspector Carey (a noted athlete, who was in charge of DMP training), giving instruction on revolvers.

"F" COY. AUX.
1. Corson. 2. Stokes Major (secret service)
3. Thompson (s.s.) 4. Reynolds. 5. Bennett.
6. Warrior.

OLIVE COX. TYPIST.

Below: the book covered both high and low society – here is Lord French, the Viceroy, at a social outing.

INSPECTOR CAREY, D.M.P.

265

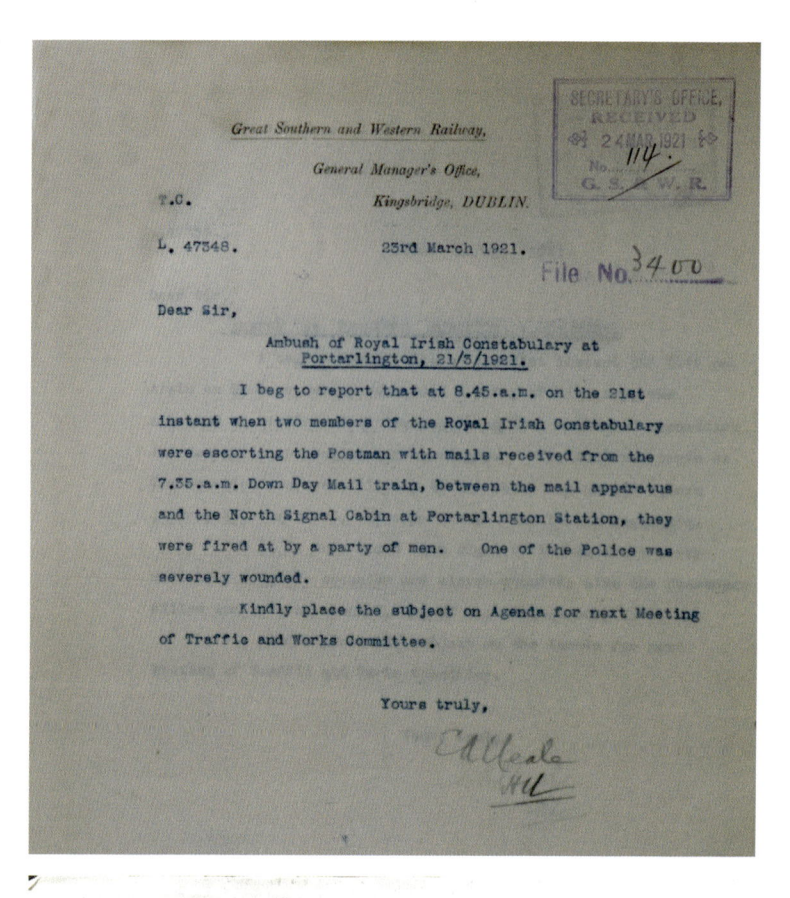

> Great Southern and Western Railway,
>
> General Manager's Office,
>
> T.C.   Kingsbridge, DUBLIN.
>
> L. 47548.   23rd March 1921.
>
> File No. 3400
>
> Dear Sir,
>
> Ambush of Royal Irish Constabulary at Portarlington, 21/3/1921.
>
> I beg to report that at 8.45.a.m. on the 21st instant when two members of the Royal Irish Constabulary were escorting the Postman with mails received from the 7.35.a.m. Down Day Mail train, between the mail apparatus and the North Signal Cabin at Portarlington Station, they were fired at by a party of men. One of the Police was severely wounded.
>
> Kindly place the subject on Agenda for next Meeting of Traffic and Works Committee.
>
> Yours truly,

Left: a GS&WR report of an incident where the IRA stole the mails from the down day mail train, after it had been deposited at the mail apparatus (for transferring the mail bags to and from the train whilst it was travelling at speed) at Portarlington on 21 March 1921. The postman and his escort, two RIC constables, were fired on – one constable was severely wounded.

Volunteers intercepted the mails with regularity all over Ireland. IRA Intelligence officers examined the mails with care and were able to unearth much information including letters to the RIC from informers. The British were aware of the dangers – hence the delivery of military mail by the RAF. Another example of this awareness was that the wave of secret service agents deployed to Ireland from London were given a secret writing course so that they could send their reports to a London address via impersonal letters.

Left: a key to a RIC code for June 1921. This was provided by a sergeant in the RIC barracks in Tralee to the Kerry Brigade.

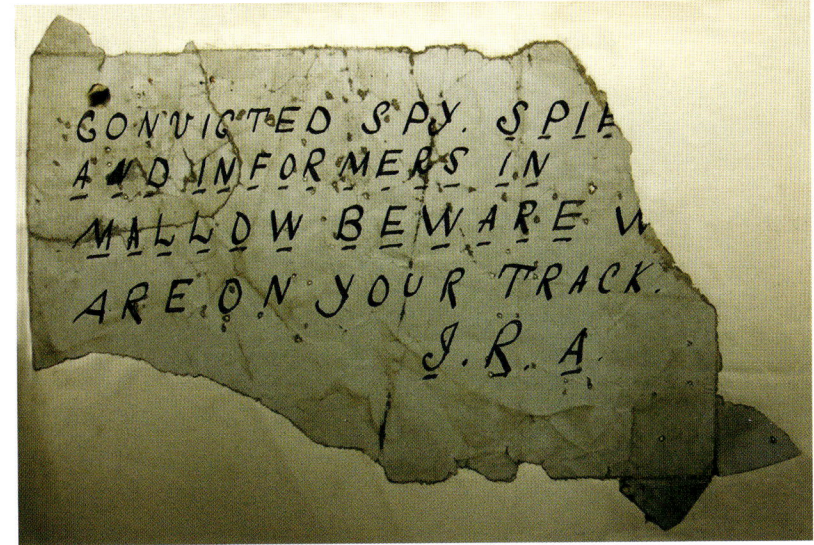

Right: 'convicted spy' – a warning note found on William Macpherson's body, dumped near Mallow, Co. Cork. A former sergeant-major in the British Army, he was suspected by the IRA. On 7 July 1921 he was detained, tried by Brigade officers, sentenced, and executed.

All over the country, informers and spies were executed by the IRA. Some were indeed guilty as charged, but – given the clandestine nature of a guerrilla war – others were innocent unfortunates who were in the wrong place and time, and subject to hasty judgement. The historian Pádraig Óg Ó Ruairc has calculated that Cork had the largest number of executions – 78 alleged spies. Tipperary came next with 16, then Dublin with 13.

Right: the 'Illustrated Police News' depicts a body with a 'spy' placard. The depiction verges on the lurid, but as the war reached its height, this became reality.

Below: IRA General Order No. 20 dealing with spies.

ALLEGED SINN FEIN "EXECUTION."

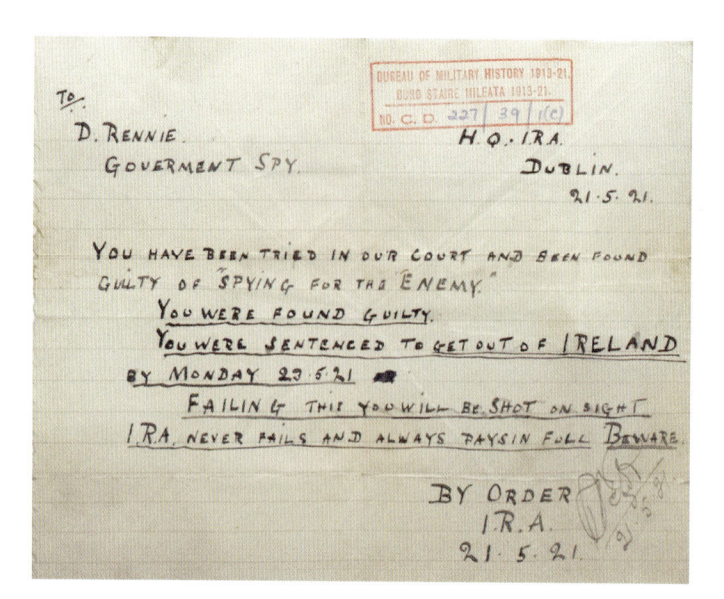

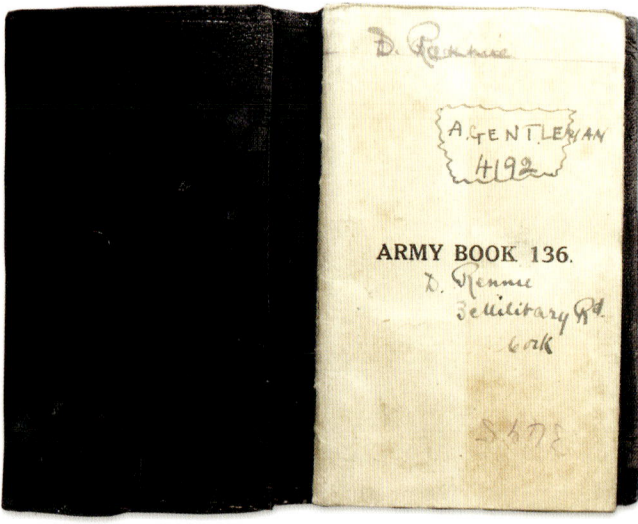

A spy's documents.

Left: Donald Rennie, found guilty as a spy by the Dublin IRA, was lucky – he was merely told to leave Ireland in this note. As encouragement it adds: 'the IRA never fails and always pays in full. Beware'.

Middle left: the title page of Rennie's notebook, where he pathetically designates himself as 'a gentleman'.

Below left: on this page of the notebook is a faded newspaper clipping of Michael Collins, with a note designating him as 'C in C, IRA'. This was inaccurate but Collins was indeed one of the highest-level persons that British intelligence had targeted.

Below: after discovery by the IRA, Rennie was obviously conscious of his potentially imminent demise – he prepared this will.

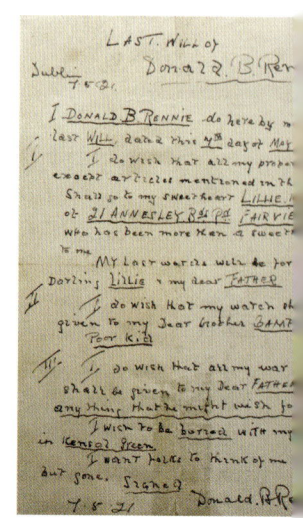

Above: Captain Stewart Chambers's sword. On 15 November 1920 Chambers and other officers, in civilian clothes, were travelling by train from Cork to Bantry. At Waterfall, the first stop, armed men boarded and seized Chambers and two other officers – all were later shot.

Right: NCO's of Casement's 'Irish Brigade' – Timothy Quinlisk is marked 'X'. Later he moved in Sinn Féin circles and was helped financially by Michael Collins. In 1919 he contacted Dublin Castle offering to be an informer. Collins heard of this from Ned Broy. Later, Quinlisk, wanting to meet Collins, was told he could see him in Cork. On 18 February 1920 the Cork IRA brought Quinlisk outside the city and shot him.

THEY ARE AWAITING "THE DAY"
Non-Commissioned Officers of 'The Irish Brigade' in Germany who discarded the red and donned the Green.

Right: the bodies of four off-duty British soldiers lie in a quarry near Cork city. On 10 July 1921, on the eve of the Truce, they were captured and executed by Volunteers of Cork No. 1 Brigade, possibly in retaliation for the killing of a Volunteer a day earlier.

Left: the crypt in the isolated Kilquane cemetery at Knockraha (around 12 kilometres north-east of Cork city).

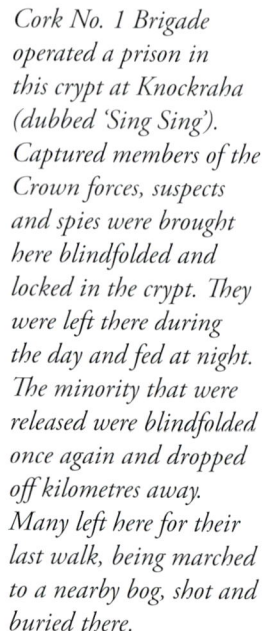

Cork No. 1 Brigade operated a prison in this crypt at Knockraha (dubbed 'Sing Sing'). Captured members of the Crown forces, suspects and spies were brought here blindfolded and locked in the crypt. They were left there during the day and fed at night. The minority that were released were blindfolded once again and dropped off kilometres away. Many left here for their last walk, being marched to a nearby bog, shot and buried there.

Left: the exit door of the crypt, probably one of the last sights for many a captive.

Below: grenade mould from Knockraha, a veritable hive of republican activity. There were two bomb factories in the locality.

The 1st Battalion Essex Regiment had been based in West Cork since February 1919. They were stationed at Bandon and Kinsale. As it turned out, this, the most pro-active of the British regiments, was now located in an area where the IRA was intensively active.

Right: an RIC Inspector and Major Arthur Percival, Essex intelligence officer, as painted from a photograph by Mick O'Dea. (Percival was over six foot, thus the Inspector was tall even by RIC standards.) Percival garnered notoriety during his service in West Cork. In 1942 he also won dishonourable attention as the general who surrendered Singapore to the Japanese.

Right: Michael Collins's birthplace at Woodfield, near Clonakilty. In April 1921 it was burnt by the Essex Regiment

Below: 'Let Essex lead the way' – a recruiting poster from WWI.

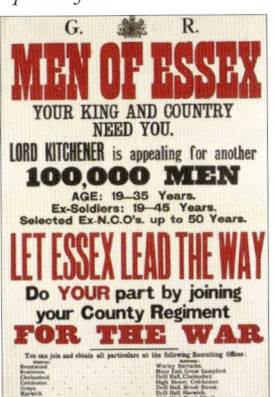

Above: soldiers mill around a partially-destroyed masonry-arch bridge near Kinsale.

Major Percival and the Essex (who won Tom Barry's particular ire) became known all over West Cork for brutality. Percival escaped an ambush in October 1920 at Newcestown Cross, where two of his fellow-officers were killed.

Percival adopted IRA flying columns' tactics. His soldiers spread out on foot in units over the countryside, sleeping in barns or tents. They surrounded houses at nightfall, closing in at daybreak.

Left: a party of the 1st Battalion, Essex Regiment resting by a road.

Above: prisoners being marched to Bandon military barracks after a round-up.

Right: Tom Hales and Pat Harte in the care of the Essex Regiment at Bandon. On 27 July 1920, Hales (then O/C 3rd West Cork Brigade) and Harte (Quartermaster) were captured at a farmhouse near Bandon, and after being beaten up, were brought to the nearby barracks. They were interrogated by several officers. After severe torture they were brought to Cork Military Hospital and then imprisoned in Britain. Harte suffered mental problems and was sent to Broadmoor asylum. He never recovered and was admitted to a Dublin asylum, dying in 1924.

Left: the Republican plot at St Finbarr's Cemetery. Amongst the many headstones, lie the fallen of the Cork Brigade, killed during the War of Independence.

Above: a Cumann na mBan unit. One estimate is that, by mid-1921, there was a membership of 20,000. Cumann na mBan provided essential support for the Irish Volunteers. They were behind the barricades in Easter 1916 and ferried ammunition and dispatches to the various garrisons. During the War of Independence, these, the eyes and ears of the IRA, formed part of the communications network. They ferried messages and weapons. They nursed wounded Volunteers as well as cooking for and maintaining the flying columns.

Right: a Cumann na mBan member, perhaps idealised by absence, in a sketch made in Frongoch camp in 1916 by Thomas Kane.

Left: IRA orders on reprisals. In the event of reprisals, a similar number of houses belonging to the 'most active Enemies of Ireland' should be destroyed. The result was that when the IRA burned down the mansions of aristocratic loyalists in response to Crown forces' reprisals, these soon tailed off.

GHQ in Dublin attempted to maintain order on the IRA – run in many places by commanders acting as local barons, some of whom felt that GHQ were 'pen pushers'. Certain strictures of a conventional army, adapted by GHQ, did not sit well with the clandestine reality of guerilla warfare. However, despite constraints, GHQ doggedly and successfully coordinated the war. It urged the Volunteers on to action, provided intelligence, training, rules and standards, as well as supplying a limited number of weapons.

Left: an tÓglach, the official paper of the IRA, combined news of the war, exhortation and advice from GHQ on tactics. Here, it gives useful guidance on how to deal with the widespread 'Republican itch' – scabies, scourge of the flying columns. 'Take a hot bath' is one of the remedies.

Right: the IRA GHQ staff, by Leo Whelan. Whelan painted each individual separately in 1921, after the Truce, only completing the composite picture a year later. Seated, left to right – Michael Collins (intelligence), Richard Mulcahy (chief-of-staff), Gearóid O'Sullivan (adjutant-general), Éamon Price (organisation), Rory O'Connor (engineering and O/C Britain), Eóin O'Duffy (assistant chief-of-staff), Seán Russell (munitions) and Seán MacMahon (quartermaster-general). Standing – JJ O'Connell (training) Emmet Dalton (operational training), James O'Donovan (chemicals), Liam Mellows (purchases) and Piaras Béaslaí (publicity).

Right: General Order No. 17 issued by IRA GHQ deals with a highly sensitive matter – written GHQ authority must be obtained to execute a Volunteer, guilty of treachery. One account says that, during the war, four Volunteers were executed for spying or informing.

NO. 17.   GENERAL ORDERS.   2nd April 1921.

DEATH PENALTY.

The penalty of death shall not be inflicted on any member of the I.R.A. without written covering authority from General Headquarters Staff.

The following are offences for the which the death penalty may be imposed on members of the army.

1. Knowingly conveying information to the enemy.
2. Disclosing to unauthorised persons particulars of plans of operations.
3. The treacherous surrender to the enemy or distruction of arms or War material.
4. Grave insubordination on active operation duty, involving danger to others and to the success of the operation.

In all such cases the written proceedings of the relative Court Martial shall be promptly forwarded to the Adjutant General.

BY ORDER.

ADJUTANT GENERAL.

WITH A SMUGGLED "BABY" TANK FOR IRELAND: THE RUSSIAN STEAMER "OLGA," STOPPED BY THE CUSTOMS, ALONGSIDE H.M.S. "LION."

Le Petit Journal illustré
12 Pages — 12 Pages
HEBDOMADAIRE, 61, rue Lafayette, Paris — PRIX : 0 fr. 30 — 3 Juillet 1921

Le Sous-Marin Fantôme

Au prix des plus grands dangers, dans les sauvages baies semées d'écueils des côtes d'Irlande, les envoyés des sinn-feiners s'embarquent pour rejoindre le mystérieux sous-marin qui leur permet d'accomplir leur mission en Amérique.

Left: 'a smuggled baby tank for Ireland'. In April 1920 the Russian steamer 'Olga' was detained at Grangemouth in Scotland with ammunition and this tank on board. The authorities were doubly nervous – about the activities of the Bolshevik government as well as possible arms smuggling to Ireland. In the event, the 'Olga' was found to be innocent – although one wonders how the IRA would have used this 'baby' tank.

Below left: 'Le Petit Journal', imaginatively tells, under the heading 'the Phantom Submarine' how the Sinn Féin envoys embark with great peril on the mysterious submarine, which will allow them to 'complete their mission in America.'

The British had long harboured an inchoate fear of submarines entering the bays of the wild Irish coast, to bring succour to Irish rebels. One actual occurrence was when a man captured in April 1918 admitted that he had been landed from a German submarine with instructions to establish contact with Sinn Féin leaders (page 36). An RAF record notes that on 21 May 1921 a plane was sent to reconnoitre Killala Bay 'for a submarine landing arms'. It found nothing.

Right: 'landing British troops on the Irish coast from a government trawler'.
On 30 May 1921, Lloyd George announced the strengthening of Crown forces in Ireland. Over the period mid-June to early July in 1921, 19 new army battalions were deployed in Ireland.

The British cabinet had a poor understanding of Ireland. They wrongly thought that the IRA enjoyed minimal support among the population. By mid-1921 the cabinet vacillated between a drive to intensify the war ('stick, not carrot') and the urge to negotiate a truce. In the peace camp were the Liberals, unhappy about the British atrocities in Ireland. Britain was earning opprobrium abroad as news of the reprisals and murders by Crown forces circulated widely.

In 1921 the British had many headaches, with Ireland being the most painful.
Right: 'Le Pélégrin' depicts Lloyd George in bad humour, smashing the crockery of Europe. British concerns included Ireland, the Ruhr and Upper Silesia, with the problems of Mesopotamia, Egypt and Palestine rumbling on.

"IT IS INTENDED TO STRENGTHEN THE CROWN FORCES IN IRELAND": LANDING BRITISH TROOPS ON THE IRISH COAST FROM A GOVERNMENT TRAWLER.

Lloyd George, dans un de ces accès de mauvaise humeur qui lui sont coutumiers, brise la vaisselle de l'Europe.

Left: the King and the Queen proceed down Donegall Place, Belfast.

On 22 June 1921, the Northern Ireland Parliament (established under the Government of Ireland Act) was formally opened by King George V. It was attended by the 40 Unionist members – but not by the 12 Sinn Féin and nationalist members.

The coming into existence of the parliament meant that the partition of Ireland was now copper-fastened, well before the Anglo-Irish Treaty (signed on 6 December) and the Civil War. Reflecting a mood for conciliation, the King made a carefully nuanced speech which did not condemn the IRA and asked for all Irishmen 'to pause...to forgive and forget'.

On 24 June Lloyd George invited de Valera and Craig, the northern premier, to go to London to explore the possibility of a settlement.

Left: the King enters City Hall for the ceremony.
Below: the King inspects the RIC.

Right: the derailed and spectacularly-destroyed wagons.

On 24 June, a train carrying 113 men and 104 horses of the 10th Hussars (part of the royal escort at the opening of parliament), departed Belfast, en route to the Curragh.
Volunteers of the 4th Northern Division, IRA (led by Frank Aiken), laid two mines and removed bolts from the outer rail at a bend on an embankment near Adavoyle station, north of Dundalk. As the train arrived, one mine was detonated under the last passenger compartment. This, the following horse vans and guard's van were derailed and smashed apart as they hit the bottom of the embankment. Three soldiers and the guard were killed. Only one horse survived afterwards.

Right: soldiers heading to the Adavoyle crash site in a Lancia armoured truck. Local civilians were drafted in, under duress, to bury the horses.

Below: the only surviving horse.

281

De Valera called a conference for 4 July to discuss Lloyd George's proposal for London talks. De Valera, 'spokesman of the nation', as he described himself, met the southern Unionists at the Mansion House. The northern premier, James Craig, had refused to come. Another meeting was held on 8 July. General Macready met de Valera and terms for a truce were agreed.

Left: southern Unionists Lord Midleton and Maurice Dockrell MP arrive.

Below: Macready (with a pistol bulging in his pocket) is cheered as he arrives on 8 July.

The Truce came into force on 11 July 1921. Under its terms, the British ended military manoeuvres, raids and searches. The IRA were to cease attacks on Crown forces.

Right: the order to all units of the IRA to suspend hostilities, issued by Richard Mulcahy, Chief of Staff.

Castleisland was the scene of the last ambush – on the night of 10 July, a party of the 2nd Battalion, Loyal Regiment set out on curfew patrol. No. 2 Kerry Brigade attacked, eventually withdrawing under machine gun fire. Four British soldiers and three Volunteers were left dead.

Right: map showing ambushes in Castleisland, (including that of 10 July) prepared by Timothy O'Connor, of the No. 2 Kerry Brigade.

Below: the regimental badge of the Loyal Regiment, which was from north Lancashire.

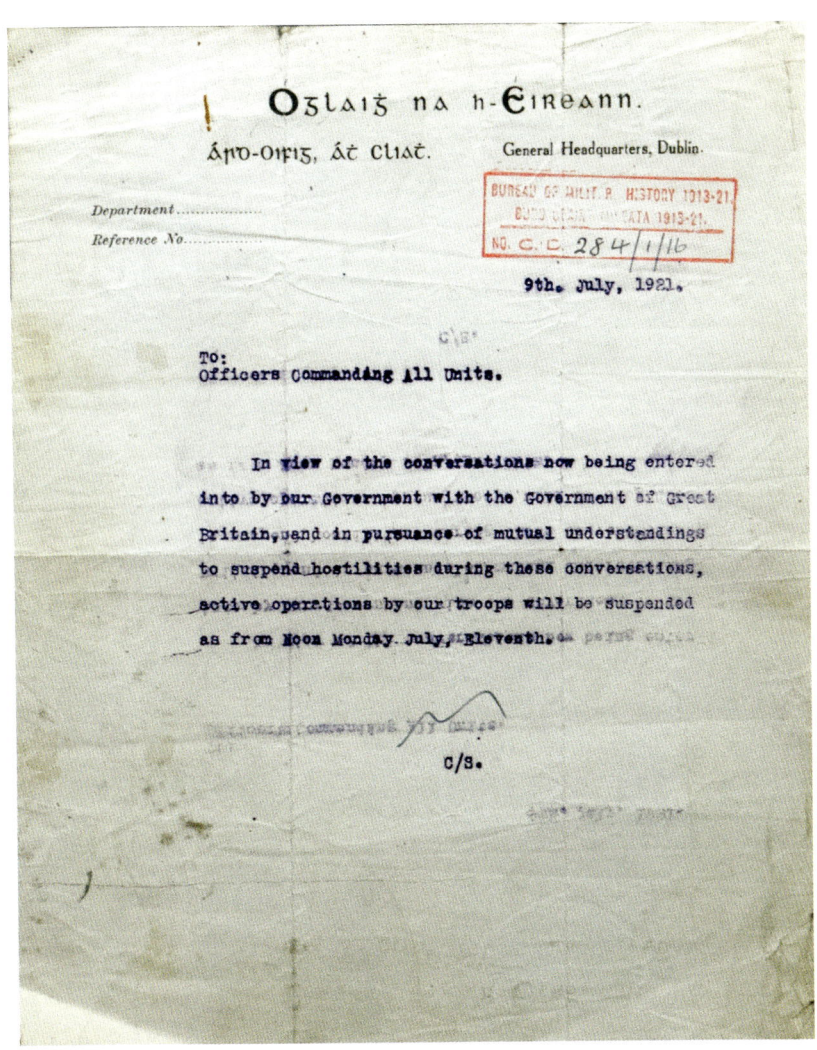

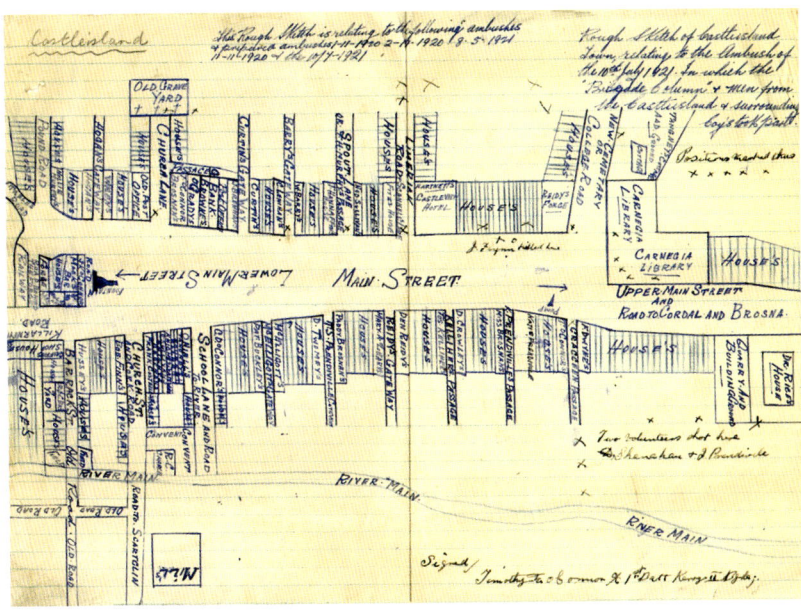

Óglaiġ na h-Éireann.

Árd-Oifig, Áṫ Cliaṫ.   General Headquarters, Dublin.

Department..................
Reference No..................

9th. July, 1921.

TO:
Officers Commanding All Units.

In view of the conversations now being entered into by our Government with the Government of Great Britain, and in pursuance of mutual understandings to suspend hostilities during these conversations, active operations by our troops will be suspended as from Noon Monday, July, Eleventh.

C/S.

Above: Auxiliaries relax after the declaration of the Truce.

Left: let joy be unconfined. Auxiliaries celebrate. The location is most likely at their HQ, Beggar's Bush Barracks.

284

Right: Éamon Duggan, IRA Chief Liaison Officer, clarifies details of the Truce for the Athlone liaison officer, Fintan Murphy.

Óglaiġ na h-Éireann.

~~Ap o Óipig AṫCliaṫ.~~ General Head-Quarters, Dublin.

Department CHIEF LIAISON OFFICE:
Reference No............

66, Dame Street,
Dublin.

Telephone 4888: 26th July, 1921.

TO:
Commandant Fintan Murphy.
Prince of Wales' Hotel,
ATHLONE.

A Chara,

Yours of the 23rd instant received this morning.

RE CARRYING OF ARMS:

I note what you say and shall take the matter up with British General Head-Quarters. I may mention for your information that there are no such armed guards operating in Dublin and I cannot therefore see why they should be necessary in other places.

RE BELFAST BOYCOTT:

The destruction of property is a distinct breach of the Truce and you should issue instructions to that effect. Of course that does not mean that the Boycott is not to continue.

RE REPUBLICAN POLICE:

The activities of the Republican Police in the discharge of the ~~other~~ ordinary civil police duties is no more a breach of the Truce than the activities of enemy police in the discharge of similar duties.

1.

Right: no Truce in Belfast – pedestrians run as bullets fly in the city centre. On 10 July loyalists attacked Catholic enclaves in the aftermath of an IRA ambush of the police. There were gun battles between the IRA, loyalists and police. Sixteen civilians were killed, mostly Catholic – more were killed in the following week. Hundreds of houses were destroyed.

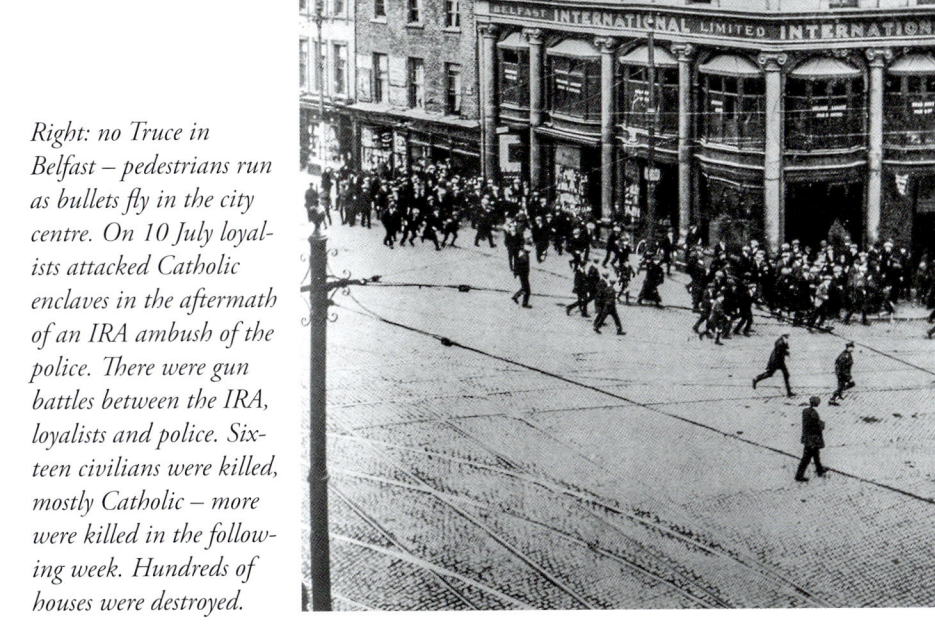

Left: Mr de Valera comes to town – arriving at London Euston on 12 July. He was accompanied by Arthur Griffith, Austin Stack, Count Plunkett, Robert Barton and Erskine Childers. (Michael Collins had been offended at not being asked to travel.) Huge and enthusiastic crowds greeted the Irish delegation as they arrived.

De Valera requested to see Lloyd George by himself, and he was received in the cabinet room at No. 10 Downing Street. Lloyd George had arranged that a large map, marked with the red of the British Empire, hung on the wall of the cabinet room. The eloquent Welshman tried to dazzle his visitor with a theatrical tour-de-force. However, de Valera remained unimpressed.

As further meetings proceeded Lloyd George carefully presented progress (or lack of it) to his colleagues in cabinet. He was politically weak in the face of Tory opposition, firm believers in the inviolability of the British Empire. At the same time as he grappled with de Valera, this adroit politician also had to manage his recalcitrant colleagues.

Left: the 'Welsh Napoleon', by Shemus.

Right: there was little meeting of minds between the two leaders. When de Valera said he would reject British proposals, Lloyd George threatened war. He noted that the reduced global commitments of Britain meant that they could now move more troops to Ireland and that 'the struggle would bear an entirely different character'. The series of meetings continued and at the end Lloyd George presented a formal offer. This gave the 26 counties dominion status (with partition and hence 'Northern Ireland' remaining in place), with control over home defence, taxation, finance and policing – but with the Royal Navy still in control of Irish waters. De Valera was displeased but brought the offer back to Dublin where there was much discussion in cabinet. Minister for Defence, Cathal Brugha, in particular, was concerned about the fundamental aspect which would mean the abandonment of the Republic, as established at Easter 1916.

THE ILLUSTRATED LONDON NEWS

SATURDAY, JULY 23, 1921.

MAKING IRISH HISTORY AT 10, DOWNING STREET: MR. LLOYD GEORGE AND MR. DE VALERA MEET ALONE, TO DISCUSS PEACE.

The first meeting between Mr. Lloyd George and Mr. de Valera took place in the drawing-room at the Premier's official residence, No. 10, Downing Street, on July 14. The official statement issued afterwards said: "Mr. Lloyd George and Mr. de Valera met as arranged at 4.30 p.m. at 10, Downing Street. They were alone, and the conversation lasted until 7 p.m. A full exchange of views took place, and relative positions were defined." Other important conferences have followed. Sir James Craig has returned to Belfast, leaving Mr. Lloyd George and Mr. de Valera to work out their own solution for the South.

DRAWN BY OUR SPECIAL ARTIST, STEVEN SPURRIER. COPYRIGHTED IN THE UNITED STATES AND CANADA.

Left: the Mid-Clare Brigade, on a training exercise, parade at Kilfenora during the Truce period. From now on, Volunteers could emerge openly from their clandestine existence.

Below left: a group of Volunteers being trained at Kilakee House, Rathfarnham Co. Dublin. A variety of weapons are laid out on the steps (including Thompson and Lewis machine guns). The array of weapons belies the fact that the IRA was woefully short of arms. GHQ redoubled its efforts to procure weapons during the Truce period.
Conscious of the need to improve discipline and standards, GHQ instituted a major programme of training during the Truce. Training camps were established all over the country. Topics included weapons instruction, ambush techniques – and even square-bashing.

Left: the Brigade Staff of Waterford Brigade at Dungarvan Castle Barracks, after the Treaty.

Right: in Autumn 1921, IRA prisoners, on a naval tender being transferred to Dartmoor prison. There were over 5,000 Republican prisoners – most had to wait until after the Treaty was signed, in December, before release.

Right: the 'Daily Sketch' of 10 August reports on Seán Mac Eoin's release. On 6 August, the British had agreed to release all members of the Dáil who were prisoners, but not Mac Eoin, who had been sentenced to death. Sinn Féin made his freedom a precondition for convening the Dáil (where the negotiation details would be debated). The British relented and allowed the release of Mac Eoin.

Following page: Dáil Éireann met on 16 August 1921 in the Mansion House, where de Valera began his report on the negotiations.

McKEOWN RELEASED: TRUCE SAFE.

Mr. J. McKeown, the Sinn Fein M.P., whose release averts a threatened rupture of the Irish truce. This photograph, taken in Mountjoy Prison, with two of his guard, appeared in yesterday's late edition.
—(Exclusive.)

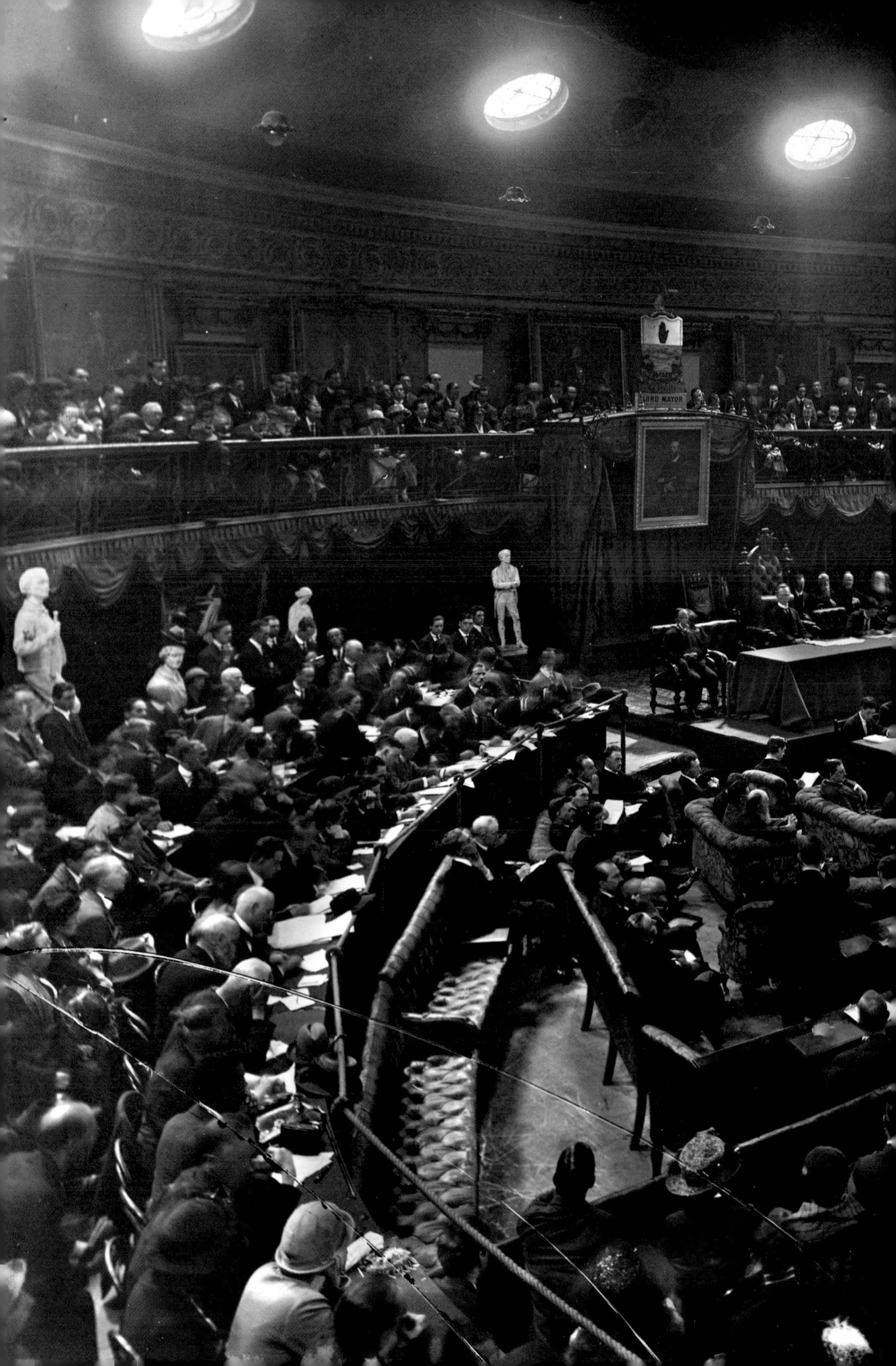
LORD MAYOR

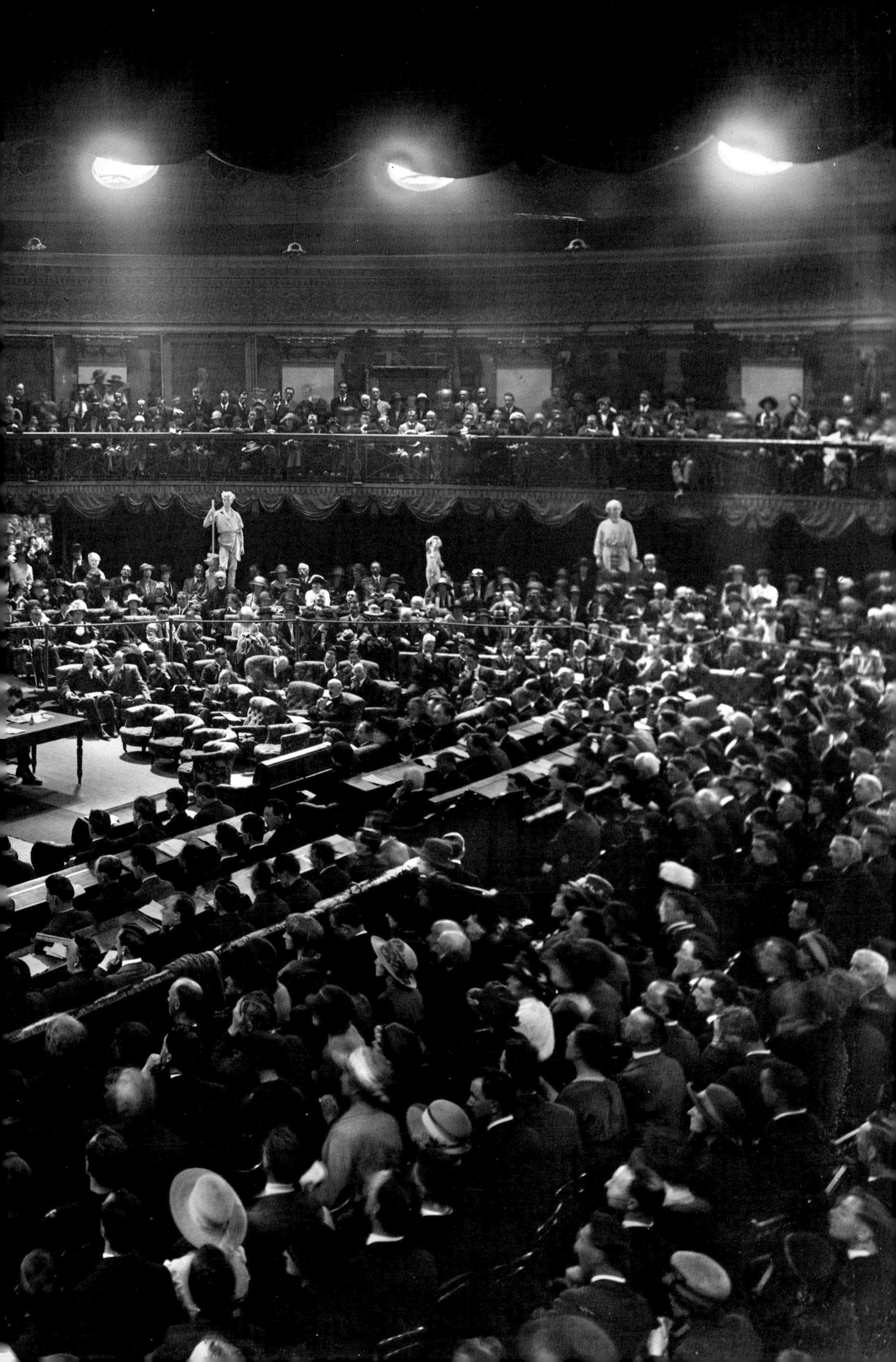

Above: the Truce period gave ample time for a Viceroy's inspection of the Auxiliaries at their HQ at Beggar's Bush Barracks in October 1921.

Left: the Truce period also gave abundant time to catch up with personal matters. On 27 October 1921, Kevin O'Higgins, rising star and Assistant Minister for Local Government, got married. Éamon de Valera was in attendance. Best man (on right) was his friend Rory O'Connor. In a cruel twist of fate during the Civil War, O'Higgins was a member of the Free State Executive Council which, on 7 December 1922, (illegally) ordered O'Connor's execution on the following morning.

In the Dáil the questions of the Republic and the North were discussed at the end of August 1921. After an exchange of letters, Lloyd George invited de Valera to 'enter a conference to ascertain how the association of Ireland with the community of nations known as the British Empire can best be reconciled with Irish national aspirations'. On 9 September the Dáil cabinet approved the sending of a delegation in response to the invitation.

Right: Punch's vision of Lloyd George in preparation for the Anglo-Irish negotiations.

PUNCH, OR THE LONDON CHARIVARI.—September 14, 1921.

THE PROBLEM PLAY.

OUR EVER-JEUNE PREMIER (*conning his part*): "NOW HERE AM I, A WELSHMAN, LOOK YOU; AND I HAF TO COME ON IN A HIGHLAND 'SET,' AND PLAY A SCENE IN ENGLISH—ALL ABOUT IRELAND—WITH A SPANISH AMERICAN—AND LEAD UP TO A HAPPY ENDING. WELL, WELL, I HOPE IT WILL BE ALL RIGHT ON THE NIGHT!"

293

Above: fateful journey – the delegates depart Kingstown (now Dún Laoghaire) for the Treaty negotiations in London.

Left: the might of the Empire – with Lloyd George in the middle, the British negotiating team.

Above: on 11 October 1921 large crowds and newsreel cameras assembled as the Irish delegation entered Downing Street to begin negotiations.

Right: the Irish delegation – (front to back) George Gavan Duffy, Robert Barton, Michael Collins, Arthur Griffith and Éamon Duggan. Standing, Erskine Childers (principal secretary to the delegation).

Lloyd George had identified Griffith and Collins as the principal movers and arranged one-to-one meetings with them. The negotiations stuck on the rock of British intransigence, on the issues of allegiance to the King and membership of the British Empire, fundamental to the imperial mind-set.

in Southern Ireland since the passing of the Government of Ireland Act, 1920, and for constituting a provisional Government, and the British Government shall take the steps necessary to transfer to such provisional Government the powers and machinery requisite for the discharge of its duties, provided that every member of such provisional Government shall have signified in writing his or her acceptance of this instrument. But this arrangement shall not continue in force beyond the expiration of twelve months from the date hereof.

18. This instrument shall be submitted forthwith by His Majesty's Government for the approval of Parliament and by the Irish signatories to a meeting summoned for the purpose of the members elected to sit in the House of Commons of Southern Ireland, and if approved shall be ratified by the necessary legislation.

On behalf of the Irish Delegation
Art Ó Gríobhtha (Arthur Griffith)
Mícheál O'Coileáin
Riobárd Bartún
Éudmonn S. O'Dugáin
Seoirse Ghabhán uí Dhubhthaigh

On behalf of the British Delegation
D Lloyd George
Austen Chamberlain
Birkenhead
Winston S. Churchill

December 6, 1921.

In the face of Lloyd George's histrionics which offered only signing the Treaty or facing renewed war, the delegation did not consult with Dublin but signed the Treaty document in London on 6 December 1921.

Left: the Anglo-Irish Treaty sets out how an Irish Free State would be formed as a self-governing dominion 'within the Community of Nations known as the British Empire'. It included: the British retaining naval ports; members of the Free State Parliament to take an oath to be faithful to the King; the right of the Northern Ireland parliament to opt out of the Irish Free State; and the sop of a Boundary Commission. In essence the Treaty comprised the same terms that Lloyd George had offered to de Valera in July 1921. A partial exit of the British from (most of) Ireland had thus been painfully achieved.

Heated debates followed in the Dáil. On 7 January 1922 it narrowly approved the Treaty. Conflict escalated between the anti-Treaty IRA (who wanted a Republic) and the new army of the Provisional Government. On 28 June 1922 the Four Courts was shelled and the Civil War began.

Bibliography

Principal Libraries, Museums & Archives consulted:
British National Archives, Kew; Cork Public Museum, Dublin City Library & Archive; Imperial War Museum, London; Irish Capuchin Provincial Archives, Dublin; Irish Railway Records Society, Dublin; Kilmainham Gaol Museum; Military Archives (Military Service Pensions Collection, Bureau of Military History Witness Statements), Dublin; Military Museum, Collins Barracks, Cork; Military Museum, the Curragh; National Archives of Ireland, Dublin; National Library of Ireland, Dublin; National Museum of Ireland, Dublin; RAF Museum, London, South Dublin Libraries, Tallaght; Trinity College Library, Dublin; UCD Archives; Ulster Folk and Transport Museum.

Periodicals:
An tÓglach
Capuchin Annual
General Irish and British newspapers
History Ireland
Irish Historical Studies
Journal of the Irish Railway Record Society
The Defence Forces Magazine: An Cosantóir
The Irish Sword

Books on the War of Independence recommended in the first instance:
Barry, T, *Guerrilla Days in Ireland*, Mercier Press, Cork, 2012
Crowley, J, Ó Drisceoil, D, Murphy, M, *Atlas of the Irish Revolution*, Cork University Press, 2017
Gillis, L, *May 25: Burning of the Custom House*, Kilmainham Tales Teo., Dublin, 2017
Hopkinson, M, *The Irish War of Independence*, McGill-Queen's University, 2004
McCall, E, *Tudor's Toughs*, Red Coat Publishing, Newtownards, 2010
O'Malley, E, *On Another Man's Wound*, Mercier Press, Cork, 2013

Books:
(No author information: NA)
(NA) *A History of the Royal Air Force and the United States Naval Reserve in Ireland*, 1913-1923, Karl Hayes and Irish Air Letter, Dublin, 1988
(NA) Iris: *Dáil Éireann, An Chéad Tionól*, 21 Ianar 1919, Baile Átha Cliath
(NA) *The forged 'Irish Bulletin'*, Aubane Historical Society, Millstreet, 2017
(NA) *The Irish Uprising, 1914-21, Papers from the British Parliamentary Archive*, The Stationery Office, London, 2000
Abbot, R, *Police casualties in Ireland*, 1919-1922, Mercier Press, Cork, 2000
Andrews, CS, *Dublin Made Me*, Lilliput Press, Dublin, 2001
Arthur, G, *General Sir John Maxwell*, John Murray, London, 1932
Balfour, G, *The armoured train, its development and usage*, Batsford, London, 1981
Barry, MB, *Courage Boys We are Winning, an Illustrated History of the 1916 Rising*, Andalus Press, Dublin, 2015
Barry, MB, *The Green Divide, an Illustrated History of the Irish Civil War*, Andalus Press, Dublin, 2014
Bateson, R, *Dead and Buried in Dublin*, Irish Graves Publications, Dublin, 2002
Béaslaí, P, *Michael Collins and the Making of a New Ireland*, Phoenix Publishing Company, Dublin, 1926
Beckett, JC, *The Making of Modern Ireland 1603-1923*, Faber & Faber, London, 1972
Begley, D, *The Road to Crossbarry*, Deso Publications, Bandon, 1999
Bennet, R, *The Black and Tans*, Edward Hulton, London, 1959
Borgonovo, J, *Spies, Informers and the 'Anti-Sinn Féin Society'*, Irish Academic Press, Dublin, 2007
Bowyer Bell, J, *The Secret Army: the IRA 1916-1979*, Poolbeg, Dublin, 1990
Breen, D, *My Fight for Irish Freedom*, Anvil Books, Dublin, 1981
Buckley, D, *The Battle of Tourmakeady: Fact or Fiction*, THP Ireland, 2008
Carey, T, *Hanged for Ireland, a Documentary History*, Blackwater Press, Dublin, 2001
Carroll, A, *Seán Moylan*, Mercier Press, Cork, 2010
Casey, C, *The Buildings of Ireland: Dublin*, Yale University Press, New Haven and London, 2005
Chambers, C, *Ireland in the Newsreels*, Irish Academic Press, Dublin, 2012
Connell, J, *Dublin in Rebellion: A Directory 1913-1923*, Lilliput Press, Dublin, 2009
Connolly, C, *Michael Collins*, Weidenfeld & Nicholson, London, 1996
Coogan, TP, *De Valera: Long Fellow, Long Shadow*, Hutchinson, London, 1993

Coogan, TP, *Michael Collins*, Arrow Books, London, 1990

Coogan, TP, *The Twelve Apostles*, Head of Zeus, London, 2016

Cooke, P, *A History of Kilmainham Gaol*, Brunswick Press, Dublin, 2005

Cottrell, P, ed., *The War for Ireland 1913-1923*, Osprey Publishing, Oxford, 2009

Cronin, S, *Frank Ryan: the Search for the Republic*, Repsol Publishing, Dublin, 1980

Crowe, C, ed., *Guide to the Military Service (1916-1923) Pensions Collection*, Óglaigh na hÉireann, Dublin, 2012

Crozier, FP, *Ireland for Ever*, Cedric Chivers, Bath, 1971

Dalton, C, *With the Dublin Brigade*, Mercier Press, 2014

Deasy, L, *Towards Ireland Free*, Mercier Press, Cork, 1973

Doherty, G, Keogh, D, ed., *Michael Collins and the Making of the Irish State*, Mercier Press, Cork, 1998

Dorney, J, *Peace after the Final Battle, the Story of the Irish Revolution*, 1912-1924, New Island, Dublin, 2014

Dwayne, D, *Life of Éamon De Valera Illustrated*, Talbot Press, Dublin, 1927

Fallon, L, *Dublin Fire Brigade and the Irish Revolution*, South Dublin Libraries, Dublin, 2012

Fanning, R, *Fatal Path: British Government and Irish Revolution 1910-1922*, Faber and Faber, London, 2013

Farrell, B, *The founding of Dáil Éireann*, Gill & Macmillan, Dublin, 1971

Farry, M, *Sligo 1914-1921, a Chronicle of Conflict*, Killoran Press, Trim, 1992

Ferriter, D, *A Nation and not a Rabble, the Irish Revolution 1913-23*, Profile Books, London, 2015

Ferriter, D, intro., *Dublin's Fighting Story 1916-1921*, Mercier Press, Cork, 2009

Fitzpatrick, D, ed., *Terror in Ireland*, Lilliput Press, Dublin, 2012

Fitzpatrick, D, *Politics and Irish Life, 1913-1921*, Gill & Macmillan, Dublin, 1998

Fox, R, *The History of the Irish Citizen Army*, James Connolly Debating Society, Belfast, 2013

Gillis, L, *Revolution in Dublin: A Photographic History 1913-23*, Mercier Press, Cork, 2013

Gillis, L, *The Hales Brothers and the Irish Revolution*, Mercier Press, Cork, 2016

Gillis, L, *Women of the Irish Revolution*, Mercier Press, Cork, 2014.

Golway, T, *Irish Rebel, John Devoy and America's Fight for Irish Freedom*, St Martin's Press, New York, 1998

Greaves, D, *Liam Mellows and the Irish Revolution*, Lawrence & Wishart, London, 1971

Griffith, K, O'Grady, T, *Curious Journey*, Mercier Press, Cork, 1998

Gwynn, D, *The History of Partition (1912-1925)*, Browne & Nolan, Dublin, 1950

Hart, P, ed., *British Intelligence in Ireland 1920-21: The Final Reports*, Cork University Press, Cork, 2002

Hart, P, *The IRA at War 1916-1923*, Oxford University Press USA, New York, 2005

Herlihy, J, *The Dublin Metropolitan Police*, Four Courts Press, Dublin, 2013

Hittle, JB, *Michael Collins and the Anglo-Irish War*, Potomac Books, Washington DC, 2011

Holt, E, *Protest in Arms, the Irish Troubles 1916-1923*, Putnam, London, 1960

Hopkinson, M, *The Last Days of Dublin Castle, the Mark Sturgis Diaries*, Irish Academic Press, 1999

Horgan, J, *Seán Lemass, the Enigmatic Patriot*, Gill & Macmillan, Dublin, 1997

Johnson, S, *Johnson's Atlas & Gazetteer of the Railways of Ireland*, Midland Publishing, Leicester, 1997

Joy, S, *The IRA in Kerry 1916-1921*, Collins Press, Cork, 2005

Keane, B, *Massacre in West Cork*, Mercier Press, Cork, 2014

Kenna, S, *War in the Shadows*, Merrion Press, Kildare, 2014

Keogh, D, *Twentieth-Century Ireland, Revolution and State Building*, Gill & Macmillan, Dublin, 2005

Laffan, M, *Judging WT Cosgrave*, Royal Irish Academy, Dublin, 2014

Laffan, M, *The Resurrection of Ireland, the Sinn Féin Party*, 1916-1923

Lawlor, P, *1920-1922, The Outrages*, Mercier Press, 2011

Lawlor, P, *The Burnings 1920*, Mercier Press, Cork, 2009

Lee, JJ, intro., *Kerry's Fighting Story 1916-1921*, Mercier Press, Cork, 2009

Lewis, M, *Frank Aiken's War*, UCD Press, Dublin, 2014

Macardle, D, *The Irish Republic*, Merlin Publishing, 1999

Mageean, J, *Man of the People, the intimate story of the Hero of Ballinalee*, Kayem Publishing Company, 1945

Martin, K, *Irish Army Vehicles, Transport & Armour since 1922*, Karl Martin, 2002

Matthews, A, *Renegades, Irish Republican Women 1900-1922*, Mercier Press, Cork, 2010

Matthews, A, *The Irish Citizen Army*, Mercier Press, Cork, 2014

Matthews, B, *The Sack of Balbriggan*, Balbriggan, 2006

Maye, B, *Arthur Griffith*, Griffith College Publications, Dublin, 1997

McCall, E, *The Auxies*, Red Coat Publishing, Newtownards, 2013

McCall, E, *The First Anti-Terrorist Unit, the Auxiliary Divsion RIC*, Red Coat Publishing, Newtownards, 2018

McCarthy, C, *Cumann na mBan and the Irish Revolution*, Collins Press, Cork, 2007

McDowell, RB, *The Irish Convention, 1917-18*, Routledge & Kegan Paul, London, 1970

McKenna, J, *Guerrilla Warfare and the Irish War of Independence, 1919-1921*, McFarland and Company, North Carolina,

McMahon, P, *British Spies and Irish Rebels*, Boydell Press, Suffolk, 2008
Mitchell, A, *Revolutionary Government in Ireland, Dáil Éireann 1919-22*, Gill & Macmillan, Dublin, 1995
Mooney, T, *Cry of the Curlew*, De Paor, Dungarvan, 2012
Morrison, G, *Revolutionary Ireland, a Photographic Record*, Gill & Macmillan, Dublin, 2013
Mulcahy, R, *My Father the General: Richard Mulcahy and the Military History of the Revolution*, Liberties Press, Dublin, 2009
Mulcahy, R, *Richard Mulcahy, a Family Memoir*, Risteard Mulcahy, 1999
Murphy, B, *The Life and Tragic Death of Winnie Barrington*, Papaver Editions, Limerick, 2018
Murphy, G, *The Year of Disappearances*, Gill & Macmillan, Dublin, 2011
Murphy, S, *Kilmichael, a Battlefield Study*, Four Roads Publishing, 2014
Neeson, E, *The Life and Death of Michael Collins*, Mercier Press, Cork, 1968
Noonan, G, *The IRA in Britain, 1919-1923*, Liverpool University Press, 2014
Ó Comhraí, C, *Revolution in Connacht, A Photographic History 1913-1923*, Mercier Press, Cork, 2013
Ó Conchubhair, B, ed., *Dublin's Fighting Story 1916-21*, Mercier Press, Cork. 2009
Ó Conchubhair, B, ed., *Rebel Cork's Fighting Story 1916-1921*, Mercier Press, 2009
Ó Drisceoil, D, *Peadar O'Donnell*, Cork University Press, Cork, 2001
Ó hÉalaithe, D, *Memoirs of an Old Warrior*, Mercier Press, Cork, 2014
Ó Ruairc, P Óg, *Blood on the Banner*, Mercier Press, Cork, 2009
Ó Ruairc, P Óg, *Revolution: A Photographic History of Revolutionary Ireland 1913-1923*, Mercier Press, Cork, 2011
Ó Ruairc, P Óg, *Truce*, Mercier Press, Cork, 2016
O'Brien, P, *Havoc: The Auxiliaries in Ireland's War of Independence*, Collins Press, Cork, 2017
O'Connor Lysaght, D, *The Communists and the Irish Revolution*, Litéreire Publishers, Dublin, 1993
O'Connor, E, *Reds and the Green*, University College Dublin Press, Dublin, 2004
O'Donnell, R, intro., *Limerick's Fighting Story 1916-1921*, Mercier Press, Cork, 2009
O'Donoghue, D, *The Devil's Deal*, New Island, Dublin, 2010
O'Faolain, S, *Constance Markievicz*, Cresset Women's Voices, London, 1987
O'Farrell, P, *Who's Who in the Irish War of Independence and Civil War, 1916-1923*, Lilliput Press, Dublin, 1997
O'Halpin, E, *The decline of the Union: British government in Ireland 1892-1920*, Gill & Macmillan
O'Malley, C, Keane, V, ed., *The men will talk to me, Mayo interviews by Ernie O'Malley*, 2014
O'Malley, E, *Raids and Rallies*, Mercier Press, Cork, 2011
O'Malley, E, *The men will talk to me: Galway Interviews*, Mercier Press, Cork, 2013
O'Malley, E, *The men will talk to me: Kerry Interviews*, Mercier Press, Cork, 2012
O'Neill, T., *The Battle of Clonmult*, Nonsuch Publishing, Dublin, 2006
O'Donoghue, F, Borgonovo, J, O'Donoghue, J, *Florence and Josephine O'Donoghue's War of Independence*, Irish Academic Press, Dublin, 2006
Osborne, C, *Michael Collins, A life in pictures*, Mercier Press, Cork, 2008
Price, D, *The Flame and the Candle, War in Mayo 1919-1924*, Collins Press, Cork, 2012
Regan, JM, *Myth and the Irish State*, Irish Academic Press, Kildare, 2013
Ring, J, *Erskine Childers, Author of the Riddle of the Sands*, Faber & Faber, London, 2011
Ryan, A, *Comrades: Inside the War of Independence*, Liberties Press, Dublin, 2007
Ryan, G, *The Works, Celebrating 150 Years of Inchicore Works*, (NP), Dublin, 1996
Ryan, M, *Tom Barry, IRA Freedom Fighter*, Mercier Press, Cork, 2013
Ryle Dwyer, T, *Tans, Terror and Troubles, Kerry's real fighting story 1913-23*, Mercier Press, Cork, 2001
Ryle Dwyer, T, *The Squad and the Intelligence Operations of Michael Collins*, Mercier Press, Cork, 2005
Scott, C, *Madame: Countess de Markievicz*, Kilmainham Tales, Dublin, 2013
Sheehan, W, *A Hard Local War, the British Army and the Guerrilla War in Cork, 1919-1921*, The History Press, Stroud, 2011
Sheehan, W, *Hearts & Mines, the British 5th Division, 1920-1922*, Collins Press, Cork, 2009
Townshend, C, *The British Campaign in Ireland, 1919-1921*, Oxford University Press, 1975
Townshend, C, *The Republic, the Fight for Irish Independence,* Allen Lane, London, 2013
White, G, O'Shea, B, *The Burning of Cork*, Mercier Press, Cork, 2006
Valiulis, M, *Portrait of a Revolutionary: General Richard Mulcahy and the Founding of the Irish Free State*, University Press of Kentucky, 1992
Williams, D, ed., *The Irish Struggle 1916-1926*, Routledge & Kegan Paul, London, 1966
Yeates, P, *A City in Turmoil: Dublin 1919-21*, Gill & Macmillan, Dublin, 2015
Yeates, P, *A City in Wartime, Dublin 1914-18*, Gill & Macmillan, Dublin, 2011
Younger, C, *Arthur Griffith*, Gill & Macmillan, Dublin, 1981

Glossary

Active Service Unit (ASU)	IRA Active Service Units were established at the end of December 1920 in Dublin. There were four companies, each assigned to one of the city battalions. These Volunteers were full-time and paid a salary.
ADRIC	Auxiliary Division of the Royal Irish Constabulary. Recruiting for this paramilitary force began in July 1920. Ex-officers were engaged at the generous pay of £1 per day. The first companies were deployed, after training, in August 1920. Each company was well armed and was allocated light lorries (tenders) and armoured cars.
Anglo-Irish Treaty	The Anglo-Irish Treaty signed on 6 December 1921 by Irish plenipotentiaries and representatives of the British Government. It provided for the establishment of an Irish Free State. The six-county entity given the name Northern Ireland was entitled to opt out, which it immediately did.
Auxiliary	A member, designated as a temporary cadet, of ADRIC.
Ballykinlar Camp	A former military barracks at Ballykinlar, Co. Down. Converted into an internment camp, it was used to house Republican prisoners after the mass round-ups following Bloody Sunday in November 1920.
Black and Tan	A nickname (after a name used for the beagles of the Scarteen Hunt, Co. Limerick) applied to the (mostly British) ex-servicemen recruited to the RIC from early 1920 onwards. They were initially clad in a mixture of khaki and green uniform, due to a shortage of RIC uniforms.
Cairo Gang	A name (not used in 1920) that became popular in the decades following the War of Independence, referring to a group of British spies. The name may have derived from the officer-spies drafted in from colonial Egypt, or from the Café Cairo, a well-known meeting place, on Grafton Street in Dublin.
Cumann na mBan	Founded in early 1914, this republican women's auxiliary corps supported the objectives of the Irish Volunteers. *Cumann na mBan* participated strongly during the Rising and War of Independence as an active, but non-combatant, support organisation.
Commandant	A military rank used in Ireland, equivalent to 'Major' in some other armies.
Crossley Tender	This rugged 1919-model Crossley 20/30 hp light truck was widely used by the Crown forces during the War of Independence.
Curragh Camp	The Curragh has been a place of military assembly on the flat plains of County Kildare for centuries. In the early years of the 20th century it was the principal base of the British Army in Ireland. It is now the main training centre for the Irish Defence Forces.
Dáil Éireann	The first *Dáil* (an assembly or parliament) met on 21 January 1919. It was established by Sinn Féin MPs (who won a majority of Irish seats) elected to the United Kingdom parliament in the December 1918 United Kingdom general election.
D&SER	Dublin & South Eastern Railway.
D/I	District Inspector of the RIC.
DMP	Dublin Metropolitan Police. An unarmed urban police force in Dublin, merged into the Garda Síochána in 1925. The 'G' Division (its detectives were popularly known as 'G-men') was a plain-clothes section which had gathered intelligence on Irish republicanism since the time of the Fenians.
Fianna Éireann	Irish nationalist youth organisation founded by Countess Markievicz and Bulmer Hobson in 1909.
Flying Column	Permanent units of the IRA engaged in fighting the guerrilla war, usually operating from remote areas in the countryside. These were established after August 1920. In essence, they were the same as the ASUs as originally established in the Dublin Brigade.
Frongoch Camp	A former POW camp for captured Germans in Merionethshire, North Wales (originally a distillery). It was used after the 1916 Rising to intern most of the Republican prisoners.
GAA	Gaelic Athletic Association. Founded in 1884, a sporting and cultural organisation, which focuses on promoting and organising Gaelic games.
Gaelic League	Founded in 1893, to promote the Irish language. (Irish: *Conradh na Gaeilge*.)
GHQ	General Headquarters.
GNR (I)	Great Northern Railway (Ireland).
Government of Ireland Act (1921)	Also titled 'An Act to provide for the better government of Ireland'. This became law on 23 December 1920. It divided Ireland into two parts. 'Northern Ireland' comprised the six north-eastern counties. 'Southern Ireland' was to comprise the remaining 26 counties. Each entity was to have a bicameral parliament with limited powers. A Northern Ireland parliament was opened on 22 June 1921, in accordance with the Act.
Great Brunswick Street	Since renamed Pearse Street. The DMP station there was the location of the 'G' Division headquarters during the early part of the War of Independence.
GS&WR	Great Southern & Western Railway.
Head Centre	The IRB secret society was organised in cells to avoid penetration by the British police and intelligence services. The basic unit was a circle, which was divided into sections of up to ten men. These elected their officer, or 'centre'. Soon after arriving at Frongoch Camp, Michael Collins was elected 'head centre' by the IRB circles there.
Home Rule	The aim of 'Home Rule' was the establishment of a parliament and government in Dublin to legislate for Irish domestic affairs, thus repatriating some aspects of government back from Westminster.
Igoe Gang	The IRA name for a group of RIC men from around the country, assembled in Dublin under the leadership of Head Constable Eugene Igoe. It had been established as 'the Intelligence Company' by Brigadier-General Ormonde Winter, chief spymaster in Dublin Castle.
Irish Parliamentary Party (IPP)	It was formed in 1882 by Charles Stewart Parnell. Its MPs promoted three Home Rule Bills in the decades that followed. After the split over Parnell, John Redmond emerged as its leader. The 1918 general election proved disastrous for the party and it was dissolved.

IRA	Irish Republican Army, which had its origins in the Irish Volunteers established in November 1913. During Easter 1916, as the Irish Citizen Army and Irish Volunteers fought as a combined force, James Connolly used the term 'Irish Republican Army', but the term came into general use at an early stage of the War of Independence. It is a title that has had many claimants over the past century.
IRB	Irish Republican Brotherhood. A secret oath-bound society, prepared to use force to establish an independent Irish Republic, which represented the continuation of the Fenian tradition. The organisation dissolved itself in 1924.
Irish Volunteers	A nationalist militia founded in November 1913 at the Rotunda in Dublin to 'secure the rights and liberties common to all the people of Ireland'. After the outbreak of WWI in 1914, as the Redmond majority departed with the objective of supporting the British war effort, the remainder reorganised and made plans for a rising.
ITGWU	Irish Transport and General Workers' Union, founded by James Larkin in 1909.
Kilmainham Gaol	Dating from 1796, this grim institution was finally decommissioned as a prison in 1924. Now it is one of Ireland's top historical sites, with a museum and tours.
Kingsbridge Railway Station	Opened in 1846, renamed Heuston Station in 1966 after Seán Heuston (executed in 1916) who worked there for the GS&WR.
Kingstown	Renamed Dún Laoghaire in 1920.
Lady Police Searchers	A contingent of British policewomen who arrived around mid-1920. These served as searchers of women suspects when accompanying the Crown forces during their operations.
L&NWR	London and North Western Railway.
Lord Lieutenant	The representative of the British sovereign in Ireland (also known as the Viceroy). His residence was the Viceregal Lodge in the Phoenix Park. (Now *Áras an Uachtaráin*, official residence of the President of Ireland.)
Marlborough Barracks, Blackhorse Avenue	Renamed McKee (after Dick McKee, murdered on Bloody Sunday) Barracks, still an operational barracks of the Irish Defence Forces.
MGWR	Midland Great Western Railway.
Mountjoy Prison	A prison located in Phibsborough, Dublin and first opened in 1850. The hanghouse added at the beginning of the twentieth century was busy during the War of Independence. Kevin Barry was executed there on 1 November 1920. Over the first half of 1921 nine other Volunteers were executed there.
MP	Member of Parliament.
Munitions Crisis	The crisis arising from the refusal of Irish railwaymen, from mid-May 1920, to carry men and equipment of the Crown forces – an initiative that lasted until December of that year.
Northern Ireland	A constituent unit of the United Kingdom of Great Britain and Northern Ireland. It comprises six Irish counties – Antrim, Armagh, Down, Fermanagh, Derry (shired as Londonderry) and Tyrone.
O/C	Officer Commanding. Ironically, the IRA utilised many of the rank and organisational designations of its principal opponent, the British Army.
Queenstown	Renamed Cobh in 1920.
RAF	The Royal Air Force, formed on 1 April 1918 (formerly the Royal Flying Corps). RAF planes were deployed at aerodromes across Ireland during the War of Independence.
RIC	The Royal Irish Constabulary, an armed police force deployed across Ireland (outside of Dublin), in existence up to 1922.
Sackville Street	Renamed O'Connell Street in 1924.
Shemus	Ernest Forbes (1879–1962), an English cartoonist who worked for the *Freeman's Journal*, published in Dublin. Over the period 1920-24 he produced some 300 cartoons. During the War of Independence his work exposed the flaws of the blundering and brutal British campaign in Ireland.
Sinn Féin	Founded in 1905, under the leadership of Arthur Griffith, who wished to establish a national legislature in Ireland. Griffith and the organisation did not participate in the Rising despite it being dubbed the 'Sinn Féin Rising'. The newly released veterans of the 1916 Rising joined in 1917 and it took a more radical nationalist and republican direction.
Sinn Féin Bank	A cooperative bank associated with *Sinn Féin*, established in August 1908, whose premises was at 6 Harcourt Street in Dublin. It was raided many times by the Crown forces during the War of Independence. Alan Bell set up his enquiry into the source of Sinn Féin's finances using documents found in a February 1920 raid on the bank. This sealed Bell's fate – he was shot in Ballsbridge by the Squad on 26 March 1920.
Squad	A small unit (of tough and resilient Volunteers, who soon gained expertise in assassination) established in 1920 by Michael Collins, to counter British intelligence efforts to crush and destroy the IRA and *Sinn Féin*.
TD	*Teachta Dála* (member of the Irish parliament, *Dáil Éireann*).
Truce	Following meetings in early July 1921, the British and the IRA agreed to a ceasefire (or 'truce'). It came into force on 11 July 1921. Post-ceasefire negotiations led to the signing of the Anglo-Irish Treaty on 6 December 1921 by Irish plenipotentiaries and their British counterparts.
Unionism	In the Irish context, it is an ideology which supports political union between Ireland and Great Britain.
Veterans and Drivers Division	A unit based within the RIC. These were assigned driving and security duties and the men were known as Temporary Constables.
Victoria Barracks, Cork	The main military barracks on the heights above the centre of Cork city. Renamed as Collins Barracks after the Civil War, it is still an operational barracks of the Irish Defence Forces.
Whippet Tank	A popular name given to the medium Mk A tank used in WWI and deployed in Ireland, so named presumably because it was faster than other types of tanks. Confusingly, the nickname was also applied to the fast and agile Rolls-Royce armoured car.

Index

A
Adavoyle 281
Aiken, Frank 281
Alfred, Father, OFMCap 120
Allman, Dan, Commandant 210
American Commission Report 171
Ames, Peter 'Ashmun', Lieutenant 150
Amiens Street (now Connolly) Station 158
Anderson, Sir John 80
Angliss, Henry, Lieutenant 147, 151
Anglo-Irish Treaty 280, 288, 289, 294, 296
An tÓglach 41, 232, 276
Arbour Hill Prison 12, 248
Ashbourne 180
Ashe, Thomas 26, 40
Ashtown 59
Askeaton 194
Austin armoured car 79, 88, 89, 90
Auxiliary Division of the RIC 65, 70, 71, 95, 96, 106-109, 114, 118, 127, 128, 135, 136, 139, 140, 144, 147, 153, 156, 158, 160, 162-168, 170, 172, 178, 179, 184, 188, 189, 193, 196, 199, 202, 203, 205, 212-214, 218, 243-245, 247-249, 255, 264, 265, 284, 292

B
Baggallay, Geoffrey, Captain 151, 200
Baggot Street, Lower 150, 151
Bailieboro 238
Balbriggan 126, 127, 128
Baldonnell 228, 231, 232
Ballincollig 186, 205
Ballingeary 39
Ballinrobe 222
Ballisodare 60
Ballsbridge 75
Ballyfermot 237
Ballykinlar camp 159
Ballylanders 98
Ballymacelligot 139
Ballyturin House 227
Ballyvourney 39
Ballyvoyle 219
Banbridge 65, 101
Bandon 192, 204-206, 259, 271, 273
Banteer 198, 255
Bantry 124, 269
Barcelona 117
Barrington, Winifrid 226
Barry, Kevin 65, 119, 120, 201, 202
Barry, Tom, Commandant-General 162-165, 204-206, 237, 272
Barton, Robert 50, 286, 295
Béal a' Ghleanna 39
Béal na Blá 93
Béaslaí, Piaras 277
Beggar's Bush Barracks 96, 107, 108, 147, 243, 284, 292
Belfast 57, 68, 91, 101, 281, 285
Bell, Alan 74, 75
Belvedere College 119
Bennett, George, Lieutenant 150
Bere Island 159
Biggs, Harry, District Inspector, Major 226
Black and Tans 65, 70, 188, 190, 194, 210
Blackrock College 147
Blackwater, river 103
Blake, Cecil, District Inspector, Captain 227
Blarney Street 215
Bloody Sunday 144, 158, 166, 185, 193, 200, 261, 264
Boast, Frederick, Second Lieutenant 64
Bodenstown 29
Boer War 61
Boland, Harry 37, 41, 44, 48, 52, 55, 237
Boland's Bakery 23
Bootle 240
Border Regiment 222
Boundary Commission 296
Breen, Dan 46, 53, 59, 134
Breeze, Donald, Lieutenant 256
Bristol F.2b fighter 229, 231-233
Britain 11-13, 18, 32, 37, 44, 49, 56, 60, 62, 240, 273, 277, 279, 287
British Army 15, 22, 32, 125, 166, 185, 207
British Cabinet 62, 106, 231, 241, 279
British Empire 15, 181, 286, 293, 295, 296
British Expeditionary Force 35
Brixton Prison 110, 112
Brooke, Frank 105
Broy, Ned 37
Brugha, Cathal 45, 52, 234, 287
Bryan, Thomas 201
Burke, Peter, District Inspector 126
Busteed, Frank 186, 187
Buttevant 133
Byrne, Robert 51
Byrne, Joseph, Sir, Brigadier-General 61
Byrne, Vinnie 56, 150

C
Café Cairo 144
Cairo 144
Cairo Gang 144
Canadian Army 88
Cape Clear island 258
Capel Street 221
Capuchin College, Rochestown 110
Carolan, John, Professor 134
Carrickmines 256
Carrigtwohill 66
Carrowkennedy 254
Casement, Roger 201
Casino, Marino, Dublin 237
Castlebar 211
Castleisland 283
Castletownbere 31
Catalonia 117
Cavan 232, 238
Chambers, Stewart, Captain 269
Childers, Erskine 286, 295
Chippewa Tribe 54
Churchill, Sir Winston 61, 81, 106
Church Street, Upper 119
City Hall 110, 114, 154, 168, 172
Civil War, Irish 181, 237, 280, 292, 296
Clancy, Peadar, Vice-Brigadier 78, 155, 264
Clancy, Seoirse 203
Clare 15, 23, 36, 86, 89, 103, 130, 173, 182, 288
Clarke, Kathleen 26
Clarke, Tom 102
Cleeves condensed milk factory 133
Clémenceau, Georges 49
Clogheen 215
Clonakilty 220, 259, 271
Clonbanin 188, 198, 199, 252
Clonfin 189
Clonliffe Road 153
Clonmult 195, 196
Clune, Conor 155
Coholan, Daniel, Judge 54, 55
Coleman, Richard 40
Collins, Michael 11, 19, 22, 26, 27, 29, 37, 41, 43, 44, 48, 52, 56, 68, 73, 75, 93, 102, 136, 145, 152, 154, 167, 176, 224, 260, 262-264, 268, 269, 277, 286, 295
Collins (previously Victoria) Barracks 167
Collinstown aerodrome 50
Connolle, Tom 131
Connolly, Seán 199, 210
Cooloreen 226
Cope, Alfred 80
Cork 53, 57, 65, 66, 71-73, 97, 100, 101, 104, 110, 112-114, 116, 133, 134, 136, 151, 159, 162, 165, 167, 168, 170-173, 182, 186, 187, 191, 192, 195, 197-199, 204, 205, 215, 219, 220, 226, 252, 255, 258, 259, 263, 267, 269-274
Cork County Club 100, 134
Cork County Gaol 187
Cork Detention Barracks 159
Cosgrave, WT 24
County Donegal Railways 197
Cox, Olive 265
Craig, James 222, 223, 280, 282
Craig, Lieutenant 222, 223
Cripps, Joseph 238
Croke Park 144, 153
Crossbarry 204-206
Crossley Tender 96, 108, 130, 158, 162, 164, 179, 189, 194, 198, 254, 255
Crowe Street 262
Crozier, Frank, Brigadier-General 218
Cullen, Tom 56
Cumann na mBan 27, 29, 45, 64, 275
Cumming, HR, Brigadier-General 188, 198, 199
Curragh 281
Custom House 242-246, 249, 252

D
Dáil Court 104
Dáil Éireann 43, 44, 52, 64, 104, 289, 293, 296
Dáil Propaganda Department 140
Dalton, Emmet 224, 225, 277
Daly, Charles 197
Dartmoor 289
Deansgrange Cemetery 74
Deasy, Liam 217
Deeds and Templar hosiery factory 128
Defence of the Realm Act 46, 78
De Loughry, Peter 48
Democratic Programme of the Dáil 45
Derry 61
De Valera, Éamon 23, 24, 26, 28, 37, 43, 48, 52, 54, 55, 176, 181, 242, 243, 280, 282, 286, 287, 289, 292, 293, 296
Devlin, Joseph 241
Devonshire Regiment 125
Devoy, John 54, 55
De Haviland 9A fighter 228, 229
Dillon's Cross 167, 168, 170
Dockrell, Maurice 282
Donegall Place 280
Donnelly, Simon 193
Donovan, Seán 277
Dowling, Charles, Major 146
Dowling, Joseph 36
Down 159
Downing Street 240, 286, 295
Doyle, Patrick 201
Dripsey 186, 187
Drishanbeg 191, 192
Dromkeen 190
Drumcondra 48, 56, 134, 184, 201
Dublin 12, 20, 23, 27, 28, 35-37, 40, 65, 68, 70, 74-77, 80, 82, 84, 85, 87, 92, 93, 95, 102, 104, 105, 108, 109, 113, 114, 119, 127, 134, 139, 140, 144-147, 150-152, 154, 156, 158, 171, 176, 177, 179-181, 183-185, 193, 202, 212, 214, 221, 224, 225, 232, 238, 241, 243, 244, 251, 256, 257, 260-269, 273, 276, 287, 288, 296
Dublin and South Eastern Railway 105
Dublin Brigade Active Service Unit 177, 184
Dublin Castle 64, 104, 139, 140, 141, 144, 145, 151, 154, 155, 158, 160, 225, 244, 256-262, 264, 265, 269
Dublin Fire Brigade 85, 171, 250
Dublin Metropolitan Police 43, 67, 68, 74, 146, 176, 244, 263-265
Duffy, George Gavan 295
Duggan, Éamon 285, 295
Duke, HE 33
Dundalk 281
Dungarvan 288
Dunmanway 162, 163, 170

E
Earlsfort Terrace 147
Easter Rising, 1916 11-13, 16-19, 21, 26, 27, 29, 31, 32, 40, 41, 43, 77, 93, 102, 275, 287
Egypt 134, 228, 279

Ellis, John 121, 201
Elphin 180
Ennis 89
Ennis, Tom 212, 244
Ennistymon 130, 131
Essex Regiment 192, 206, 220, 271, 272, 273
Exchange Court 154

F

Fastnet lighthouse 258
Fenian 22, 27
Fermoy 57, 112, 124, 133
Fianna Éireann 27
First Southern Division, IRA 217, 238, 252
Fitzalan, Edmund, Viscount 218
Fitzgerald, John, Captain 147
Fitzgerald, Michael 112
Fitzpatrick, Matt 235
Flood, Frank 201
Foley, Edmond 202
Forbes Redmond, William, Assistant-Commissioner 68, 74
Four Courts 179, 296
Foynes 194
Franco, Francisco, General 141
French, John, Field Marshal, Lord 35, 43, 57, 59, 60, 61, 64, 73, 74, 105, 134, 265
Frongoch Camp 18, 19, 20, 26, 275
Furlong, Matt 239

G

Gaelic Athletic Association 64
Gaelic League 64
Gallagher, Frank 140
Galway 109, 160, 227, 232, 260
Gardiner Row 177
'G' Division, DMP 43, 68, 74, 146, 262, 263
George V, King 280
German Plot 11, 36, 40, 52
Germany 13, 32, 49
Germ warfare 178
GHQ 66, 76, 102, 154, 155, 178, 180, 262, 276, 277, 288
GHQ Intelligence 262
Glanmire railway station 197
Glasnevin Cemetery 27, 202
Glen of Aherlow 118
Glenties 197
Gloucestershire Regiment 252
Gorey 102
Gormanston Camp 126
Gort 160, 227, 233
Gortatlea 31, 36
Government of Ireland Act 174, 181, 241, 280
Granard 136, 166, 189
Grangemouth 278
Grazebrook, RM, Lieutenant 252
Great Brunswick (now Pearse) Street 263
Great Northern Railway (I) 84
Green Howard Regiment 220
Greenwood, Sir Hamar 81, 96, 113, 128, 172, 193
Gresham Hotel 152, 200
Greville Arms 136
Greystones 37
Griffin, Fr Michael 160
Griffith, Arthur 21, 286, 295
Great Southern and Western Railway 85, 188, 197, 209, 266

H

Hales, Tom 273
Harcourt Street 64, 68, 154
Harte, Pat 273
Headford Junction 208, 209, 210
Higginson, HW, Brigadier-General 170, 172, 182
HMS *Sea-Wolf* 156
HMS *Truro* 258
Hoboken, New Jersey 237
Hoey, Daniel, Detective 56
Hogan, Michael 153
Hogan, Seán 46, 53

Holmes, Jonathan 99
Holyhead 114, 156
Home Rule 11, 16, 30, 33, 63, 175
Hotchkiss light machine gun 80, 132, 199
Houlihan, Garry 213
Hue-and-Cry 180
Hunger strike 65, 78, 80, 110, 112, 113
Hurley, Charlie 192, 205, 206

I

Ibberson, Geoffrey, Lieutenant 222, 223
Igoe, Eugene, Head Constable 260
Igoe Gang 260
India 117, 228
Inishannon 192
Inistioge 193
Intelligence activities 56, 134, 144, 145, 146, 147, 150, 184, 260
Iraq 228, 231
Irish Brigade 269
Irish Bulletin 140, 141
Irish Citizen Army 12, 20
Irish Convention 11, 25, 30
Irish Crown Jewels 214
Irish Free State 296
Irish Parliamentary Party 11, 16, 21, 22, 23, 24, 25, 30, 33, 34, 42, 44
Irish Republican Army 47, 51, 56, 65, 67, 73, 76, 98-100, 103, 110, 113, 118, 130, 132-137, 144, 145, 147, 151, 153, 164, 166, 167, 170, 173, 178, 180, 181, 184, 186, 187, 191-194, 196, 197, 199, 206, 209, 210, 212, 214, 215, 217, 222, 223, 226, 227, 229, 232-240, 244-247, 250-252, 255, 256, 258-260, 262-264, 266-269, 271, 272, 275-278, 280, 281, 283, 285, 288, 289, 296
Irish Republican Brotherhood 19, 41, 263
Irish Transport and General Workers' Union 131, 202
Irish Volunteers 11, 12, 28, 29, 31, 38, 41, 64, 275

J

Jameson Raid 218
Jeffery Quad armoured car 88
Jervis Street Hospital 153
Johnson, Thomas 45, 158

K

Kavanagh, Ernest 32
Kelleher, Jeremiah, Doctor 166
Kelleher, Philip, District Inspector 136, 166
Kelly's public house 59
Kenmare 208, 209
Keogh, Tom 56
Kerry 173, 198, 199, 208, 214, 226, 233, 266, 283
Kiernan, Kitty 136
Kilbarry 103
Kildare Street 257
Kilkenny 24, 48, 182, 193
Killala Bay 278
Killarney 137, 191, 198, 208
Kilmainham Gaol 193
Kilmallock 98, 99, 104
Kilmichael 65, 136, 162, 163, 165, 166, 168, 196
Kilmorna House 214
Kilquane cemetery 270
Kilroy, Michael 211, 254
Kingsbridge (now Heuston) Railway Station 85
Kingstown (now Dún Laoghaire) 294
King, William, County Inspector 188
Kinsale 192, 204, 205, 206, 271, 272
Knocklong 53, 134, 202
Knockraha 270

L

Labour Commission to Ireland 128, 183
Labour Party, British 183
Labour Party, Irish 45, 158
Lacey, Denis 118
Lady police searcher 71
Lahinch 131
Lancia armoured personnel carrier 97, 239, 250, 251, 255, 281

Lea-Wilson, Percival, Captain 102
Lee Enfield bolt-action SMLE Mk III 108, 171, 207, 235
Lee Metford bolt-action carbine 67
Leenane 254
Lemass, Seán 151
Lenaboy Castle 160
Leonard, Joe 224, 225
Lewis machine gun 207, 211-223, 233, 244, 253
Liberty Hall 20, 158, 185
Liffey, river 152, 179, 250
Limerick 51, 53, 70, 98, 103, 104, 124, 151, 171, 173, 190, 194, 203, 220, 226, 229
Limerick Soviet 51
Lincoln Prison 43, 48
Lindsay, Mary 186, 187
Lisburn 73, 124
Listowel 100, 214
Liverpool 176, 240
Lloyd George, David 16, 25, 33, 35, 61, 63, 73, 84, 105, 113, 174, 181, 279, 280, 282, 286, 287, 293-296
London 113, 133, 152, 156, 178, 181, 198, 199, 212, 236, 241, 248, 266, 280, 282, 286, 294, 296
London & North Western Railway Hotel 212, 245
Long, Walter 63
Longford 118, 136, 189, 199, 210
Lorraine King, Captain 264
Loughnane, Harry 160
Loughnane, Patrick 160
Loyal Regiment 283
Lucas, Charles, Brigadier-General 103, 118
Luger Parabellum 119, 135, 235
Lynch, John 147, 151
Lynch, Liam 57, 132, 133, 151, 217
Lynch, Patrick 23

M

Mac Curtain, Tomás, Lord Mayor 72, 73, 117
Mac Eoin, Seán 118, 136, 189, 224, 225, 289
MacCormack, Patrick 152
MacDermott, Seán 102
Macroom 136, 162, 164, 186, 205
MacKinnon, Ernest, Major 214
Maclean, Donald, Captain 150
MacMahon, Seán 234, 277
MacNeill, Eóin 52
MacPherson, Ian 174
Macpherson, William 267
Macready, Nevil, General, Sir 80, 282
MacSwiney, Muriel 112
MacSwiney, Terence, Lord Mayor 65, 110, 112-114, 116, 117
Maher, Patrick 202
Maguire, Tom, Commandant 222
Mallow 132, 133, 188, 191, 208, 209, 267
Manchester 240
Mannix, Daniel, Archbishop 105, 112
Mansion House, Dublin 28, 34, 217, 282, 289
Mark IV tank 51, 86, 87, 167, 221
Marlborough (now McKee) Barracks 119, 154
Martial Law 173, 182
Martini-Henry carbine 67
Mater Hospital 79, 134
Mauser C96 semi-automatic pistol 236, 245
Maxwell, John, General, Sir 16
Mayo 211, 222, 232, 254, 260
McDonnell, Mick 56, 59, 75
McGarrity, JJ 55
McGarry, Seán 48
McKee, Richard, Brigadier 19, 154, 155, 264
McKenna, Kathleen 140
McLean, Michael, Lieutenant 259
Meade, Maurice 190
Meath 218, 239
Meelin 182
Mellows, Liam 277
Messines Ridge 23
Midleton 182, 195
Midleton, Lord, St John Brodrick 282
Military Service Act 32, 33

Mills bomb 98, 207
Millstreet 191, 255
Milltown Malbay 130, 131
Minh, Ho Chi 117
Mohill 199
Monaghan 109
Monk's Bakery 119
Monkstown 264
Montgomery, Hugh, Lieutenant-Colonel 146
Moran, Patrick 193, 200, 202
Morehampton Road 150
Mountjoy Jail 27, 50, 78, 113, 120, 184, 200-202, 224, 225, 248
Mount Street, Lower 147, 193
Mount Street, Upper 200
Moylan, Seán 182, 199, 217, 252
Mulcahy, Richard 29, 37, 47, 50, 110, 176, 178, 263, 277, 283
Munitions crisis, 1919 82, 96
Murphy, Fintan 285
Murphy, Séamus 165
Myers, Jack 171

N
Nassau Street 256
National Pledge, 1918 34
National Union of Railwaymen 84
Nenagh 124
Newberry, William, Captain 150
Newport, Co. Tipperary 226
New York 54, 105, 145, 215
North Circular Road 224
'Northern Ireland' 63, 175, 231, 241, 280, 296
Northern Ireland Parliament 280
North Roscommon 21
Northumberland Road 147
North Wall 212

O
O'Brien, Michael 223
O'Callaghan, Michael 203
O'Connell, JJ 277
O'Connor, Pádraig 237, 256
O'Connor, Rory 277, 292
O'Daly, Paddy 56, 68, 105
O'Donnell, Patrick, Bishop 30
O'Donoghue, Florrie 217
O'Donovan, Dan 'Sandow' 100
O'Donovan, James 179
O'Donovan Rossa, Jeremiah 27
O'Duffy, Eóin 277
O'Dwyer, Edward, Bishop 16
O'Hannigan, Donncha 190
O'Higgins, Kevin 292
O'Kelly, Seán T. 49
O'Malley, Ernie 132, 193
O'Sullivan, Gearóid 277
Oola 118
Order of St Patrick 214

P
Pallasgreen 190
Paris 43, 49, 63, 117
Paris Peace Conference 42, 43, 45, 49
Parliament Street 151
Parnell Street 239
Partry Mountains 222
Pearse, Patrick 27
Peerless armoured car 90, 194, 221, 224, 225, 245
Pembroke Street, Upper 146
Penzance 105
'Peppercanister' Church 150
Percival, Arthur, Major 271, 272
Phoenix Park 64, 74, 81, 88
Piggott Forgeries 74
Plunkett, George Noble, Count 21, 45, 286
Pollard, HB, Captain 139, 141
Portarlington 266
Price, Éamon 277
Price, Leonard, Captain 146

Q
Queenstown (Cobh) 114
Quinlisk, Timothy 269

R
Rathcoole, Co. Cork 191, 239, 255
Rathfarnham 288
Rathmore 226, 233
Redmond, John 15, 22, 23, 30
Redmond, William 15
Rennie, Donald 268
Rhodes, Cecil 218
Rineen 130
Robinson, Séamus 46
Rogers Brothers foundry 238
Rolls-Royce armoured car 93, 95, 173, 198
Roscommon 59, 180, 210
Rotunda Hospital 102
Royal Air Force 79, 228, 229, 231-233, 266, 278
Royal Engineers 82
Royal Exchange Hotel 151
Royal Flying Corps 147
Royal Fusiliers 198, 208, 209
Royal Hampshire Regiment 195, 253
Royal Irish Constabulary 31, 37, 39, 43, 46, 51, 53, 57-59, 61, 62, 65-68, 70, 71, 73, 74, 76, 81, 89, 97-102, 106, 107, 118, 124, 126, 130, 141, 160, 166, 171, 172, 180, 182, 184, 188, 190, 194, 210, 215, 220, 222, 226, 233, 234, 254, 259, 260, 264, 266, 271, 280
Royal Navy 105, 287
Royal Tank Corps 87
Royal Ulster Constabulary 97
Russell, Seán 238, 277
Russia 32
Ryan, Bernard 201

S
Sackville (now O'Connell) Street 92
Sallins 38
Salthill 109
Savage, Martin 59, 60
Schull 258, 259
Scramogue 210
Scully, Liam 98, 99
Selton Hill 199, 210
Shannon, river 51
Shelbourne Hotel 183
Shemus, cartoonist 86, 193, 286
Shortt, Edward 35
Schultze, Charles 170
Singapore 271
Sinn Féin 11, 13, 21-26, 28, 34, 36, 37, 41, 42-45, 47, 49, 62, 64, 72, 74, 75, 79, 82, 154, 181, 240, 241, 269, 278, 280, 289
Sixth Infantry Division 125, 173
Slattery, Jim 56, 105
Sliabh na mBan 93, 95
Sligo 60, 109, 159
Smith, Thomas 150
Smith, TJ 61
Smyth, George Osbert, Major 134
Smyth, Gerald, Lieutenant-Colonel 100, 101, 134
Smyth, Patrick, Detective-Sergeant 56, 235
Soloheadbeg 43, 46, 47, 53, 59, 134
'Southern Ireland' 175, 241
South Lancashire Regiment 62
Southwark Cathedral 113
Spanish Civil War 141
Spencer Dock 213
Spike Island 159, 252
Spies 261, 264, 267, 268, 270
Squad, the 43, 56, 68, 75, 105, 134, 135, 145, 146, 150, 154, 155, 201, 235, 237, 244, 260
Stack, Austin 286
Stafford Detention barracks 19
Stevenson, Edward, District Inspector 254
St Finbarr's Cemetery 72, 116, 117, 274
St Kearn's Quay, Saltmills 135
St Patrick's Street 116, 168
Stranorlar 197

Strickland Report 172
Strickland, Peter, Major-General 173, 187
Strokestown 210
Sturgis, Mark 80
Swanzy, Oswald, District Inspector 73

T
Talbot Street 135, 155
Teeling, Frank 193
Templemore 124
Tetuan 141
The Dawn 137
The Kerryman 214
Thomastown 118
Thompson submachine gun 211, 237
Thornton, Frank 56, 68, 102, 262, 264
Tipperary 46, 58, 118, 134, 147, 153, 173, 219, 226, 267
'TNT Mick' 238
Tobin, Liam 56, 102
Tolka Bridge, Drumcondra 184
Tourmakeady 222, 223
Townsend Street 56
Tralee 139, 191, 208, 214
Traynor, Thomas 202
Treacy, Seán 46, 53, 118, 134, 135, 155
Trim 218
Trinity College, Dublin 25, 30, 241, 256
Truce of 11 July 1921 109, 181, 232, 234, 237, 238, 269, 277, 283-285, 288, 292
Tudor, Henry, Major-General, Sir 81, 100, 106, 218, 261

U
Ulster Folk and Transport Museum 97
Unionists 11, 16, 25, 30, 33, 42, 174, 175, 181, 241, 280
United States of America 54, 240
Upton 192, 204, 205
Usk Prison 40

V
Vanston, Sir George 251
Vaughan's Hotel 155
Viceregal Lodge 59, 64, 219
Vickers water-cooled machine gun 95, 207
Vicars, Sir Arthur 214
Vico Road, Killiney 139
Victoria (now Collins) Barracks, Cork 167, 168, 173, 187
Volunteers 11, 12, 18, 24, 26, 27, 28, 29, 31, 38, 41

W
Waterfall 269
Waterford 182, 219, 228, 288
Webley firearms 67, 108, 207, 235
Wellington (now Griffith) Barracks 62
Wesleyan Chapel, Fermoy 57
West Cork Railway 192
Westland Row (now Pearse) Station 105
Westminster Abbey 156
Westport 254
Wexford 102, 135, 182, 232
Whelan, Thomas 200, 202
Wicklow 232, 241
Wilde, Leonard, Lieutenant 152
Wilson, Sir Henry, Field Marshal 106
Wilson, Thomas Woodrow 49
Winchester pump-action shotgun 108
Winter, Ormonde de l'Épée, Brigadier-General 155, 178, 260, 261
Wolfe Tone, Theobald 29
Wood, EA, Brigadier-General 218
Woodfield 271
WWI ('Great' War) 11, 15, 23, 32, 41, 57, 81, 87, 88, 90, 96, 136, 151, 228, 229, 231, 271
Wright, Kathleen 256

Y
Youghal 253